A Book of Remarkable Criminals

by

H. B. Irving

The Echo Library 2006

Published by

The Echo Library

Echo Library
131 High St.
Teddington
Middlesex TW11 8HH

www.echo-library.com

Please report serious faults in the text to complaints@echo-library.com

ISBN 1-40681-453-9

CONTENTS

INTRODUCTION

"The silent workings, and still more the explosions, of human passion which bring to light the darker elements of man's nature present to the philosophical observer considerations of intrinsic interest; while to the jurist, the study of human nature and human character with its infinite varieties, especially as affecting the connection between motive and action, between irregular desire or evil disposition and crime itself, is equally indispensable and difficult."—*Wills on Circumstantial Evidence.*

I REMEMBER my father telling me that sitting up late one night talking with Tennyson, the latter remarked that he had not kept such late hours since a recent visit of Jowett. On that occasion the poet and the philosopher had talked together well into the small hours of the morning. My father asked Tennyson what was the subject of conversation that had so engrossed them. "Murders," replied Tennyson. It would have been interesting to have heard Tennyson and Jowett discussing such a theme. The fact is a tribute to the interest that crime has for many men of intellect and imagination. Indeed, how could it be otherwise? Rob history and fiction of crime, how tame and colourless would be the residue! We who are living and enduring in the presence of one of the greatest crimes on record, must realise that trying as this period of the world's history is to those who are passing through it, in the hands of some great historian it may make very good reading for posterity. Perhaps we may find some little consolation in this fact, like the unhappy victims of famous freebooters such as Jack Sheppard or Charley Peace.

But do not let us flatter ourselves. Do not let us, in all the pomp and circumstance of stately history, blind ourselves to the fact that the crimes of Frederick, or Napoleon, or their successors, are in essence no different from those of Sheppard or Peace. We must not imagine that the bad man who happens to offend against those particular laws which constitute the criminal code belongs to a peculiar or atavistic type, that he is a man set apart from the rest of his fellow-men by mental or physical peculiarities. That comforting theory of the Lombroso school has been exploded, and the ordinary inmates of our prisons shown to be only in a very slight degree below the average in mental and physical fitness of the normal man, a difference easily explained by the environment and conditions in which the ordinary criminal is bred.

A certain English judge, asked as to the general characteristics of the prisoners tried before him, said: "They are just like other people; in fact, I often think that, but for different opportunities and other accidents, the prisoner and I might very well be in one another's places." "Greed, love of pleasure," writes a French judge, "lust, idleness, anger, hatred, revenge, these are the chief causes of crime. These passions and desires are shared by rich and poor alike, by the educated and uneducated. They are inherent in human nature; the germ is in every man."

Convicts represent those wrong-doers who have taken to a particular form of wrong-doing punishable by law. Of the larger army of bad men they represent a minority, who have been found out in a peculiarly unsatisfactory kind of misconduct. There are many men, some lying, unscrupulous, dishonest, others cruel, selfish, vicious, who go through life without ever doing anything that brings them within the scope of the criminal code, for whose offences the laws of society provide no punishment. And so it is with some of those heroes of history who have been made the theme of fine writing by gifted historians.

Mr. Basil Thomson, the present head of the Criminal Investigation Department, has said recently that a great deal of crime is due to a spirit of "perverse adventure" on the part of the criminal. The same might be said with equal justice of the exploits of Alexander the Great and half the monarchs and conquerors of the world, whom we are taught in our childhood's days to look up to as shining examples of all that a great man should be. Because crimes are played on a great stage instead of a small, that is no reason why our moral judgment should be suspended or silenced. Class Machiavelli and Frederick the Great as a couple of rascals fit to rank with Jonathan Wild, and we are getting nearer a perception of what constitutes the real criminal. "If," said Frederick the Great to his minister, Radziwill, "there is anything to be gained by it, we will be honest; if deception is necessary, let us be cheats." These are the very sentiments of Jonathan Wild.

Crime, broadly speaking, is the attempt by fraud or violence to possess oneself of something belonging to another, and as such the cases of it in history are as clear as those dealt with in criminal courts. Germany to-day has been guilty of a perverse and criminal adventure, the outcome of that false morality applied to historical transactions, of which Carlyle's life of Frederick is a monumental example. In that book we have a man whose instincts in more ways than one were those of a criminal, held up for our admiration, in the same way that the same writer fell into dithyrambic praise over a villain called Francia, a former President of Paraguay. A most interesting work might be written on the great criminals of history, and might do something towards restoring that balance of moral judgment in historical transactions, for the perversion of which we are suffering to-day.

In the meantime we must be content to study in the microcosm of ordinary crime those instincts, selfish, greedy, brutal which, exploited often by bad men in the so-called cause of nations, have wrought such havoc to the happiness of mankind. It is not too much to say that in every man there dwell the seeds of crime; whether they grow or are stifled in their growth by the good that is in us is a chance mysteriously determined. As children of nature we must not be surprised if our instincts are not all that they should be. "In sober truth," writes John Stuart Mill, "nearly all the things for which men are hanged or imprisoned for doing to one another are nature's everyday performances," and in another passage: "The course of natural phenomena being replete with everything which when committed by human beings is most worthy of abhorrence, anyone who endeavoured in his actions to imitate the natural course of things would be universally seen and acknowledged to be the wickedest of men."

Here is explanation enough for the presence of evil in our natures, that instinct to destroy which finds comparatively harmless expression in certain forms of taking life, which is at its worst when we fall to taking each other's. It is to check an inconvenient form of the expression of this instinct that we punish murderers with death. We must carry the definition of murder a step farther before we can count on peace or happiness??{in}??this world. We must concentrate all our strength on?? fighting criminal nature, both in ourselves and in the world around us. With the destructive forces of nature we are waging a perpetual struggle for our very existence. Why dissipate our strength by fighting among ourselves? By enlarging our conception of crime we move towards that end. What is anti- social, whether it be written in the pages of the historian or those of the Newgate Calendar, must in the future be regarded with equal abhorrence and subjected to equally sure punishment. Every professor of history should now and then climb down from the giddy heights of Thucydides and Gibbon and restore his moral balance by comparing the acts of some of his puppets with those of their less fortunate brethren who have dangled at the end of a rope. If this war is to mean anything to posterity, the crime against humanity must be judged in the future by the same rigid standard as the crime against the person.

The individual criminals whose careers are given in this book have been chosen from among their fellows for their pre-eminence in character or achievement. Some of the cases, such as Butler, Castaing and Holmes, are new to most English readers.

Charles Peace is the outstanding popular figure in nineteenth- century crime. He is the type of the professional criminal who makes crime a business and sets about it methodically and persistently to the end. Here is a man, possessing many of those qualities which go to make the successful man of action in all walks of life, driven by circumstances to squander them on a criminal career. Yet it is a curious circumstance that this determined and ruthless burglar should have suffered for what would be classed in France as a "crime passionel." There is more than a possibility that a French jury would have ?? ing circumstances in the murder of Dyson. ?? Peace is only another instance of the wreck- ?? ong man's career by his passion for a ??

?? bert Butler we have the criminal by conviction, a conviction which finds the ground ready prepared for its growth in the natural laziness and idleness of the man's disposition. The desire to acquire things by a short cut, without taking the trouble to work for them honestly, is perhaps the most fruitful of all sources of crime. Butler, a bit of a pedant, is pleased to justify his conduct by reason and philosophy—he finds in the acts of unscrupulous monarchs an analogy to his own attitude towards life. What is good enough for Caesar Borgia is good enough for Robert Butler. Like Borgia he comes to grief; criminals succeed and criminals fail. In the case of historical criminals their crimes are open; we can estimate the successes and failures. With ordinary criminals, we know only those who fail. The successful, the real geniuses in crime, those whose guilt remains undiscovered, are for the most part unknown to us. Occasionally in society a man or woman is pointed out as having once murdered somebody or other, and at times, no doubt, with truth. But the matter can only be referred to clandestinely; they are gazed at with awe or curiosity, mute witnesses to their own achievement. Some years ago James Payn, the novelist, hazarded the reckoning that one person in every five hundred was an undiscovered murderer. This gives us all a hope, almost a certainty, that we may reckon one such person at least among our acquaintances.[1]

[1] The author was one of three men discussing this subject in a London club. They were able to name six persons of their various acquaintance who were, or had been, suspected of being successful murderers.

Derues is remarkable for the extent of his social ambition, the daring and impudent character of his attempts to gratify it, the skill, the consummate hypocrisy with which he played on the credulity of honest folk, and his flagrant employment of that weapon known and recognised to-day in the most exalted spheres by the expressive name of "bluff." He is remarkable, too, for his mirth and high spirits, his genial buffoonery; the merry murderer is a rare bird.

Professor Webster belongs to that order of criminal of which Eugene Aram and the Rev. John Selby Watson are our English examples, men of culture and studious habits who suddenly burst on the astonished gaze of their fellowmen as murderers. The exact process of mind by which these hitherto harmless citizens are converted into assassins is to a great extent hidden from us.

Perhaps Webster's case is the clearest of the three. Here we have a selfish, self-indulgent and spendthrift gentleman who has landed himself in serious financial embarrassment, seeking by murder to escape from an importunate and relentless creditor. He has not, apparently, the moral courage to face the consequences of his own weakness. He forgets the happiness of his home, the love of those dear to him, in the desire to free himself from a disgrace insignificent{sic} in comparison with that entailed by committing the highest of all crimes. One would wish to believe that Webster's deed was unpremeditated, the result of a sudden gust of passion caused by his victim's acrimonious pursuit of his debtor. But there are circumstances in the case which tell powerfully against such a view. The character of the murderer seems curiously contradictory; both cunning and simplicity mark his proceedings; he makes a determined attempt to escape from the horrors of his situation and shows at the same time a curious insensibility to its real gravity. Webster was a man of refined tastes and seemingly gentle character, loved by those near to him, well liked by his friends.

The mystery that surrounds the real character of Eugene Aram is greater, and we possess little or no means of solving it. From what motive this silent, arrogant man, despising his ineffectual wife, this reserved and moody scholar stooped to fraud and murder the facts of the case help us little to determine. Was it the hope of leaving the narrow surroundings of Knaresborough, his tiresome belongings, his own poor way of life, and seeking a wider field for the exercise of those gifts of scholarship which he undoubtedly possessed that drove him to commit fraud in company with Clark and Houseman, and then, with the help of the latter, murder the unsuspecting Clark? The fact of his humble origin makes his association with so low a ruffian as Houseman the less remarkable. Vanity in all probability played a considerable part in Aram's disposition. He would seem to have thought himself a superior person, above the laws that bind ordinary men. He showed at the end no consciousness of his guilt. Being something of a philosopher, he had no doubt constructed for himself a philosophy of life which served to justify his own actions. He was a deist, believing in "one almighty Being the God of Nature," to whom he recommended himself at the last in the event of his "having done amiss." He emphasised the fact that his life had been unpolluted and his morals irreproachable. But his views as to the murder of Clark he left unexpressed. He suggested as justification of it that Clark had carried on an intrigue with his neglected wife, but he never urged this circumstance in his defence, and beyond his own statement there is no evidence of such a connection.

The Revd. John Selby Watson, headmaster of the Stockwell Grammar School, at the age of sixty-five killed his wife in his library one Sunday afternoon. Things had been going badly with the unfortunate man. After more than twenty-five years' service as headmaster of the school at a meagre salary of L400 a year, he was about to be dismissed; the number of scholars had been declining steadily and a change in the headmastership thought necessary; there was no suggestion of his receiving any kind of pension. The future for a man of his years was dark enough. The author of several learned books, painstaking, scholarly, dull, he could hope to make but little money from literary work. Under a cold, reserved and silent exterior, Selby Watson concealed a violence of temper which he sought diligently to repress. His wife's temper was none of the best. Worried, depressed, hopeless of his future, he in all probability killed his wife in a sudden access of rage, provoked by some taunt or reproach on her part, and then, instead of calling in a policeman and telling him what he had done, made clumsy and ineffectual efforts to conceal his crime. Medical opinion was divided as to his mental condition. Those doctors called for the prosecution could find no trace of insanity about him, those called for the defence said that he was suffering from melancholia. The unhappy man would appear hardly to have realised the gravity of his situation. To a friend who visited him in prison he said: "Here's a man who can write Latin, which the Bishop of Winchester would commend, shut up in a place like this." Coming from a man who had spent all his life buried in books and knowing little of the world the remark is not so greatly to be wondered at. Profound scholars are apt to be impatient of mundane things. Professor Webster showed a similar want of appreciation of the circumstances of a person charged with wilful murder. Selby Watson was convicted of murder and sentenced to death. The sentence was afterwards commuted to one of penal servitude for life, the Home Secretary of the day showing by his decision that, though not satisfied of the prisoner's insanity, he recognised certain extenuating circumstances in his guilt.[2]

[2] Selby Watson was tried at the Central Criminal Court January, 1872.

In Castaing much ingenuity is shown in the conception of the crime, but the man is weak and timid; he is not the stuff of which the great criminal is made; Holmes is cast in the true mould of the instinctive murderer. Castaing is a man of sensibility, capable of domestic affection; Holmes completely insensible to all feelings of humanity. Taking life is a mere incident in the accomplishment of his schemes; men, women and children are sacrificed with equal mercilessness to the necessary end. A consummate liar and hypocrite, he has that strange power of fascination over others, women in particular, which is often independent altogether of moral or even physical attractiveness. We are accustomed to look for a certain vastness, grandeur of scale in the achievements of America. A study of American crime will show that it does not disappoint us in this expectation. The extent and audacity of the crimes of Holmes are proof of it.

To find a counterpart in imaginative literature to the complete criminal of the Holmes type we must turn to the pages of Shakespeare. In the number of his victims, the cruelty and insensibility with which he attains his ends, his unblushing hypocrisy, the fascination he can exercise at will over others, the Richard III. of Shakespeare shows how clearly the poet understood the instinctive criminal of real life. The Richard of history was no doubt less instinctively and deliberately an assassin than the Richard of Shakespeare. In the former we can trace the gradual temptation to crime to which circumstances provoke him. The murder of the Princes, if, as one writer contends, it was not the work of Henry VII.—in which case that monarch deserves to be hailed as one of the most consummate criminals that ever breathed and the worthy father of a criminal son—was no doubt forced to a certain extent on Richard by the exigencies of his situation, one of those crimes to which bad men are driven in order to secure the fruits of other crimes. But the Richard of Shakespeare is no child of circumstance. He espouses deliberately a career of crime, as deliberately as Peace or Holmes or Butler; he sets out "determined to prove a villain," to be "subtle, false and treacherous," to employ to gain his ends "stern murder in the dir'st degree." The character is sometimes criticised as being overdrawn and unreal. It may not be true to the Richard of history, but it is very true to crime, and to the historical criminal of the Borgian or Prussian type, in which fraud and violence are made part of a deliberate system of so- called statecraft.

Shakespeare got nearer to what we may term the domestic as opposed to the political criminal when he created Iago. In their envy and dislike of their fellowmen, their contempt for humanity in general, their callousness to the ordinary sympathies of human nature, Robert Butler, Lacenaire, Ruloff are witnesses to the poet's fidelity to criminal character in his drawing of the Ancient. But there is a weakness in the character of Iago regarded as a purely instinctive and malignant criminal; indeed it is a weakness in the consistency of the play. On two occasions Iago states explicitly that Othello is more than suspected of having committed adultery with his wife, Emilia, and that therefore he has a strong and justifiable motive for being revenged on the Moor. The thought of it he describes as "gnawing his inwards." Emilia's conversation with Desdemona in the last act lends some colour to the correctness of Iago's belief.

If this belief be well-founded it must greatly modify his character as a purely wanton and mischievous criminal, a supreme villain, and lower correspondingly the character of Othello as an honourable and high-minded man. If it be a morbid suspicion, having no ground in fact, a mental obsession, then Iago becomes abnormal and consequently more or less irre-

sponsible. But this suggestion of Emilia's faithlessness made in the early part of the play is never followed up by the dramatist, and the spectator is left in complete uncertainty as to whether there be any truth or not in Iago's suspicion. If Othello has played his Ancient false, that is an extenuating circumstance in the otherwise extraordinary guilt of Iago, and would no doubt be accorded to him as such, were he on trial before a French jury.

The most successful, and therefore perhaps the greatest, criminal in Shakespeare is King Claudius of Denmark. His murder of his brother by pouring a deadly poison into his ear while sleeping, is so skilfully perpetrated as to leave no suspicion of foul play. But for a supernatural intervention, a contingency against which no murderer could be expected to have provided, the crime of Claudius would never have been discovered. Smiling, jovial, genial as M. Derues or Dr. Palmer, King Claudius might have gone down to his grave in peace as the bluff hearty man of action, while his introspective nephew would in all probability have ended his days in the cloister, regarded with amiable contempt by his bustling fellowmen. How Claudius got over the great dif-

ficulty of all poisoners, that of procuring the necessary poison without detection, we are not told; by what means he distilled the "juice of cursed hebenon"; how the strange appearance of the late King's body, which "an instant tetter" had barked about with "vile and loathsome crust," was explained to the multitude we are left to imagine. There is no real evidence to show that Queen Gertrude was her lover's accomplice in her husband's murder. If that had been so, she would no doubt have been of considerable assistance to Claudius in the preparation of the crime. But in the absence of more definite proof we must assume Claudius' murder of his brother to have been a solitary achievement, skilfully carried out by one whose genial good- fellowship and convivial habits gave the lie to any suggestion of criminality. Whatever may have been his inward feelings of remorse or self-reproach, Claudius masked them successfully from the eyes of all. Hamlet's instinctive dislike of his uncle was not shared by the members of the Danish court. The "witchcraft of his wit," his "traitorous gifts," were powerful aids to Claudius, not only in the seduction of his sister-in-law, but the perpetration of secret murder.

The case of the murder of King Duncan of Scotland by Macbeth and his wife belongs to a different class of crime. It is a striking example of dual crime, four instances of which are given towards the end of this book. An Italian advocate, Scipio Sighele, has devoted a monograph to the subject of dual crime, in which he examines a number of cases in which two persons have jointly committed heinous crimes.[3] He finds that in couples of this kind there is usually an incubus and a succubus, the one who suggests the crime, the other on whom the suggestion works until he or she becomes the accomplice or instrument of the stronger will; "the one playing the Mephistophelian part of tempter, preaching evil, urging to crime, the other allowing himself to be overcome by his evil genius." In some cases these two roles are clearly differentiated; it is easy, as in the case of Iago and Othello, Cassius and Brutus, to say who prompted the crime. In others the guilt seems equally divided and the original suggestion of crime to spring from a mutual tendency towards the adoption of such an expedient. In Macbeth and his wife we have a perfect instance of the latter class. No sooner have the witches prophesied that Macbeth shall be a king than the "horrid image" of the suggestion to murder Duncan presents itself to his mind, and, on returning to his wife, he answers her question as to when Duncan is to leave their house by the significant remark, "To-morrow—as he proposes." To Lady Macbeth from the moment she has received her husband's letter telling of the prophecy of the weird sisters, murder occurs as a means of accomplishing their prediction. In the minds of Macbeth and his wife the suggestion of murder is originally an auto-suggestion, coming to them independently of each other as soon as they learn from the witches that Macbeth is one day to be a king. To Banquo a somewhat similar intimation is given, but no foul thought of crime suggests itself for an instant to his loyal nature. What Macbeth and his wife lack at first as thorough-going murderers is that complete insensibility to taking human life that marks the really ruthless assassin. Lady Macbeth has the stronger will of the two for the commission of the deed. It is doubtful whether without her help Macbeth would ever have undertaken it. But even she, when her husband hesitates to strike, cannot bring herself to murder the aged Duncan with her own hands because of his resemblance as he sleeps to her father. It is only after a deal of boggling and at serious risk of untimely interruption that the two contrive to do the murder, and plaster with blood the "surfeited grooms." In thus putting suspicion on the servants of Duncan the assassins cunningly avert suspicion from themselves, and Macbeth's killing of the unfortunate men in seeming indigna- tion at the discovery of their crime is a master-stroke of ingenuity. "Who," he asks in a splendid burst of feigned horror, "can be wise, amazed, temperate and furious, loyal and natural in a moment?" At the same time Lady Macbeth affects to swoon away in the presence of so awful a crime. For the time all suspicion of guilt, except in the mind of Banquo, is averted from the real murderers. But, like so many criminals, Macbeth finds it impossible to rest on his first success in crime. His sensibility grows dulled; he "forgets the taste of fear"; the murder of Banquo and his son is diabolically planned, and that is soon followed by the outrageous slaughter of the wife and children of Macduff. Ferri, the Italian writer on crime, describes the psychical condition favourable to the commission of murder as an absence of both moral repugnance to the crime itself and the fear of the consequences following it. In the murder of Duncan, it is the first of these two states of mind to which Macbeth and his wife have only partially attained. The moral repugnance stronger in the man has not been wholly lost by the woman. But as soon as the crime is successfully accomplished, this repugnance begins to wear off until the King and Queen are able calmly and deliberately to contemplate those further crimes necessary to their peace of mind. But now Macbeth, at first the more compunctious of the two, has become the more ruthless; the germ of crime, developed by suggestion, has spread through his whole being; he has begun to acquire that indifference to human suffering with which Richard III. and Iago were gifted from the first. In both Macbeth and Lady Macbeth the germ of crime was latent; they wanted only favourable circumstances to convert them into one of those criminal couples who are the more dangerous for the fact that the temptation to crime has come to each spontaneously and grown and been fostered by mutual understanding, an elective affinity for evil. Such couples are frequent in the history of crime. Eyraud and Bompard, Mr. and Mrs. Manning, Burke and Hare, the Peltzer brothers, Barre and Lebiez, are instances of those collaborations in crime which find their counterpart in history, literature, drama and business. Antoninus and Aurelius, Ferdinand and Isabella, the De Goncourt brothers, Besant and Rice, Gilbert and Sullivan, Swan and Edgar leap to the memory.

[3] "Le Crime a Deux," by Scipio Sighele (translated from the Italian), Lyons, 1893.

In the cases of Eyraud and Bompard, both man and woman are idle, vicious criminals by instinct. They come together, lead an abandoned life, sinking lower and lower in moral degradation. In the hour of need, crime presents itself as a simple expedient for which neither of them has any natural aversion. The repugnance to evil, if they ever felt it, has long since disappeared from their natures. The man is serious, the woman frivolous, but the criminal tendency in both cases is the same; each performs his or her part in the crime with characteristic aptitude. Mrs. Manning was a creature of much firmer character than her husband, a woman of strong passions, a redoubtable murderess. Without her dominating force Manning might never have committed murder. But he was a criminal before the crime, more than suspected as a railway official of complicity in a considerable train robbery; in his case the suggestion of murder involved only the taking of a step farther in a criminal career. Manning suffered from nerves almost as badly as Macbeth; after the deed he sought to drown the prickings of terror and remorse by heavy drinking Mrs. Manning was never troubled with any feelings of this kind; after the murder of O'Connor the gratification of her sexual passion seemed uppermost in her mind; and she met the consequences of her crime fearlessly. Burke and Hare were a couple of ruffians, tempted by what must have seemed almost fabulous wealth to men of their wretched poverty to commit a series of cruel murders. Hare, with his queer, Mephistophelian countenance, was the wickeder of the two. Burke became haunted as time went on and flew to drink to banish horror, but Hare would seem to have been free from such "compunctious visitings of Nature." He kept his head and turned King's evidence.

In the case of the Peltzer brothers we have a man who is of good social position, falling desperately in love with the wife of a successful barrister. The wife, though unhappy in her domestic life, refuses to become her lover's mistress; marriage is the only way to secure her. So Armand Peltzer plots to murder the husband. For this purpose he calls in the help of a brother, a ne'er-do-well, who has left his native country under a cloud. He sends for this dubious person to Europe, and there between them they plan the murder of the inconvenient husband. Though the idea of the crime comes from the one brother, the other receives the idea without repugnance and enters wholeheartedly into the commission of the murder. The ascendency of the one is evident, but he knows his man, is sure that he will have no difficulty in securing the other's co-operation in his felonious purpose. Armand Peltzer should have lived in the Italy of the Renaissance.

The crime was cunningly devised, and methodically and successfully accomplished. Only an over-anxiety to secure the fruits of it led to its detection. Barre and Lebiez are a perfect criminal couple, both young men of good education, trained to better things, but the one idle, greedy and vicious, the other cynical, indifferent, inclined at best to a lazy sentimentalism. Barre is a needy stockbroker at the end of his tether, desperate to find an expedient for raising the wind, Lebiez a medical student who writes morbid verses to a skull and lectures on Darwinism. To Barre belongs the original suggestion to murder an old woman who sells milk and is reputed to have savings. But his friend and former schoolfellow, Lebiez, accepts the suggestion placidly, and reconciles himself to the murder of an unnecessary old woman by the same argument as that used by Raskolnikoff in "Crime and Punishment" to justify the killing of his victim.

In all the cases here quoted the couples are essentially criminal couples. From whichever of the two comes the first suggestion of crime, it falls on soil already prepared to receive it; the response to the suggestion is immediate. In degree of guilt there is little or nothing to choose between them. But the more interesting instances of dual crime are those in which one innocent hitherto of crime, to whom it is morally repugnant, is persuaded by another to the commission of a criminal act, as Cassius persuades Brutus; Iago, Othello. Cassius is a criminal by instinct. Placed in a social position which removes him from the temptation to ordinary crime, circumstances combine in his case to bring out the criminal tendency and give it free play in the projected murder of Caesar. Sour, envious, unscrupulous, the suggestion to kill Caesar under the guise of the public weal is in reality a gratification to Cassius of his own ignoble instincts, and the deliberate unscrupulousness with which he seeks to corrupt the honourable metal, seduce the noble mind of his friend, is typical of the man's innate dishonesty. Cassius belongs to that particular type of the envious nature which Shakespeare is fond of exemplifying with more or less degree of villainy in such characters as Iago, Edmund, and Don John, of which Robert Butler, whose career is given in this book, is a living instance. Cassius on public grounds tempts Brutus to crime as subtly as on private grounds Iago tempts Othello, and with something of the same malicious satisfaction; the soliloquy of Cassius at the end of the second scene of the first act is that of a bad man and a false friend. Indeed, the quarrel between Brutus and Cassius after the murder of Caesar loses much of its sincerity and pathos unless we can forget for the moment the real character of Cassius. But the interest in the cases of Cassius and Brutus, Iago and Othello, lies not so much in the nature of the prompter of the crime. The instances in which an honest, honourable man is by force of another's suggestion converted into a criminal are psychologically remarkable. It is to be expected that we should look in the annals of real crime for confirmation of the truth to life of stories such as these, told in fiction or drama.

The strongest influence, under which the naturally non-criminal person may be tempted in violation of instinct and better nature to the commission of a crime, is that of love or passion. Examples of this kind are frequent in the annals of crime. There is none more striking than that of the Widow Gras and Natalis Gaudry. Here a man, brave, honest, of hitherto irreproachable character, is tempted by a woman to commit the most cruel and infamous of crimes. At first he repels the suggestion; at last, when his senses have been excited, his passion inflamed by the cunning of the woman, as the jealous passion of Othello is played on and excited by Iago, the patriotism of Brutus artfully exploited by Cassius, he yields to the repeated solicitation and does a deed in every way repugnant to his normal character. Nothing seems so blinding in its effect on the moral sense as passion. It obscures all sense of humour, proportion, congruity; the murder of the man or woman who stands in the way of its full enjoyment becomes an act of inverted justice to the perpetrators; they reconcile themselves to it by the most perverse reasoning until they come to regard it as an act, in which they may justifiably invoke the help of God; eroticism and religion are often jumbled up together in this strange medley of conflicting emotions.

A woman, urging her lover to the murder of her husband, writes of the roses that are to deck the path of the lovers as soon as the crime is accomplished; she sends him flowers and in the same letter asks if he has got the necessary cartridges. Her husband has been ill; she hopes that it is God helping them to the desired end; she burns a candle on the altar of a saint for the success of their murderous plan.[4] A jealous husband setting out to kill his wife carries in his pockets, beside a knife and a service revolver, a rosary, a medal of the Virgin and a holy image.[5] Marie Boyer in the blindness of her passion and jealousy believes God to be helping her to get rid of her mother.

[4] Case of Garnier and the woman Aveline, 1884. [5] Case of the Comte de Cornulier: "Un An de Justice," Henri Varennes, 1901.

A lover persuades the wife to get rid of her husband. For a whole year he instils the poison into her soul until she can struggle no longer against the obsession; he offers to do the deed, but she writes that she would rather suffer all the risks and consequences herself. "How many times," she writes, "have I wished to go away, leave home, but it meant leaving my children, losing them for ever . . that made my lover jealous, he believed that I could not bring myself to leave my husband. But if my husband were out of the way then I would keep my children, and my lover would see in my crime a striking proof of my devotion." A curious farrago of slavish passion, motherly love and murder.[6]

[6] Case of Madame Weiss and the engineer Roques. If I may be permitted the reference, there is an account of this case and that of Barre and Lebiez in my book "French Criminals of the Nineteenth Century."

There are some women such as Marie Boyer and Gabrielle Fenayrou, who may be described as passively criminal, chameleon-like, taking colour from their surroundings. By the force of a man's influence they commit a dreadful crime, in the one instance it is matricide, in the other the murder of a former lover, but neither of the women is profoundly vicious or criminal in her instincts. In prison they become exemplary, their crime a thing of the past.

Gabrielle Fenayrou during her imprisonment, having won the confidence of the religious sisters in charge of the convicts, is appointed head of one of the workshops. Marie Boyer is so contrite, exemplary in her behaviour that she is released after fifteen years' imprisonment. In some ways, perhaps, these malleable types of women, "soft paste" as one authority has described them, "effacees" in the words of another, are the most dangerous material of all for the commission of crime, their obedience is so complete, so cold and relentless.

There are cases into which no element of passion enters, in which one will stronger than the other can so influence, so dominate the weaker as to persuade the individual against his or her better inclination to an act of crime, just as in the relations of ordinary life we see a man or woman led and controlled for good or ill by one stronger than themselves. There is no more extraordinary instance of this than the case of Catherine Hayes, immortalised by Thackeray, which occurred as long ago as the year 1726. This singular woman by her artful insinuations, by representing her husband as an atheist and a murderer, persuaded a young man of the name of Wood, of hitherto exemplary character, to assist her in murdering him. It was unquestionably the sinister influence of Captain Cranstoun that later in the same century persuaded the respectable Miss Mary Blandy to the murder of her father. The assassin of an old woman in Paris recounts thus the arguments used by his mistress to induce him to commit the crime: "She began by telling me about the money and jewellery in the old woman's possession which could no longer be of any use to her"—the argument of Raskolnikoff—"I resisted, but next day she began again, pointing out that one killed people in war, which was not considered a crime, and therefore one should not be afraid to kill a miserable old woman. I urged that the old woman had done us no harm, and that I did not see why one should kill her; she reproached me for my weakness and said that, had she been strong enough, she would soon have done this abominable deed herself. 'God,' she added, 'will forgive us because He knows how poor we are.'" When he came to do the murder, this determined woman plied her lover with brandy and put rouge on his cheeks lest his pallor should betray him.[7]

[7] Case of Albert and the woman Lavoitte, Paris, 1877.

There are occasions when those feelings of compunction which troubled Macbeth and his wife are wellnigh proof against the utmost powers of suggestion, or, as in the case of Hubert and Prince Arthur, compel the criminal to desist from his enterprise.

A man desires to get rid of his father and mother-in-law. By means of threats, reproaches and inducements he persuades another man to commit the crime. Taking a gun, the latter sets out to do the deed; but he realises the heinousness of it and turns back. "The next day," he says, "at four o'clock in the morning I started again. I passed the village church. At the sight of the place where I had celebrated my first communion I was filled with remorse. I knelt down and prayed to God to make me good. But some unknown force urged me to the crime. I started again—ten times I turned back, but the more I hesitated the stronger was the desire to go on." At length the faltering assassin arrived at the house, and in his painful anxiety of mind shot a servant instead of the intended victims.[8]

[8] Case of Porcher and Hardouin cited in Despine. "Psychologie Naturelle."

In a town in Austria there dwelt a happy and contented married couple, poor and hard-working. A charming young lady, a rich relation and an orphan, comes to live with them. She brings to their modest home wealth and comfort. But as time goes on, it is likely that the young lady will fall in love and marry. What then? Her hosts will have to return to their original poverty. The idea of how to secure to himself the advantages of his young kinswoman's fortune takes possession of the husband's mind. He revolves all manner of means, and gradually murder presents itself as the only way. The horrid suggestion fixes itself in his mind, and at last he communicates it to his wife. At first she resists, then yields to the temptation. The plan is ingenious. The wife is to disappear to America and be given out as dead. The husband will then marry his attractive kinswoman, persuade her to make a will in his favour, poison her and, the fortune secured, rejoin his wife. As if to help this cruel plan, the young lady has developed a sentimental affection for her relative. The wife goes to America, the husband marries the young lady. He commences to poison her, but, in the presence of her youth, beauty and affection for him, relents, hesitates to commit a possibly unnecessary crime. He decides to forget and ignore utterly his wife who is waiting patiently in America. A year passes. The expectant wife gets no sign of her husband's existence. She comes back to Europe, visits under a false name the town in which her faithless husband and his bride are living, discovers the truth and divulges the intended crime to the authorities. A sentence of penal servitude for life rewards this perfidious criminal.[9]

[9] Case of the Scheffer couple at Linz, cited by Sighele.

Derues said to a man who was looking at a picture in the Palais de Justice: "Why study copies of Nature when you can look at such a remarkable original as I?" A judge once told the present writer that he did not go often to the theatre because none of the dramas which he saw on the stage, seemed to him equal in in-

tensity to those of real life which came before him in the course of his duties. The saying that truth is stranger than fiction applies more forcibly to crime than to anything else. But the ordinary man and woman prefer to take their crime romanticised, as it is administered to them in novel or play. The true stories told in this book represent the raw material from which works of art have been and may be yet created. The murder of Mr. Arden of Faversham inspired an Elizabethan tragedy attributed by some critics to Shakespeare. The Peltzer trial helped to inspire Paul Bourget's remarkable novel, "Andre Cornelis." To Italian crime we owe Shelley's "Cenci" and Browning's "The Ring and the Book." Mrs. Manning was the original of the maid Hortense in "Bleak House." Jonathan Wild, Eugene Aram, Deacon Brodie, Thomas Griffiths Wainewright have all been made the heroes of books or plays of varying merit. But it is not only in its stories that crime has served to inspire romance. In the investigation of crime, especially on the broader lines of Continental procedure, we can track to the source the springs of conduct and character, and come near to solving as far as is humanly possible the mystery of human motive. There is always and must be in every crime a terra incognita which, unless we could enter into the very soul of a man, we cannot hope to reach. Thus far may we go, no farther. It is rarely indeed that a man lays bare his whole soul, and even when he does we can never be quite sure that he is telling us all the truth, that he is not keeping back some vital secret. It is no doubt better so, and that it should be left to the writer of imagination to picture for us a man's inmost soul. The study of crime will help him to that end. It will help us also in the ethical appreciation of good and evil in individual conduct, about which our notions have been somewhat obscured by too narrow a definition of what constitutes crime. These themes, touched on but lightly and imperfectly in these pages, are rich in human interest.

And so it is hardly a matter for surprise that the poet and the philosopher sat up late one night talking about murders.

THE LIFE OF CHARLES PEACE

"Charles Peace, or the Adventures of a Notorious Burglar," a large volume published at the time of his death, gives a full and accurate account of the career of Peace side by side with a story of the Family Herald type, of which he is made the hero. "The Life and Trial of Charles Peace" (Sheffield, 1879), "The Romantic Career of a Great Criminal" (by N. Kynaston Gaskell, London 1906), and "The Master Criminal," published recently in London give useful information. I have also consulted some of the newspapers of the time. There is a delightful sketch of Peace in Mr. Charles Whibley's "Book of Scoundrels."

I

HIS EARLY YEARS

Charles Peace told a clergyman who had an interview with him in prison shortly before his execution that he hoped that, after he was gone, he would be entirely forgotten by everybody and his name never mentioned again.

Posterity, in calling over its muster-roll of famous men, has refused to fulfil this pious hope, and Charley Peace stands out as the one great personality among English criminals of the nineteenth century. In Charley Peace alone is revived that good- humoured popularity which in the seventeenth and eighteenth centuries fell to the lot of Claude Duval, Dick Turpin and Jack Sheppard. But Peace has one grievance against posterity; he has endured one humiliation which these heroes have been spared. His name has been omitted from the pages of the "Dictionary of National Biography." From Duval, in the seventeenth, down to the Mannings, Palmer, Arthur Orton, Morgan and Kelly, the bushrangers, in the nineteenth century, many a criminal, far less notable or individual than Charley Peace, finds his or her place in that great record of the past achievements of our countrymen. Room has been denied to perhaps the greatest and most naturally gifted criminal England has produced, one whose character is all the more remarkable for its modesty, its entire freedom from that vanity and vain-gloriousness so common among his class.

The only possible reason that can be suggested for so singular an omission is the fact that in the strict order of alphabetical succession the biography of Charles Peace would have followed immediately on that of George Peabody. It may have been thought that the contrast was too glaring, that even the exigencies of national biography had no right to make the philanthropist Pea-body rub shoulders with man's constant enemy, Peace. To the memory of Peace these few pages can make but poor amends for the supreme injustice, but, by giving a particular and authentic account of his career, they may serve as material for the correction of this grave omission should remorse overtake those responsible for so undeserved a slur on one of the most unruly of England's famous sons.

From the literary point of view Peace was unfortunate even in the hour of his notoriety. In the very year of his trial and execution, the Annual Register, seized with a fit of respectability from which it has never recovered, announced that "the appetite for the strange and marvellous" having considerably abated since the year 1757 when the Register was first published, its "Chronicle," hitherto a rich mine of extraordinary and sensational occurrences, would become henceforth a mere diary of important events. Simultaneously with the curtailment of its "Chronicle," it ceased to give those excellent summaries of celebrated trials which for many years had been a feature of its volumes. The question whether "the appetite for the strange and marvellous" has abated in an appreciable degree with the passing of time and is not perhaps keener than it ever was, is a debatable one. But it is undeniable that the present volumes of the Annual Register have fallen away dismally from the variety and human interest of their predecessors. Of the trial and execution of Peace the volume for 1879 gives but the barest record.

Charles Peace was not born of criminal parents. His father, John Peace, began work as a collier at Burton-on-Trent. Losing his leg in an accident, he joined Wombwell's wild beast show and soon acquired some reputation for his remarkable powers as a tamer of wild animals. About this time Peace married at Rotherham the daughter of a surgeon in the Navy. On the death of a favourite son to whom he had imparted successfully the secrets of his wonderful control over wild beasts of every kind, Mr. Peace gave up lion-taming and settled in Sheffield as a shoemaker.

It was at Sheffield, in the county of Yorkshire, already famous in the annals of crime as the county of John Nevison and Eugene Aram, that Peace first saw the light. On May 14, 1832, there was born to John Peace in Sheffield a son, Charles, the youngest of his family of four. When he grew to boyhood Charles was sent to two schools near Sheffield, where he soon made himself remarkable, not as a scholar, but for his singular aptitude in a variety of other employments such as making paper models, taming cats, constructing a peep-show, and throwing up a heavy ball of shot which he would catch in a leather socket fixed on to his forehead.

The course of many famous men's lives has been changed by what appeared at the time to be an unhappy accident. Who knows what may have been the effect on Charles Peace's subsequent career of an accident he met with in 1846 at some rolling mills, in which he was employed? A piece of red hot steel entered his leg just below the knee, and after eighteen months spent in the Sheffield Infirmary he left it a cripple for life. About this time Peace's father died. Peace and his family were fond of commemorating events of this kind in suitable verse; the death of John Peace was celebrated in the following lines:
"In peace he lived;
In peace he died;
Life was our desire,
But God denied."

Of the circumstances that first led Peace to the commission of crime we know nothing. How far enforced idleness, bad companionship, according to some accounts the influence of a criminally disposed mother, how far his own daring and adventurous temper provoked him to robbery, cannot be determined accurately. His first exploit was the stealing of an old gentleman's gold watch, but he soon passed to greater things. On October 26, 1851, the house of a lady living in Sheffield was broken into and a quantity of her property stolen. Some of it was found in the possession of Peace, and he was arrested. Owing no doubt to a good character for honesty given him by his late employer Peace was let off lightly with a month's imprisonment.

After his release Peace would seem to have devoted himself for a time to music, for which he had always a genuine passion. He taught himself to play tunes on a violin with one string, and at entertainments which he attended was described as "the modern Paganini." In later life when he had attained to wealth and prosperity the violin and the harmonium were a constant source of solace during long winter evenings in Greenwich and Peckham. But playing a one-stringed violin at fairs and public-houses could not be more than a relaxation to a man of Peace's active temper, who had once tasted what many of those who have practised it, describe as the fascination of that particular form of nocturnal adventure known by the unsympathetic name of burglary. Among the exponents of the art Peace was at this time known as a "portico- thief," that is to say one who contrived to get himself on to the portico of a house and from that point of vantage make his entrance into the premises. During the year 1854 the houses of a number of well-to-do residents in and about Sheffield were entered after this fashion, and much valuable property stolen. Peace was arrested, and with him a girl with whom he was keeping company, and his sister, Mary Ann, at that time Mrs. Neil. On October 20, 1854, Peace was sentenced at Doncaster Sessions to four years' penal servitude, and the ladies who had been found in possession of the stolen property to six months apiece. Mrs. Neil did not long survive her misfortune. She would seem to have been married to a brutal and drunken husband, whom Peace thrashed on more than one occasion for ill-treating his sister. After one of these punishments Neil set a bull-dog on to Peace; but Peace caught the dog by the lower jaw and punched it into a state of coma. The death in 1859 of the unhappy Mrs. Neil was lamented in appropriate verse, probably the work of her brother:
"I was so long with pain opprest
That wore my strength away;
It made me long for endless rest
Which never can decay."

On coming out of prison in 1858, Peace resumed his fiddling, but it was now no more than a musical accompaniment to burglary. This had become the serious business of Peace's life, to be pursued, should necessity arise, even to the peril of men's lives. His operations extended beyond the bounds of his native town. The house of a lady living in Manchester was broken into on the night of August 11, 1859, and a substantial booty carried away. This was found the following day concealed in a hole in a field. The police left it undisturbed and awaited the return of the robber. When Peace and another man arrived to carry it away, the officers sprang out on them. Peace, after nearly killing the officer who was trying to arrest him, would have made his escape, had not other policemen come to the rescue. For this crime Peace was sentenced to six years' penal servitude, in spite of a loyal act of perjury on the part of his aged mother, who came all the way from Sheffield to swear that he had been with her there on the night of the crime.

He was released from prison again in 1864, and returned to Sheffield. Things did not prosper with him there, and he went back to Manchester. In 1866 he was caught in the act of burglary at a house in Lower Broughton. He admitted that at the time he was fuddled with whisky; otherwise his capture would have been more difficult and dangerous. Usually a temperate man, Peace realised on this occasion the value of sobriety even in burglary, and never after allowed intemperance to interfere with his success. A sentence of eight years' penal servitude at Manchester Assizes on December 3, 1866, emphasised this wholesome lesson.

Whilst serving this sentence Peace emulated Jack Sheppard in a daring attempt to escape from Wakefield prison. Being engaged on some repairs, he smuggled a small ladder into his cell. With the help of a saw made out of some tin, he cut a hole through the ceiling of the cell, and was about to get out on to the roof when a warder came in. As the latter attempted to seize the ladder Peace knocked him down, ran along the wall of the prison, fell off on the inside owing to the looseness of the bricks, slipped into the governor's house where he changed his clothes, and there, for an hour and a half, waited for an opportunity to escape. This was denied him, and he was recaptured in the governor's bedroom. The prisons at Millbank, Chatham and Gibraltar were all visited by Peace before his final release in 1872. At Chatham he is said to have taken part in a mutiny and been flogged for his pains.

On his liberation from prison Peace rejoined his family in Sheffield. He was now a husband and father. In 1859 he had taken to wife a widow of the name of Hannah Ward. Mrs. Ward was already the mother of a son, Willie. Shortly after her marriage with Peace she gave birth to a daughter, and during his fourth term of imprisonment presented him with a son. Peace never saw this child, who died before his release. But, true to the family custom, on his return from prison the untimely death of little "John Charles" was commemorated by the printing of a funeral card in his honour, bearing the following sanguine verses:
"Farewell, my dear son, by us all beloved,
Thou art gone to dwell in the mansions above.
In the bosom of Jesus Who sits on the throne
Thou art anxiously waiting to welcome us home."

Whether from a desire not to disappoint little John Charles, for some reason or other the next two or three years of Peace's career would seem to have been spent in an endeavour to earn an honest living by picture framing, a trade in which Peace, with that skill he displayed in whatever he turned his hand to, was remarkably proficient. In Sheffield his children attended the Sunday School. Though he never went to church himself, he was an avowed believer in both God and the devil. As he said, however, that he feared neither, no great reliance could be placed on the restraining force of such a belief to a man of Peace's daring spirit. There was only too good reason to fear that little John Charles' period of waiting would be a prolonged one.

In 1875 Peace moved from Sheffield itself to the suburb of Darnall. Here Peace made the acquaintance—a fatal acquaintance, as it turned out—of a Mr. and Mrs. Dyson. Dyson was a civil engineer. He had spent some years in America, where, in 1866, he married.

Toward the end of 1873 or the beginning of 1874, he came to England with his wife, and obtained a post on the North Eastern Railway. He was a tall man, over six feet in height, extremely thin, and gentlemanly in his bearing. His engagement with the North Eastern Railway terminated abruptly owing to Dyson's failing to appear at a station to which he had been sent on duty.

It was believed at the time by those associated with Dyson that this unlooked-for dereliction of duty had its cause in domestic trouble. Since the year 1875, the year in which Peace came to Darnall, the domestic peace of Mr. Dyson had been rudely disturbed by this same ugly little picture-framer who lived a few doors away from the Dysons' house. Peace had got to know the Dysons, first as a tradesman, then as a friend. To what degree of intimacy he attained with Mrs. Dyson it is difficult to determine. In that lies the mystery of the case Mrs. Dyson is described as an attractive woman, "buxom and blooming"; she was dark-haired, and about twenty-five years of age. In an interview with the Vicar of Darnall a few days before his execution, Peace asserted positively that Mrs. Dyson had been his mistress. Mrs. Dyson as strenuously denied the fact. There was no question that on one occasion Peace and Mrs. Dyson had been photographed together, that he had given her a ring, and that he had been in the habit of going to music halls and public-houses with Mrs. Dyson, who was a woman of intemperate habits.

Peace had introduced Mrs. Dyson to his wife and daughter, and on one occasion was said to have taken her to his mother's house, much to the old lady's indignation. If there were not many instances of ugly men who have been notably successful with women, one might doubt the likelihood of Mrs. Dyson falling a victim to the charms of Charles Peace. But Peace, for all his ugliness, could be wonderfully ingratiating when he chose. According to Mrs. Dyson, Peace was a demon, "beyond the power of even a Shakespeare to paint," who persecuted her with his attentions, and, when he found them rejected, devoted all his malignant energies to making the lives of her husband and herself unbearable. According to Peace's story he was a slighted lover who had been treated by Mrs. Dyson with contumely and ingratitude.

Whether to put a stop to his wife's intimacy with Peace, or to protect himself against the latter's wanton persecution, sometime about the end of June, 1876, Dyson threw over into the garden of Peace's house a card, on which was written: "Charles Peace is requested not to interfere with my family." On July 1

Peace met Mr. Dyson in the street, and tried to trip him up. The same night he came up to Mrs. Dyson, who was talking with some friends, and threatened in coarse and violent language to blow out her brains and those of her husband. In consequence of these incidents Mr. Dyson took out a summons against Peace, for whose apprehension a warrant was issued. To avoid the consequences of this last step Peace left Darnall for Hull, where he opened an eating-shop, presided over by Mrs. Peace.

But he himself was not idle. From Hull he went to Manchester on business, and in Manchester he committed his first murder. Entering the grounds of a gentleman's home at Whalley Range, about midnight on August 1, he was seen by two policemen. One of them, Constable Cock, intercepted him as he was trying to escape.

Peace took out his revolver and warned Cock to stand back. The policeman came on. Peace fired, but deliberately wide of him. Cock, undismayed, drew out his truncheon, and made for the burglar. Peace, desperate, determined not to be caught, fired again, this time fatally. Cock's comrade heard the shots, but before he could reach the side of the dying man, Peace had made off. He returned to Hull, and there learned shortly after, to his intense relief, that two brothers, John and William Habron, living near the scene of the murder, had been arrested and charged with the killing of Constable Cock.

If the Dysons thought that they had seen the last of Peace, they were soon to be convinced to the contrary. Peace had not forgotten his friends at Darnall. By some means or other he was kept informed of all their doings, and on one occasion was seen by Mrs. Dyson lurking near her home. To get away from him the Dysons determined to leave Darnall. They took a house at Banner Cross, another suburb of Sheffield, and on October 29 moved into their new home. One of the first persons Mrs. Dyson saw on arriving at Banner Cross was Peace himself. "You see," he said, "I am here to annoy you, and I'll annoy you wherever you go." Later, Peace and a friend passed Mr. Dyson in the street. Peace took out his revolver. "If he offers to come near me," said he, "I will make him stand back." But Mr. Dyson took no notice of Peace and passed on. He had another month to live.

Whatever the other motives of Peace may have been—unreasoning passion, spite, jealousy, or revenge it must not be forgotten that Dyson, by procuring a warrant against Peace, had driven him from his home in Sheffield. This Peace resented bitterly. According to the statements of many witnesses, he was at this time in a state of constant irritation and excitement on the Dyson's account. He struck his daughter because she alluded in a way he did not like to his relations with Mrs. Dyson. Peace always believed in corporal chastisement as a means of keeping order at home. Pleasant and entertaining as he could be, he was feared. It was very dangerous to incur his resentment. "Be sure," said his wife, "you do nothing to offend our Charley, or you will suffer for it." Dyson beyond a doubt had offended "our Charley." But for the moment Peace was interested more immediately in the fate of John and William Habron, who were about to stand their trial for the murder of Constable Cock at Whalley Range.

The trial commenced at the Manchester Assizes before Mr. Justice (now Lord) Lindley on Monday, November 27. John Habron was acquitted.

The case against William Habron depended to a great extent on the fact that he, as well as his brother, had been heard to threaten to "do for" the murdered man, to shoot the "little bobby." Cock was a zealous young officer of twenty-three years of age, rather too eager perhaps in the discharge of his duty. In July of 1876 he had taken out summonses against John and William Habron, young fellows who had been several years in the employment of a nurseryman in Whalley Range, for being drunk and disorderly. On July 27 William was fined five shillings, and on August 1, the day of Cock's murder, John had been fined half a sovereign. Between these two dates the Habrons had been heard to threaten to "do for" Cock if he were not more careful. Other facts relied upon by the prosecution were that William Habron had inquired from a gunsmith the price of some cartridges a day or two before the murder; that two cartridge percussion caps had been found in the pocket of a waistcoat given to William Habron by his employer, who swore that they could not have been there while it was in his possession; that the other constable on duty with Cock stated that a man he had seen lurking near the house about twelve o'clock on the night of the murder appeared to be William Habron's age, height and complexion, and resembled him in general appearance; and that the boot on Habron's left foot, which was "wet and sludgy" at the time of his arrest, corresponded in certain respects with the footprints of the murderer. The prisoner did not help himself by an ineffective attempt to prove an alibi. The Judge was clearly not impressed by the strength of the case for the prosecution. He pointed out to the jury that neither the evidence of identification nor that of the footprint went very far. As to the latter, what evidence was there to show that it had been made on the night of the murder? If it had been made the day before, then the defence had proved that it could not have been Habron's. He called their attention to the facts that Habron bore a good character, that, when arrested on the night of the murder, he was in bed, and that no firearms had been traced to him. In spite, however, of the summing-up the jury convicted William Habron, but recommended him to mercy. The Judge without comment sentenced him to death. The Manchester Guardian expressed its entire concurrence with the verdict of the jury. "Few persons," it wrote, "will be found to dispute the justice of the conclusions reached." However, a few days later it opened its columns to a number of letters protesting against the unsatisfactory nature of the conviction. On December 6 a meeting of some forty gentlemen was held, at which it was resolved to petition Mr. Cross, the Home Secretary, to reconsider the sentence. Two days before the day of execution Habron was granted a respite, and later his sentence commuted to one of penal servitude for life. And so a tragic and irrevocable miscarriage of justice was happily averted.

Peace liked attending trials. The fact that in Habron's case he was the real murderer would seem to have made him the more eager not to miss so unique an experience. Accordingly he went from Hull to Manchester, and was present in court during the two days that the trial lasted. No sooner had he heard the innocent man condemned to death than he left Manchester for Sheffield—now for all he knew a double murderer.

It is a question whether, on the night of November 28, Peace met Mrs. Dyson at an inn in one of the suburbs of Sheffield. In any case, the next morning, Wednesday, the 29th, to his mother's surprise Peace walked into her house. He said that he had come to Sheffield for the fair. The afternoon of that day Peace spent in a public-house at Ecclesall, entertaining the customers by playing tunes on a poker suspended from a piece of strong string, from which he made music by beating it with a short stick. The musician was rewarded by drinks. It took very little drink to excite Peace. There was dancing, the fun grew fast and furious, as the strange musician beat out tune after tune on his fantastic instrument.

At six o'clock the same evening a thin, grey-haired, insignificant-looking man in an evident state of unusual excitement called to see the Rev. Mr. Newman, Vicar of Ecclesall, near Banner Cross. Some five weeks before, this insignificant-looking man had visited Mr. Newman, and made certain statements in regard to the character of a Mr. and Mrs. Dyson who had come to live in the parish. The vicar had asked for proof of these statements. These proofs his visitor now produced. They consisted of a number of calling cards and photographs, some of them alleged to be in the handwriting of Mrs. Dyson, and showing her intimacy with Peace. The man made what purported to be a confession to Mr. Newman. Dyson, he said, had become jealous of him, whereupon Peace had suggested to Mrs. Dyson that they should give her husband something to be jealous about. Out of this proposal their intimacy had sprung. Peace spoke of Mrs. Dyson in terms of forgiveness, but his wrath against Dyson was extreme. He complained bitterly that by taking proceedings against him, Dyson had driven him to break up his home and become a fugitive in the land. He should follow the Dysons, he said, wherever they might go; he believed that they were at that moment intending to take further proceedings against him. As he left, Peace said that he should not go and see the Dysons that night, but would call on a friend of his, Gregory, who lived next door to them in Banner Cross Terrace. It was now about a quarter to seven.

Peace went to Gregory's house, but his friend was not at home. The lure of the Dysons was irresistible. A little after eight o'clock Peace was watching the house from a passage-way that led up to the backs of the houses on the terrace. He saw Mrs. Dyson come out of the back door, and go to an outhouse some few yards distant. He waited. As soon as she opened the door to come out, Mrs. Dyson found herself confronted by Peace, holding his revolver in his hand. "Speak," he said, "or I'll fire." Mrs. Dyson in terror went back. In the meantime Dyson, hearing the disturbance, came quickly into the yard. Peace made for the passage. Dyson followed him. Peace fired once, the shot striking the lintel of the passage doorway. Dyson undaunted, still pursued. Then Peace, according to his custom, fired a second time, and Dyson fell, shot through the temple. Mrs. Dyson, who had come into the yard again on hearing the first shot, rushed to her husband's side, calling out: "Murder! You villain! You have shot my husband." Two hours later Dyson was dead.

After firing the second shot Peace had hurried down; the passage into the roadway. He stood there hesitating a moment, until the cries of Mrs. Dyson warned him of his danger. He crossed the road, climbed a wall, and made his way back to Sheffield. There he saw his mother and brother, told them that he had shot Mr. Dyson, and bade them a hasty good-bye. He then walked to Attercliffe Railway Station, and took a ticket for Beverley. Something suspicious in the manner of the booking-clerk made him change his place of destination. Instead of going to Beverley that night he got out of the train at Normanton and went on to York. He spent the remainder of the night in the station yard. He took the first train in the morning for Beverley, and from there travelled via Collingham to Hull. He went straight to the eating-house kept by his wife, and demanded some dinner. He had hardly commenced to eat it when he heard two detectives come into the front shop and ask his wife if a man called Charles Peace was lodging with her. Mrs. Peace said that that was her husband's name, but that she had not seen him for two months. The detectives proposed to search the house. Some customers in the shop told them that if they had any business with Mrs. Peace, they ought to go round to the side door. The polite susceptibility of these customers gave Peace time to slip up to a back room, get out on to an adjoining roof, and hide behind a chimney stack, where he remained until the detectives had finished an exhaustive search. So importunate were the officers in Hull that once again during the day Peace had to repeat this experience. For some three weeks, however, he contrived to remain in Hull. He shaved the grey beard he was wearing at the time of Dyson's murder, dyed his hair, put on a pair of spectacles, and for the first time made use of his singular power of contorting his features in such a way as to change altogether the character of his face. But the hue and cry after him was unremitting. There was a price of L100 on his head, and the following description of him was circulated by the police:

"Charles Peace wanted for murder on the night of the 29th inst. He is thin and slightly built, from fifty-five to sixty years of age. Five feet four inches or five feet high; grey (nearly white) hair, beard and whiskers. He lacks use of three fingers of left hand, walks with his legs rather wide apart, speaks somewhat peculiarly as though his tongue were too large for his mouth, and is a great boaster. He is a picture-frame maker. He occasionally cleans and repairs clocks and watches and sometimes deals in oleographs, engravings and pictures. He has been in penal servitude for burglary in Manchester. He has lived in Manchester, Salford, and Liverpool and Hull."

This description was altered later and Peace's age given as forty-six. As a matter of fact he was only forty-four at this time, but he looked very much older. Peace had lost one of his fingers. He said that it had been shot off by a man with whom he had quarrelled, but it was believed to be more likely that he had himself shot it off accidentally in handling one of his revolvers. It was to conceal this obvious means of identification that Peace made himself the false arm which he was in the habit of wearing. This was of gutta percha, with a hole down the middle of it into which he passed his arm; at the end was a steel plate to which was fixed a hook; by means of this hook Peace could wield a fork and do other dexterous feats.

Marked man as he was, Peace felt it dangerous to stay longer in Hull than he could help. During the closing days of the year 1876 and the beginning of 1877, Peace was perpetually on the move. He left Hull for Doncaster, and from there travelled to London. On arriving at King's Cross he took the underground railway to Paddington, and from there a train to Bristol. At the beginning of January he left Bristol for Bath, and from Bath, in the company of a sergeant of police, travelled by way of Didcot to Oxford. The officer had in his custody a young woman charged with stealing L40. Peace and the sergeant discussed the case during the journey. "He seemed a smart chap," said Peace in re-lating the circumstances, "but not smart enough to know me." From Oxford he went to Birmingham, where he stayed four or five days, then a week in Derby, and on January 9th he arrived in Nottingham.

Here Peace found a convenient lodging at the house of one, Mrs. Adamson, a lady who received stolen goods and on occasion indicated or organised suitable opportunities for acquiring them.

She lived in a low part of the town known as the Marsh. It was at her house that Peace met the woman who was to become his mistress and subsequently betray his identity to the police. Her maiden name was Susan Gray.

She was at this time about thirty-five years of age, described as "taking" in appearance, of a fair complexion, and rather well educated. She had led a somewhat chequered married life with a gentleman named Bailey, from whom she continued in receipt of a weekly allowance until she passed under the protection of Peace. Her first meeting with her future lover took place on the occasion of Peace inviting Mrs. Adamson to dispose of a box of cigars for him, which that good woman did at a charge of something like thirty per cent. At first Peace gave himself out to Mrs. Bailey as a hawker, but before long he openly acknowledged his real character as an accomplished burglar. With characteristic insistence Peace declared his passion for Mrs. Bailey by threatening to shoot her if she did not become his. Anxious friends sent for her to soothe the distracted man. Peace had been drowning care with the help of Irish whiskey. He asked "his pet" if she were not glad to see him, to which the lady replied with possible sarcasm: "Oh, particularly, very, I like you so much." Next day Peace apologised for his rude behaviour of the previous evening, and so melted the heart of Mrs. Bailey that she consented to become his mistress, and from that moment discarding the name of Bailey is known to history as Mrs. Thompson.

Life in Nottingham was varied pleasantly by burglaries carried out with the help of information supplied by Mrs. Adamson. In the June of 1877 Peace was nearly detected in stealing, at the request of that worthy, some blankets, but by flourishing his revolver he contrived to get away, and, soon after, returned for a season to Hull. Here this hunted murderer, with L100 reward on his head, took rooms for Mrs. Thompson and himself at the house of a sergeant of police. One day Mrs. Peace, who was still keeping her shop in Hull, received a pencilled note saying, "I am waiting to see you just up Anlaby Road." She and her stepson, Willie Ward, went to the appointed spot, and there to their astonishment stood her husband, a distinguished figure in black coat and trousers, top hat, velvet waistcoat, with stick, kid gloves, and a pretty little fox terrier by his side. Peace told them of his whereabouts in the town, but did not disclose to them the fact that his mistress was there also. To the police sergeant with whom he lodged, Peace described himself as an agent. But a number of sensational and successful burglaries at the houses of Town Councillors and other well-to-do citizens of Hull revealed the presence in their midst of no ordinary robber. Peace had some narrow escapes, but with the help of his revolver, and on one occasion the pusillanimity of a policeman, he succeeded in getting away in safety. The bills offering a reward for his capture were still to be seen in the shop windows of Hull, so after a brief but brilliant adventure Peace and Mrs. Thompson returned to Nottingham.

Here, as the result of further successful exploits, Peace found a reward of L50 offered for his capture. On one occasion the detectives came into the room where Peace and his mistress were in bed. After politely expressing his surprise at seeing "Mrs. Bailey" in such a situation, one of the officers asked Peace his name. He gave it as John Ward, and described himself as a hawker of spectacles. He refused to get up and dress in the presence of the detectives who were obliging enough to go downstairs and wait his convenience. Peace seized the opportunity to slip out of the house and get away to another part of the town. From there he sent a note to Mrs. Thompson insisting on her joining him. He soon after left Nottingham, paid another brief visit to Hull, but finding that his wife's shop was still frequented by the police, whom he designated freely as "a lot of fools," determined to quit the North for good and begin life afresh in the ampler and safer field of London.

II

PEACE IN LONDON

Peace's career in London extended over nearly two years, but they were years of copious achievement. In that comparatively short space of time, by the exercise of that art, to his natural gifts for which he had now added the wholesome tonic of experience, Peace passed from a poor and obscure lodging in a slum in Lambeth to the state and opulence of a comfortable suburban residence in Peckham. These were the halcyon days of Peace's enterprise in life. From No. 25 Stangate Street, Lambeth, the dealer in musical instruments, as Peace now described himself, sallied forth night after night, and in Camberwell and other parts of South London reaped the reward of skill and vigilance in entering other people's houses and carrying off their property. Though in the beginning there appeared to be but few musical instruments in Stangate Street to justify his reputed business, "Mr. Thompson," as he now called himself, explained that he was not wholly dependent on his business, as Mrs. Thompson "had money."

So successful did the business prove that at the Christmas of 1877 Peace invited his daughter and her betrothed to come from Hull and spend the festive season with him. This, in spite of the presence of Mrs. Thompson, they consented to do. Peace, in a top hat and grey ulster, showed them the sights of London, always inquiring politely of a policeman if he found himself in any difficulty. At the end of the visit Peace gave his consent to his daughter's marriage with Mr. Bolsover, and before parting gave the young couple some excellent advice. For more reasons than one Peace was anxious to unite under the same roof Mrs. Peace and Mrs. Thompson. Things still prospering, Peace found himself able to remove from Lambeth to Crane Court, Greenwich, and before long to take a couple of adjoining houses in Billingsgate Street in the same district. These he furnished in style. In one he lived with Mrs. Thompson, while Mrs. Peace and her son, Willie, were persuaded after some difficulty to leave Hull and come to London to dwell in the other.

But Greenwich was not to the taste of Mrs. Thompson. To gratify her wish, Peace, some time in May, 1877, removed the whole party to a house, No. 5, East Terrace, Evelina Road, Peckham. He paid thirty pounds a year for it, and obtained permission to build a stable for his pony and trap. When asked for his references, Peace replied by inviting the agent to dine with him at his house in Greenwich, a proceeding that seems to have removed all doubt from the agent's mind as to the desirability of the tenant.

This now famous house in Peckham was of the ordinary type of suburban villa, with basement, ground floor, and one above; there were steps up to the front door, and a bow window to the front sitting-room. A garden at the back of the house ran down to the Chatham and Dover railway line. It was by an entrance at the back that Peace drove his horse and trap into the stable which he had erected in the garden. Though all living in the same house, Mrs. Peace, who passed as Mrs. Ward, and her son, Willie, inhabited the basement, while Peace and Mrs. Thompson occupied the best rooms on the ground floor. The house was fitted with Venetian blinds. In the drawing-room stood a good walnut suite of furniture; a Turkey carpet, gilded mirrors, a piano, an inlaid Spanish guitar, and, by the side of an elegant table, the beaded slippers of the good master of the house completed the elegance of the apartment. Everything confirmed Mr. Thompson's description of himself as a gentleman of independent means with a taste for scientific inventions. In association with a person of the name of Brion, Peace did, as a fact, patent an invention for raising sunken vessels, and it is said that in pursuing their project, the two men had obtained an interview with Mr. Plimsoll at the House of Commons. In any case, the Patent Gazette records the following grant:

"2635 Henry Fersey Brion, 22 Philip Road, Peckham Rye, London, S.E., and John Thompson, 5 East Terrace, Evelina Road, Peckham Rye, London, S.E., for an invention for raising sunken vessels by the displacement of water within the vessels by air and gases."

At the time of his final capture Peace was engaged on other inventions, among them a smoke helmet for firemen, an improved brush for washing railway carriages, and a form of hydraulic tank. To the anxious policeman who, seeing a light in Mr. Thompson's house in the small hours of the morning, rang the bell to warn the old gentleman of the possible presence of burglars, this business of scientific inventions was sufficient explana- tion.

Socially Mr. Thompson became quite a figure in the neighbourhood. He attended regularly the Sunday evening services at the parish church, and it must have been a matter of anxious concern to dear Mr. Thompson that during his stay in Peckham the vicarage was broken into by a burglar and an unsuccessful attempt made to steal the communion plate which was kept there.

Mr. Thompson was generous in giving and punctual in paying. He had his eccentricities. His love of birds and animals was remarkable. Cats, dogs, rabbits, guinea-pigs, canaries, parrots and cockatoos all found hospitality under his roof. It was certainly eccentricity in Mr. Thompson that he should wear different coloured wigs; and that his dark complexion should suggest the use of walnut juice. His love of music was evinced by the number of violins, banjoes, guitars, and other musical instruments that adorned his drawing-room. Tea and music formed the staple of the evening entertainments which Mr. and Mrs. Thompson would give occasionally to friendly neighbours. Not that the pleasures of conversation were neglected wholly in favour of art. The host was a voluble and animated talker, his face and body illustrating by appropriate twists and turns the force of his comments. The Russo-Turkish war, then raging, was a favourite theme of Mr. Thompson's. He asked, as we are still asking, what Christianity and civilisation mean by countenancing the horrors of war. He considered the British Government in the highest degree guilty in supporting the cruel Turks, a people whose sobriety seemed to him to be their only virtue, against the Christian Russians. He was confident that our Ministers would be punished for opposing the only Power which had shown any sympathy with suffering races. About ten o'clock Mr. Thompson, whose health, he said, could not stand late hours, would bid his guests good night, and by half-past ten the front door of No. 5, East Terrace, Evelina Road, would be locked and bolted, and the house plunged in darkness.

Not that it must be supposed that family life at No. 5, East Terrace, was without its jars. These were due chiefly to the drunken habits of Mrs. Thompson. Peace was willing to overlook his mistress' failing as long as it was confined to the house. But Mrs. Thompson had an unfortunate habit of slipping out in an intoxicated condition, and chattering with the neighbours. As she was the repository of many a dangerous secret the inconvenience of her habit was serious. Peace was not the man to hesitate in the face of danger. On these occasions Mrs. Thompson was followed by Peace or his wife, brought back home and soundly beaten. To Hannah Peace there must have been some satisfaction in spying on her successful rival, for, in her own words, Peace never refused his mistress anything; he did not care what she cost him in dress; "she could swim in gold if she liked." Mrs. Thompson herself admitted that with the exception of such punishment as she brought on herself by her inebriety, Peace was always fond of her, and treated her with great kindness. It was she to whom he would show with pride the proceeds of his nightly labours, to whom he would look for a smile when he returned home from his expeditions, haggard and exhausted

Through all dangers and difficulties the master was busy in the practice of his art. Night after night, with few intervals of repose, he would sally forth on a plundering adventure. If the job was a distant one, he would take his pony and trap. Peace was devoted to his pony, Tommy, and great was his grief when at the end of six months' devotion to duty Tommy died after a few days' sickness, during which his master attended him with un-

remitting care. Tommy had been bought in Greenwich for fourteen guineas, part of a sum of two hundred and fifty pounds which Peace netted from a rich haul of silver and bank-notes taken from a house in Denmark Hill. Besides the pony and trap, Peace would take with him on these expeditions a violin case containing his tools; at other times they would be stuffed into odd pockets made for the purpose in his trousers. These tools consisted of ten in all—a skeleton key, two pick-locks, a centre-bit, gimlet, gouge, chisel, vice jemmy and knife; a portable ladder, a revolver and life preserver completed his equipment.

The range of Peace's activities extended as far as Southampton, Portsmouth and Southsea; but the bulk of his work was done in Blackheath, Streatham, Denmark Hill, and other suburbs of South London. Many dramatic stories are told of his exploits, but they rest for the most part on slender foundation. On one occasion, in getting on to a portico, he fell, and was impaled on some railings, fortunately in no vital part. His career as a burglar in London lasted from the beginning of the year 1877 until October, 1878. During that time this wanted man, under the very noses of the police, exercised with complete success his art as a burglar, working alone, depending wholly on his own mental and physical gifts, disposing in absolute secrecy of the proceeds of his work, and living openly the life of a respectable and industrious old gentleman.

All the while the police were busily seeking Charles Peace, the murderer of Mr. Dyson. Once or twice they came near to capturing him. On one occasion a detective who had known Peace in Yorkshire met him in Farringdon Road, and pursued him up the steps of Holborn Viaduct, but just as the officer, at the top of the steps, reached out and was on the point of grabbing his man, Peace with lightning agility slipped through his fingers and disappeared. The police never had a shadow of suspicion that Mr. Thompson of Peckham was Charles Peace of Sheffield. They knew the former only as a polite and chatty old gentleman of a scientific turn of mind, who drove his own pony and trap, and had a fondness for music and keeping pet animals.

Peace made the mistake of outstaying his welcome in the neighbourhood of South-East London. Perhaps he hardly realised the extent to which his fame was spreading. During the last three months of Peace's career, Blackheath was agog at the number of successful burglaries committed in the very midst of its peaceful residents. The vigilance of the local police was aroused, the officers on night duty were only too anxious to ef- fect the capture of the mysterious criminal.

About two o'clock in the morning of October 10, 1878, a police constable, Robinson by name, saw a light appear suddenly in a window at the back of a house in St. John's Park, Blackheath, the residence of a Mr. Burness. Had the looked-for opportunity arrived? Was the mysterious visitor, the disturber of the peace of Blackheath, at his burglarious employment? Without delay Robinson summoned to his aid two of his colleagues. One of them went round to the front of the house and rang the bell, the other waited in the road outside, while Robinson stayed in the garden at the back. No sooner had the bell rung than Robinson saw a man come from the dining-room window which opened on to the garden, and make quickly down the path. Robinson followed him. The man turned; "Keep back!" he said, "or by God I'll shoot you!" Robinson came on. The man fired three shots from a revolver, all of which passed close to the officer's head. Robinson made another rush for him, the man fired another shot. It missed its mark. The constable closed with his would-be assassin, and struck him in the face. "I'll settle you this time," cried the man, and fired a fifth shot, which went through Robinson's arm just above the elbow. But, in spite of his wound, the valiant officer held his prisoner, succeeded in flinging him to the ground, and catching hold of the revolver that hung round the burglar's wrist, hit him on the head with it. Immediately after the other two constables came to the help of their colleague, and the struggling desperado was secured.

Little did the police as they searched their battered and moaning prisoner realise the importance of their capture. When next morning Peace appeared before the magistrate at Greenwich Police Court he was not described by name—he had refused to give any— but as a half-caste about sixty years of age, of repellant aspect. He was remanded for a week. The first clue to the identity of their prisoner was afforded by a letter which Peace, unable apparently to endure the loneliness and suspense of prison any longer, wrote to his co-inventor Mr. Brion. It is dated November 2, and is signed "John Ward." Peace was disturbed at the absence of all news from his family. Immediately after his arrest, the home in Peckham had been broken up. Mrs. Thompson and Mrs. Peace, taking with them some large boxes, had gone first to the house of a sister of Mrs. Thompson's in Nottingham, and a day or two later Mrs. Peace had left Nottingham for Sheffield. There she went to a house in Hazel Road, occupied by her son-in- law Bolsover, a working collier.[10]

[10] Later, Mrs. Peace was arrested and charged with being in possession of stolen property. She was taken to London and tried at the Old Bailey before Mr. Commissioner Kerr, but acquitted on the ground of her having acted under the compulsion of her husband.

It was no doubt to get news of his family that Peace wrote to Brion. But the letters are sufficiently ingenious. Peace represents himself as a truly penitent sinner who has got himself into a most unfortunate and unexpected "mess" by giving way to drink. The spelling of the letters is exaggeratedly illiterate. He asks Mr. Brion to take pity on him and not despise him as "his own famery has don," to write him a letter to "hease his trobel hart," if possible to come and see him. Mr. Brion complied with the request of the mysterious "John Ward," and on arriving at Newgate where Peace was awaiting trial, found himself in the presence of his friend and colleague, Mr. Thompson.

In the meantime the police were getting hot on the scent of the identity of "John Ward" with the great criminal who in spite of all their efforts had eluded them for two years. The honour and profit of putting the police on the right scent were claimed by Mrs. Thompson. To her Peace had contrived to get a letter conveyed about the same time that he wrote to Mr. Brion. It is addressed to his "dearly beloved wife." He asks pardon for the "drunken madness" that has involved him in his present trouble, and gives her the names of certain witnesses whom he would wish to be called to prove his independent means and his dealings in musical instruments. It is, he writes, his first offence, and as he has "never been in prison before," begs her not to feel it a disgrace to come and see him there. But Peace was leaning on a broken reed. Loyalty does not appear to have been Susan Thompson's strong point. In her own words she "was not of the sentimental sort." The "traitress Sue," as she is called by chroniclers of the time, had fallen a victim to the wiles of the police. Since, after Peace's arrest, she had been in possession of a certain amount of stolen property, it was easier no doubt to persuade her to be frank.

In any case, we find that on February 5, 1879, the day after Peace had been sentenced to death for the murder of Dyson, Mrs. Thompson appealed to the Treasury for the reward of L100 offered for Peace's conviction. She based her application on information which she said she had supplied to the police officers in charge of the case on November 5 in the previous year, the very day on which Peace had first written to her from Newgate. In reply to her letter the Treasury referred "Mrs. S. Bailey, alias Thompson," to the Home Office, but whether she received from that office the price of blood history does not relate.

The police scouted the idea that any revelation of hers had assisted them to identify "John Ward" with Charles Peace. They said that it was information given them in Peckham, no doubt by Mr. Brion, who, on learning the deplorable character of his coadjutor, had placed himself unreservedly in their hands, which first set them on the track. From Peckham they went to Nottingham, where they no doubt came across Sue Thompson, and thence to Sheffield, where on November 6 they visited the house in Hazel Road, occupied by Mrs. Peace and her daughter, Mrs. Bolsover. There they found two of the boxes which Mrs. Peace had brought with her from Peckham. Besides stolen property, these boxes contained evidence of the identity of Ward with Peace. A constable who had known Peace well in Sheffield was sent to Newgate, and taken into the yard where the prisoners awaiting trial were exercising. As they passed round, the constable pointed to the fifth man: "That's Peace," he said, "I'd know him anywhere." The man left the ranks and, coming up to the constable, asked earnestly, "What do you want me for?" but the Governor ordered him to go on with his walk.

It was as John Ward, alias Charles Peace, that Peace, on November 19, 1878, was put on his trial for burglary and the attempted murder of Police Constable Robinson, at the Old Bailey before Mr. Justice Hawkins. His age was given in the calendar as sixty, though Peace was actually forty-six. The evidence against the prisoner was clear enough. All Mr. Montagu Williams could urge in his defence was that Peace had never intended to kill the officer, merely to frighten him. The jury found Peace guilty of attempted murder. Asked if he had anything to say why judgment should not be passed upon him, he addressed the Judge. He protested that he had not been fairly dealt with, that he never intended to kill the prosecutor, that the pistol was one that went off very easily, and that the last shot had been fired by accident. "I really did not know," he said, "that the pistol was loaded, and I hope, my lord, that you will have mercy on me. I feel that I have disgraced myself, I am not fit either to live or die. I am not prepared to meet my God, but still I feel that my career has been made to appear much worse than it really is. Oh, my lord, do have mercy on me; do give me one chance of repenting and of preparing to meet my God. Do, my lord, have mercy on me; and I assure you that you shall never repent it. As you hope for mercy yourself at the hands of the great God, do have mercy on me, and give me a chance of redeeming my character and preparing myself to meet my God. I pray, and beseech you to have mercy upon me."

Peace's assumption of pitiable senility, sustained throughout the trial, though it imposed on Sir Henry Hawkins, failed to melt his heart. He told Peace that he did not believe his statement that he had fired the pistol merely to frighten the constable; had not Robinson guarded his head with his arm he would have been wounded fatally, and Peace condemned to death. He did not consider it necessary, he said, to make an inquiry into Peace's antecedents; he was a desperate burglar, and there was an end of the matter. Notwithstanding his age,

Mr. Justice Hawkins felt it his duty to sentence him to penal servitude for life. The severity of the sentence was undoubtedly a painful surprise to Peace; to a man of sixty years of age it would be no doubt less terrible, but to a man of forty-six it was crushing.

Not that Peace was fated to serve any great part of his sentence.

With as little delay as possible he was to be called on to answer to the murder of Arthur Dyson. The buxom widow of the murdered man had been found in America, whither she had returned after her husband's death. She was quite ready to come to England to give evidence against her husband's murderer. On January 17, 1879, Peace was taken from Pentonville prison, where he was serving his sentence, and conveyed by an early morning train to Sheffield. There at the Town Hall he appeared before the stipendiary magistrate, and was charged with the murder of Arthur Dyson. When he saw Mrs. Dyson enter the witness box and tell her story of the crime, he must have realised that his case was desperate. Her cross-examination was adjourned to the next hearing, and Peace was taken back to London. On the 22nd, the day of the second hearing in Sheffield, an enormous crowd had assembled outside the Town Hall. Inside the court an anxious and expectant audiience{sic}, among them Mrs. Dyson, in the words of a con-

temporary reporter, "stylish and cheerful," awaited the appearance of the protagonist. Great was the disappointment and eager the excitement when the stipendiary came into the court about a quarter past ten and stated that Peace had attempted to escape that morning on the journey from London to Sheffield, and that in consequence of his injuries the case would be adjourned for eight days.

What had happened was this. Peace had left King's Cross by the 5.15 train that morning, due to arrive at Sheffield at 8.45. From the very commencement of the journey he had been wilful and troublesome. He kept making excuses for leaving the carriage whenever the train stopped. To obviate this nuisance the two warders, in whose charge he was, had provided themselves with little bags which Peace could use when he wished and then throw out of the window. Just after the train passed Worksop, Peace asked for one of the bags. When the window was lowered to allow the bag to be thrown away, Peace with lightning agility took a flying leap through it. One of the warders caught him by the left foot. Peace, hanging from the carriage, grasped the footboard with his hands and kept kicking the warder as hard as he could with his right foot. The other warder, unable to get to the window to help his colleague, was making vain efforts to stop the train by pulling the communication cord. For two miles the train ran on, Peace struggling desperately to escape. At last he succeeded in kicking off his left shoe, and dropped on to the line. The train ran on another mile until, with the assistance of some gentlemen in other carriages, the warders were able to get it pulled up. They immediately hurried back along the line, and there, near a place called Kineton Park, they found their prisoner lying in the footway, apparently unconscious and bleeding from a severe wound in the scalp. A slow train from Sheffield stopped to pick up the injured man. As he was lifted into the guard's van, he asked them to cover him up as he was cold. On arriving at Sheffield, Peace was taken to the Police Station and there made as comfortable as possible in one of the cells. Even then he had energy enough to be troublesome over taking the brandy ordered for him by the surgeon, until one of the officers told "Charley" they would have none of his hanky- panky, and he had got to take it. "All right," said Peace, "give me a minute," after which he swallowed contentedly a couple of gills of the genial spirit.

Peace's daring feat was not, according to his own account, a mere attempt to escape from the clutches of the law; it was noble and Roman in its purpose. This is what he told his stepson, Willie Ward: "I saw from the way I was guarded all the way down from London and all the way back, when I came for my first trial, that I could not get away from the warders, and I knew I could not jump from an express train without being killed. I took a look at Darnall as I went down and as I went back, and after I was put in my cell, I thought it all over. I felt that I could not get away, and then I made up my mind to kill myself. I got two bits of paper and pricked on them the words, 'Bury me at Darnall. God bless you all!' With a bit of black dirt that I found on the floor of my cell I wrote the same words on another piece of paper, and then I hid them in my clothes. My hope was that, when I jumped from the train I should be cut to pieces under the wheels. Then I should have been taken to the Duke of York (a public-house at Darnall) and there would have been an inquest over me. As soon as the inquest was over you would have claimed my body, found the pieces of paper, and then you would have buried me at Darnall."

This statement of Peace is no doubt in the main correct. But it is difficult to believe that there was not present to his mind the sporting chance that he might not be killed in leaping from the train, in which event he would no doubt have done his best to get away, trusting to his considerable powers of ingenious disguise to elude pursuit. But such a chance was remote. Peace had faced boldly the possibility of a dreadful death.

With that strain of domestic sentiment, which would appear to have been a marked characteristic of his family, Peace was the more ready to cheat the gallows in the hope of being by that means buried decently at Darnall. It was at Darnall that he had spent some months of comparative calm in his tempestuous career, and it was at Darnall that he had first met Mrs. Dyson. Another and more practical motive that may have urged Peace to attempt to injure seriously, if not kill himself, was the hope of thereby delaying his trial. If the magisterial investigation in Sheffield were completed before the end of January, Peace could be committed for trial to the ensuing Leeds Assizes which commenced in the first week in February. If he were injured too seriously, this would not be possible. Here again he was doomed to disappointment.

Peace recovered so well from the results of his adventure on the railway that the doctor pronounced him fit to appear for his second examination before the magistrate on January 30. To avoid excitement, both on the part of the prisoner and the public, the court sat in one of the corridors of the Town Hall. The scene is described as dismal, dark and cheerless. The proceedings took place by candlelight, and Peace, who was seated in an armchair, complained frequently of the cold. At other times he moaned and groaned and protested against the injustice with which he was being treated. But the absence of any audience rather dashed the effect of his laments.

The most interesting part of the proceedings was the cross- examination of Mrs. Dyson by Mr. Clegg, the prisoner's solicitor.

Its purpose was to show that Mrs. Dyson had been on more intimate terms with Peace than she was ready to admit, and that Dyson had been shot by Peace in the course of a struggle, in which the former had been the aggressor.

In the first part of his task Mr. Clegg met with some success. Mrs. Dyson, whose memory was certainly eccentric—she could not, she said, remember the year in which she had been married—was obliged to admit that she had been in the habit of going to Peace's house, that she had been alone with him to public-houses and places of entertainment, and that she and Peace had been photographed together during the summer fair at Sheffield. She could not "to her knowledge" recollect having told the landlord of a public-house to charge her drink to Peace.

A great deal of Mrs. Dyson's cross-examination turned on a bundle of letters that had been found near the scene of Dyson's murder on the morning following the crime. These letters consisted for the most part of notes, written in pencil on scraps of paper, purporting to have been sent from Mrs. Dyson to Peace. In many of them she asks for money to get drink, others refer to oppor-tunities for their meetings in the absence of Dyson; there are kind messages to members of Peace's family, his wife and daughter, and urgent directions to Peace to hold his tongue and not give ground for suspicion as to their relations. This bundle of letters contained also the card which Dyson had thrown into Peace's garden requesting him not to interfere with his family. According to the theory of the defence, these letters had been written by Mrs. Dyson to Peace, and went to prove the intimacy of their relations. At the inquest after her husband's murder, Mrs. Dyson had been questioned by the coroner about these letters. She denied that she had ever written to Peace; in fact, she said, she "never did write." It was stated that Dyson himself had seen the letters, and declared them to be forgeries written by Peace or members of his family for the purpose of annoyance. Neverthe-less, before the Sheffield magistrate Mr. Clegg thought it his duty to cross-examine Mrs. Dyson closely as to their authorship. He asked her to write out a passage from one of them: "You can give me something as a keepsake if you like, but I don't like to be covetous, and to take them from your wife and daughter. Love to all!" Mrs. Dyson refused to admit any likeness between what she had written and the handwriting of the letter in ques-tion. Another passage ran: "Will see you as soon as I possibly can. I think it would be easier after you move; he won't watch so. The r—g fits the little finger. Many thanks and love to— Jennie (Peace's daughter Jane). I will tell you what I thought of when I see you about arranging matters. Excuse this scribbling." In answer to Mr. Clegg, Mrs. Dyson admitted that Peace had given her a ring, which she had worn for a short time on her little finger.

Another letter ran: "If you have a note for me, send now whilst he is out; but you must not venture, for he is watching, and you cannot be too careful. Hope your foot is better. I went to Sheffield yesterday, but I could not see you anywhere. Were you out? Love to Jane." Mrs. Dyson denied that she had known of an accident which Peace had had to his foot at this time. In spite of the ruling of the magistrate that Mr. Clegg had put forward quite enough, if true, to damage Mrs. Dyson's credibility, he continued to press her as to her authorship of these notes and letters, but Mrs. Dyson was firm in her repudiation of them. She was equally firm in denying that anything in the nature of a struggle had taken place between Peace and her husband previous to his murder.

At the conclusion of Mrs. Dyson's evidence the prisoner was committed to take his trial at the Leeds Assizes, which commenced the week following. Peace, who had groaned and moaned and constantly interrupted the proceedings, protested his innocence, and complained that his witnesses had not been called. The apprehension with which this daring malefactor was regarded by the authorities is shown by this clandestine hearing of his case in a cold corridor of the Town Hall, and the rapidity with which his trial followed on his committal. There is an appearance almost of precipitation in the haste with which Peace was bustled to his doom. After his committal he was taken to Wakefield Prison, and a few days later to Armley Jail, there to await his trial.

This began on February 4, and lasted one day. Mr. Justice Lopes, who had tried vainly to persuade the Manchester Grand Jury to throw out the bill in the case of the brothers Habron, was the presiding judge. Mr. Campbell Foster, Q.C., led for the prosecution. Peace was defended by Mr. Frank Lockwood, then rising into that popular success at the bar which some fifteen years later made him Solicitor-General, and but for his premature death would have raised him to even higher honours in his profession.

In addressing the jury, both Mr. Campbell Foster and Mr. Lockwood took occasion to protest against the recklessness with which the press of the day, both high and low, had circulated stories and rumours about the interesting convict. As early as November in 1878 one leading London daily newspaper had said that "it was now established beyond doubt that the burglar captured by Police Constable Robinson was one and the same as the Banner Cross murderer." Since then, as the public excitement grew and the facts of Peace's extraordinary career came to light, the press had responded loyally to the demands of the greedy lovers of sensation, and piled fiction on fact with generous profusion. "Never," said Mr. Lockwood, "in the whole course of his experience—and he defied any of his learned friends to quote an experience— had there been such an attempt made on the part of those who should be most careful of all others to preserve the liberties of their fellowmen and to preserve the dignity of the tribunals of justice to determine the guilt of a man." Peace exclaimed "Hear, hear!" as Mr. Lockwood went on to say that "for the sake of snatching paltry pence from the public, these persons had wickedly sought to prejudice the prisoner's life." Allowing for Mr. Lockwood's zeal as an advocate, there can be no question that, had Peace chosen or been in a position to take proceedings, more than one newspaper had at this time laid itself open to prosecution for contempt of Court. The Times was not far wrong in saying that, since Muller murdered Mr. Briggs on the North London Railway and the poisonings of William Palmer, no criminal case had created such excitement as that of Charles Peace. The fact that property seemed to be no more sacred to him than life aggravated in a singular degree the resentment of a commercial people.

The first witness called by the prosecution was Mrs. Dyson. She described how on the night of November 29, 1876, she had come out of the outhouse in the yard at the back of her house, and found herself confronted by Peace holding a revolver; how he said: "Speak, or I'll fire!" and the sequence of events already related up to the moment when Dyson fell, shot in the temple.

Mr. Lockwood commenced his cross-examination of Mrs. Dyson by endeavouring to get from her an admission; the most important to the defence, that Dyson had caught hold of Peace after the first shot had been fired, and that in the struggle which ensued, the revolver had gone off by accident. But he was not very successful. He put it to Mrs. Dyson that before the magistrate at Sheffield she had said: "I can't say my husband did not get hold of the prisoner." "Put in the little word `try,' please," answered Mrs. Dyson. In spite of Mr. Lockwood's questions, she maintained that, though her husband may have attempted to get hold of Peace, he did not succeed in doing so. As she was the only witness to the shooting there was no one to contradict her statement.

Mr. Lockwood fared better when he came to deal with the relations of Mrs. Dyson with Peace previous to the crime. Mrs. Dyson admitted that in the spring of 1876 her husband had objected to her friendship with Peace, and that nevertheless, in the following summer, she and Peace had been photographed together at the Sheffield fair. She made a vain attempt to escape from such an admission by trying to shift the occasion of the summer fair to the previous year, 1875, but Mr. Lockwood put it to her that she had not come to Darnall, where she first met Peace, until the end of that year. Finally he drove her to say that she could not remember when she came to Darnall, whether in 1873, 1874, 1875, or 1876. She admitted that she had accepted a ring from Peace, but could not remember whether she had shown it to her husband. She had been perhaps twice with Peace to the Marquis of Waterford public-house, and once to the Star Music Hall. She could not swear one way or the other whether she had charged to Peace's account drink consumed by her at an inn in Darnall called the Half-way House. Confronted with a little girl and a man, whom Mr. Lockwood suggested she had employed to carry notes to Peace, Mrs. Dyson said that these were merely receipts for pictures which he had framed for her. On the day before her husband's murder, Mrs. Dyson was at the Stag Hotel at Sharrow with a little boy belonging to a neighbour. A man followed her in and sat beside her, and afterwards followed her out. In answer to Mr. Lockwood, Mrs. Dyson would "almost swear" the man was not Peace; he had spoken to her, but she could not remember whether she had spoken to him or not. She denied that this man had said to her that he would come and see her the next night. As the result of a parting shot Mr. Lockwood obtained from Mrs. Dyson a reluc-

tant admission that she had been "slightly inebriated" at the Half-way House in Darnall, but had not to her knowledge" been turned out of the house on that account. "You may not have known you were inebriated? suggested Mr. Lockwood. "I always know what I am doing," was Mrs. Dyson's reply, to which an unfriendly critic might have replied that she did not apparently know with anything like certainty what she had been doing during the last three or four years. In commenting on the trial the following day, the Times stigmatised as "feeble" the prevarications by which Mrs. Dyson tried to explain away her intimacy with Peace. In this part of his cross-examination Mr. Lockwood had made it appear at least highly probable that there had been a much closer relationship between Mrs. Dyson and Peace than the former was willing to acknowledge.

The evidence of Mrs. Dyson was followed by that of five persons who had either seen Peace in the neighbourhood of Banner Cross Terrace on the night of the murder, or heard the screams and shots that accompanied it. A woman, Mrs. Gregory, whose house was between that of the Dysons and the passage in which Dyson was shot, said that she had heard the noise of the clogs Mrs. Dyson was wearing as she went across the yard. A minute later she heard a scream. She opened her back door and saw Dyson standing by his own. She told him to go to his wife. She then went back into her house, and almost directly after heard two shots, followed by another scream, but no sound as of any scuffling.

Another witness was a labourer named Brassington. He was a stranger to Peace, but stated that about eight o'clock on the night of the murder a man came up to him outside the Banner Cross Hotel, a few yards from Dyson's house. He was standing under a gas lamp, and it was a bright moonlight night. The man asked him if he knew of any strange people who had come to live in the neighbourhood. Brassington answered that he did not. The man then produced a bundle of letters which he asked Brassington to read. But Brassington declined, as reading was not one of his accomplishments. The man then said that "he would make it a warm 'un for those strange folks before morning—he would shoot both of them," and went off in the direction of Dyson's house. Brassington swore positively that Peace was the stranger who had accosted him that night, and Mr. Lockwood failed to shake him in his evidence. Nor could Mr. Lockwood persuade the surgeon who was called to Dyson at the time of his death to admit that the marks on the nose and chin of the dead man could have been caused by a blow; they were merely abrasions of the skin caused by the wounded man falling to the ground.

Evidence was then given as to threats uttered by Peace against the Dysons in the July of 1876, and as to his arrest at Blackheath in the October of 1878. The revolver taken from Peace that night was produced, and it was shown that the rifling of the bullet extracted from Dyson's head was the same as that of the bullet fired from the revolver carried by Peace at the time of his capture.

Mr. Campbell Foster wanted to put in as evidence the card that Dyson had flung into Peace's garden at Darnall requesting him not to interfere with his family. This card had been found among the bundle of letters dropped by Peace near the scene of the murder. Mr. Lockwood objected to the admission of the card unless all the letters were admitted at the same time. The Judge ruled that both the card and the letters were inadmissible, as irrelevant to the issue; Mr. Lockwood had, he said, very properly cross- examined Mrs. Dyson on these letters to test her credibility, but he was bound by her answers and could not contradict her by introducing them as evidence in the case.

Mr. Lockwood in his address to the jury did his best to persuade them that the death of Dyson was the accidental result of a struggle between Peace and himself. He suggested that Mrs. Dyson had left her house that night for the purpose of meeting Peace, and that Dyson, who was jealous of his wife's intimacy with him, had gone out to find her; that Dyson, seeing Peace, had caught hold of him; and that the revolver had gone off accidentally as Dyson tried to wrest it from his adversary. He repudiated the suggestion of Mr. Foster that the persons he had confronted with Mrs. Dyson in the course of his cross-examination had been hired for a paltry sum to come into court and lie.

Twice, both at the beginning and the end of his speech, Mr. Lockwood urged as a reason for the jury being tender in taking Peace's life that he was in such a state of wickedness as to be quite unprepared to meet death. Both times that his counsel put forward this curious plea, Peace raised his eyes to heaven and exclaimed "I am not fit to die."

Mr. Justice Lopes in summing up described as an "absolute surmise" the theory of the accidental discharge of the pistol. He asked the jury to take Peace's revolver in their hands and try the trigger, so as to see for themselves whether it was likely to go off accidentally or not. He pointed out that the pistol produced might not have been the pistol used at Banner Cross; at the same time the bullet fired in November, 1876, bore marks such as would have been produced had it been fired from the pistol taken from Peace at Blackheath in October, 1878. He said that Mr. Lockwood had been perfectly justified in his attempt to discredit the evidence of Mrs. Dyson, but the case did not rest on her evidence alone. In her evidence as to the threats uttered by Peace in July, 1876, Mrs. Dyson was corroborated by three other witnesses. In the Judge's opinion it was clearly proved that no struggle or scuffle had taken place before the murder. If the defence, he concluded, rested on no solid founda-

tion, then the jury must do their duty to the community at large and by the oath they had sworn.

It was a quarter past seven when the jury retired. Ten minutes later they came back into court with a verdict of guilty. Asked if he had anything to say, Peace in a faint voice replied, "It is no use my saying anything." The Judge, declining very properly to aggravate the prisoner's feelings by "a recapitulation of any portion of the details of what I fear, I can only call your criminal career," passed on him sentence of death. Peace accepted his fate with composure.

Before we proceed to describe the last days of Peace on earth, let us finish with the two women who had succeeded Mrs. Peace in his ardent affections.

A few days after Peace's execution Mrs. Dyson left England for America, but before going she left behind her a narrative intended to contradict the imputations which she felt had been made against her moral character. An Irishwoman by birth, she said that she had gone to America when she was fifteen years old.

There she met and married Dyson, a civil engineer on the Atlantic and Great Western Railway. Theirs was a rough and arduous life. But Mrs. Dyson was thoroughly happy in driving her husband about in a buggy among bears and creeks. She did not know fear and loved danger: "My husband loved me and I loved him, and in his company and in driving him about in this wild kind of fashion I derived much pleasure." However, Mr. Dyson's health broke down, and he was obliged to return to England. It was at Darnall that the fatal acquaintance with Peace began. Living next door but one to the Dysons, Peace took the opportunity of introducing himself, and Mr. Dyson "being a gentleman," took polite notice of his advances. He became a constant visitor at the house. But after a time Peace began to show that he was not the gentleman Mr. Dyson was. He disgusted the latter by offering to show him improper pictures and "the sights of the town" of Sheffield.

The Dysons tried to shake off the unwelcome acquaintance, but that was easier said than done. By this time Peace had set his heart on making Mrs. Dyson leave her husband. He kept trying to persuade her to go to Manchester with him, where he would take a cigar or picture shop, to which Mrs. Dyson, in fine clothes and jewelry, should lend the charm of her comely presence. He offered her a sealskin jacket, yards of silk, a gold watch. She should, he said, live in Manchester like a lady, to which Mrs. Dyson replied coldly that she had always lived like one and should continue to do so quite independently of him. But Peace would listen to no refusal, however decided its tone. Dyson threw over the card into Peace's garden. This only served to aggravate his determination to possess himself of the wife. He would listen at keyholes, leer in at the window, and follow Mrs. Dyson wherever she went. When she was photographed at the fair, she found that Peace had stood behind her chair and by that means got himself included in the picture. At times he had threatened her with a revolver. On one occasion when he was more insulting than usual, Mrs. Dyson forgot her fear of him and gave him a thrashing. Peace threatened "to make her so that neither man nor woman should look at her, and then he would have her all to himself." It was with some purpose of this kind, Mrs. Dyson suggested, that Peace stole a photograph of herself out of a locket, intending to make some improper use of it. At last, in desperation, the Dysons moved to Banner Cross. From the day of their arrival there until the murder, Mrs. Dyson never saw Peace. She denied altogether having been in his company ght before the murder. The letters were "bare forgeries," written by Peace mbers of his family to get her into their power.

Against the advice of all her friends Mrs. Dyson had come back from America to give evidence against Peace. To the detective who saw her at Cleveland she said, "I will go back if I have to walk on my head all the way"; and though she little knew what she would have to go through in giving her evidence, she would do it again under the circumstances. "My opinion is," she said, "that Peace is a perfect demon—not a man. I am told that since he has been sentenced to death he has become a changed character. That I don't believe. The place to which the wicked go is not bad enough for him. I think its occupants, bad as they might be, are too good to be where he is. No matter where he goes, I am satis-

fied that there will be hell. Not even a Shakespeare could adequately paint such a man as he has been. My lifelong regret will be that I ever knew him."

With these few earnest words Mrs. Dyson quitted the shores of England, hardly clearing up the mystery of her actual relations with Peace.

A woman with whom Mrs. Dyson very much resented finding herself classed—inebriety would appear to have been their only common weakness—was Mrs. Thompson, the "traitress Sue." In spite of the fact that on February 5 Mrs. Thompson had applied to the Treasury for L100, blood money due her for assisting the police in the identification of Peace, she was at the same time carrying on a friendly correspondence with her lover and making attempts to see him. Peace had written to her before his trial hoping she would not forsake him; "you have been my bosom friend, and you have ofttimes said you loved me, that you would die for me." He asked her to sell some goods which he had left with her in order to raise money for his defence. The traitress replied on January 27 that she had already sold everything and shared the proceeds with Mrs. Peace. "You are doing me great injustice," she wrote, "by saying that I have been out to `work' with you. Do not die with such a base falsehood on your conscience, for you know I am young and have my living and character to redeem. I pity you and myself to think we should have met." After his condemnation Mrs. Thompson made repeated efforts to see Peace, coming to Leeds for the purpose. Peace wrote a letter on February 9 to his "poor Sue," asking her to come to the prison. But, partly at the wish of Peace's relatives and for reasons of their own, a permission given Mrs. Thompson by the authorities to visit the convict was suddenly withdrawn, and she never saw him again.

III

HIS TRIAL AND EXECUTION

In the lives of those famous men who have perished on the scaffold their behaviour during the interval between their condemnation and their execution has always been the subject of curiosity and interest.

It may be said at once that nothing could have been more deeply religious, more sincerely repentant, more Christian to all appearances than Peace's conduct and demeanour in the last weeks of his life. He threw himself into the work of atonement with the same uncompromising zeal and energy that he had displayed as a burglar. By his death a truly welcome and effective re-cruit was lost to the ranks of the contrite and converted sinners. However powerless as a controlling force—and he admitted it—his belief in God and the devil may have been in the past, that belief was assured and confident, and in the presence of death proclaimed itself with vigour, not in words merely, but in deeds.

In obedience to the wishes of his family, Peace had refrained from seeing Sue Thompson. This was at some sacrifice, for he wished very much to see her and to the last, though he knew that she had betrayed him, sent her affectionate and forgiving messages. These were transmitted to Sue by Mr. Brion. This disingenuous gentleman was a fellow-applicant with Sue to the Treasury for pecuniary recognition of his efforts in bringing about the identification of Peace, and furnishing the police with information as to the convict's disposal of his stolen property. In his zeal he had even gone so far as to play the role of an accomplice of Peace, and by this means discovered a place in Petticoat Lane where the burglar got rid of some of his booty.

After Peace's condemnation Mr. Brion visited him in Armley Jail. His purpose in doing so was to wring from his co-inventor an admission that the inventions which they had patented together were his work alone. Peace denied this, but offered to sell his share for L50. Brion refused the offer, and persisted in his assertion that Peace had got his name attached to the patents by undue influence, whatever that might mean. Peace, after wres-tling with the spirit, gave way. "Very well, my friend," he said, "let it be as you say. I have not cheated you, Heaven knows. But I also know that this infamy of mine has been the cause of bringing harm to you, which is the last thing I should have wished to have caused to my friend." A deed of gift was drawn up, making over to Brion Peace's share in their inventions; this Peace handed to Brion as the price of the latter's precious forgiveness and a token of the sincerity of his colleague's repentance. Thus, as has often happened in this sad world, was disreputable genius exploited once again by smug mediocrity. Mr. Brion, having got all he wanted, left the prison, assuring the Governor that Peace's repentance was "all bunkum," and advising, with commendable anxiety for the public good, that the warders in the condemned cell should be doubled.

Peace had one act of atonement to discharge more urgent than displaying Christian forbearance towards ignoble associates. That was the righting of William Habron, who was now serving the third year of his life sentence for the murder of Constable Cock at Whalley Range. Peace sent for the Governor of the jail a few days before his execution and obtained from him the materials necessary for drawing up a plan. Peace was quite an adept at making plans; he had already made an excellent one of the scene of Dyson's murder. He now drew a plan of the place where Cock had been shot, gave a detailed account of how he came by his death, and made a full confession of his own guilt.

In the confession he described how, some days before the burglary, he had, according to his custom, "spotted" the house at Whalley Range. In order to do this he always dressed himself respectably, because he had found that the police never suspected anyone who wore good clothes. On the night of the crime he passed two policemen on the road to the house. He had gone into the grounds and was about to begin operations when he heard a rustle behind him and saw a policeman, whom he recognised as one of those he had met in the road, enter the garden. With his well-known agility Peace climbed on to the wall, and dropped on to the other side, only to find himself almost in the arms of the second policeman. Peace warned the officer to stand back and fired his revolver wide of him. But, as Peace said, "these Manchester policemen are a very obstinate lot." The constable took out his truncheon. Peace fired again and killed him.

Soon after the murderer saw in the newspapers that two men had been arrested for the crime. "This greatly interested me," said Peace. "I always had a liking to be present at trials, as the public no doubt know by this time." So he went to Manchester Assizes and saw William Habron sentenced to death. "People will say," he said, "that I was a hardened wretch for allowing an innocent man to suffer for the crime of which I was guilty but what man would have given himself up under such circumstances, knowing as I did that I should certainly be hanged?" Peace's view of the question was a purely practical one: "Now that I am going to forfeit my own life and feel that I have nothing to gain by further secrecy, I think it is right in the sight of God and man to clear this innocent young man." It would have been more right in the sight of God and man to have done it before, but then Peace admitted that during all his career he had allowed neither God nor man to influence his actions.

How many men in the situation of Peace at the time, with the certainty of death before him if he confessed, would have sacrificed themselves to save an innocent man? Cold-blooded heroism of this kind is rare in the annals of crime. Nor did Peace claim to have anything of the hero about him.

"Lion-hearted I've lived,

And when my time comes

Lion-hearted I'll die."

Though fond of repeating this piece of doggerel, Peace would have been the last man to have attributed to himself all those qualities associated symbolically with the lion.

A few days before his execution Peace was visited in his prison by Mr. Littlewood, the Vicar of Darnall. Mr. Littlewood had known Peace a few years before, when he had been chaplain at Wakefield Prison. "Well, my old friend Peace," he said as he entered the cell, "how are you to-day?" "`I am very poorly, sir," replied the convict, "but I am exceedingly pleased to see you." Mr. Littlewood assured Peace that there was at any rate one person in the world who had deep sympathy with him, and that was himself. Peace burst into tears. He expressed a wish to unburden himself to the vicar, but before doing so, asked for his assurance that he believed in the truth and sincerity of what he was about to say to him. He said that he preferred to be hanged to lingering out his life in penal servitude, that he was grieved and repentant for his past life. "If I could undo, or make amends for anything I have done, I would suffer my body as I now stand to be cut in pieces inch by inch. I feel, sir, that I am too bad to live or die, and having this feeling I cannot think that either you or anyone else would believe me, and that is the reason why I ask you so much to try to be assured that you do not think I am telling lies. I call my God to witness that all I am saying and wish to say shall be the truth—the whole truth— nothing but the truth." Mr. Littlewood said that, after carefully watching Peace and having regard to his experience of some of the most hardened of criminals during his service in Wakefield Prison, he felt convinced that Peace was in earnest and as sincere as any man could be; he spoke rationally, coherently, and without excitement.

Peace was determined to test the extent of the reverend gentleman's faith in his asseverations. "Now, sir," he said, "I understand that you still have the impression that I stole the clock from your day-schools." Mr. Littlewood admitted that such was his impression. "I thought so," replied Peace, "and this has caused me much grief and pain, for I can assure you I have so much respect for you personally that I would rather have given you a clock and much more besides than have taken it. At the time your clock was stolen I had reason for suspecting that it was taken by some colliers whom I knew." There was a pause. Mr. Littlewood thought that Peace was going to give him the name of the colliers. But that was not Peace's way. He said sharply: "Do you now believe that I have spoken the truth in denying that I took your clock, and will you leave me to-day fully believing that I am innocent of doing that?" Mr. Littlewood looked at him closely and appeared to be deliberating on his reply. Peace watched him intently. At last Mr. Littlewood said, "Peace, I am convinced that you did not take the clock. I cannot believe that you dare deny it now in your position, if you really did." Once more Peace burst into tears, and was unable for some time to speak.

Having recovered his self-possession, Peace turned to the serious business of confession. He dealt first with the murder of Dyson.

He maintained that his relations with Mrs. Dyson had been of an intimate character. He wanted to see her on the night of the crime in order to get her to induce her husband to withdraw the warrant which he had procured against him; he was tired, he said, of being hunted about from place to place. He intercepted Mrs. Dyson as she crossed the yard. Instead of listening to him quietly Mrs.

Dyson became violent and threatening in her language. Peace took out his revolver, and, holding it close to her head, warned her that he was not to be trifled with. She refused to be warned. Dyson, hearing the loud voices, came out of his house. Peace tried to get away down the passage into Banner Cross Road, but Dyson followed and caught hold of him. In the struggle Peace fired one barrel of his revolver wide. Dyson seized the hand in which Peace was holding the weapon. "Then I knew," said Peace, "I had not a moment to spare. I made a desperate effort, wrenched the arm from him and fired again. All that was in my head at the time was to get away. I never did intend, either there or anywhere else, to take a man's life; but I was determined that I should not be caught at that time, as the result, knowing what I had done before, would have been worse even than had I stayed under the warrant." If he had intended to murder Dyson, Peace pointed out that he would have set about it in quite a different and more secret way; it was as unintentional a thing as ever was done; Mrs. Dyson had committed the grossest perjury in saying that no struggle had taken place between her husband and himself.

It is to be remembered that Peace and Mrs. Dyson were the sole witnesses of what took place that night between the two men. In point of credibility there may be little to choose between them, but Peace can claim for his account that it was the statement of a dying, and, to all appearances, sincerely repentant sinner.

Peace then repeated to Mr. Littlewood his confession of the killing of Constable Cock, and his desire that Habron should be set free.[11] As to this part of his career Peace indulged in some general reflections. "My great mistake, sir," he said, "and I can see it now as my end approaches, has been this—in all my career I have used ball cartridge. I can see now that in using ball cartridge I did wrong I ought to have used blank cartridge; then I would not have taken life." Peace said that he hoped he would meet his death like a hero. "I do not say this in any kind of bravado. I do not mean such a hero as some persons will understand when they read this. I mean such a hero as my God might wish me to be. I am deeply grieved for all I have done, and would atone for it to the utmost of my power." To Mr. Littlewood the moment seemed convenient to suggest that as a practical means of atonement Peace should reveal to him the names of the persons with whom he had disposed of the greater part of his stolen property. But in spite of much attempted persuasion by the reverend gentleman Peace explained that he was a man and meant to be a man to the end.

[11] William Habron was subsequently given a free pardon and L800 by way of compensation.

Earlier in their interview Peace had expressed to Mr. Littlewood a hope that after his execution his name would never be mentioned again, but before they parted he asked Mr. Littlewood, as a favour, to preach a sermon on him after his death to the good people of Darnall. He wished his career held up to them as a beacon, in order that all who saw might avoid his example, and so his death be of some service to society.

Before Mr. Littlewood left, Peace asked him to hear him pray. Having requested the warders to kneel down, Peace began a prayer that lasted twenty minutes. He prayed for himself, his family, his victims, Mr. Littlewood, society generally, and all classes of the community. Mr. Littlewood described the prayer as earnest, fervent and fluent. At the end Peace asked Mr. Littlewood if he ought to see Mrs. Dyson and beg her forgiveness for having killed her husband. Mr. Littlewood, believing er-

roneously that Mrs. Dyson had already left the country, told Peace that he should direct all his attention to asking forgiveness of his Maker. At the close of their interview Peace was lifted into bed and, turning his face to the wall, wept.

Tuesday, February 25, was the day fixed for the, execution of Peace. As the time drew near, the convict's confidence in ultimate salvation increased. A Dr. Potter of Sheffield had declared in a sermon that "all hope of Peace's salvation was gone for ever." Peace replied curtly, "Well, Dr. Potter may think so, but I don't." Though his health had improved, Peace was still very feeble in body. But his soul was hopeful and undismayed. On the Saturday before his death his brother and sister-in-law, a nephew and niece visited him for the last time. He spoke with some emotion of his approaching end. He said he should die about eight o'clock, and that at four o'clock an inquest would be held on his body; he would then be thrown into his grave without service or sermon of any kind. He asked his relatives to plant a flower on a certain grave in a cemetery in Sheffield on the day of his execution. He was very weak, he said, but hoped he should have strength enough to walk to the scaffold. He sent messages to friends and warnings to avoid gambling and drinking. He begged his brother to change his manner of life and "become religious." His good counsel was not apparently very well received. Peace's visitors took a depressing view of their relative's condition. They found him "a poor, wretched, haggard man," and, meeting Mrs. Thompson who was waiting outside the gaol for news of "dear Jack," wondered how she could have taken up with such a man.

When, the day before his execution, Peace was visited for the last time by his wife, his stepson, his daughter, Mrs. Bolsover, and her husband, he was in much better spirits. He asked his visitors to restrain themselves from displays of emotion, as he felt very happy and did not wish to be disturbed. He advised them to sell or exhibit for money certain works of art of his own devising. Among them was a design in paper for a monument to be placed over his grave. The design is elaborate but well and ingeniously executed; in the opinion of Frith, the painter, it showed "the true feeling of an artist." It is somewhat in the style of the Albert Memorial, and figures of angels are prominent in the scheme. The whole conception is typical of the artist's sanguine and confident assurance of his ultimate destiny. A model boat and a fiddle made out of a hollow bamboo cane he wished also to be made the means of raising money. He was describing with some detail the ceremony of his approaching death and burial when he was interrupted by a sound of hammering. Peace listened for a moment and then said, "That's a noise that would make some men fall on the floor. They are working at my own scaffold." A warder said that he was mistaken. "No, I am not," answered Peace, "I have not worked so long with wood without knowing the sound of deals; and they don't have deals inside a prison for anything else than scaffolds." But the noise, he said, did not disturb him in the least, as he was quite prepared to meet his fate. He would like to have seen his grave and coffin; he knew that his body would be treated with scant ceremony after his death. But what of that? By that time his soul would be in Heaven. He was pleased that one sinner who had seen him on his way from Pentonville to Sheffield, had written to tell him that the sight of the convict had brought home to him the sins of his own past life, and by this means he had found salvation.

The time had come to say good-bye for the last time. Peace asked his weeping relatives whether they had anything more that they wished to ask him. Mrs. Peace reminded him that he had promised to pray with them at the last. Peace, ever ready, knelt with them and prayed for half an hour. He then shook hands with them, prayed for and blessed each one singly, and himself gave way to tears as they left his presence. To his wife as she departed Peace gave a funeral card of his own designing. It ran:

In
Memory
of
Charles Peace
Who was executed in
Armley Prison
Tuesday February 25th,
1879 Aged 47
For that I don but never
Intended.

The same day there arrived in the prison one who in his own trade had something of the personality and assurance of the culprit he was to execute. William Marwood—unlike his celebrated victim, he has his place in the Dictionary of National Biography—is perhaps the most remarkable of these persons who have held at different times the office of public executioner. As the inventor of the "long drop," he has done a lasting service to humanity by enabling the death-sentence passed by the judge to be carried out with the minimum of possible suffering. Marwood took a lofty view of the office he held, and refused his assent to the somewhat hypocritical loathing, with which those who sanction and profit by his exertions are pleased to regard this servant of the law. "I am doing God's work," said Marwood, "according to the divine command and the law of the British Crown. I do it simply as a matter of duty and as a Christian. I sleep as soundly as a child and am never disturbed by phantoms. Where there is guilt there is bad sleeping, but I am conscious that I try to live a blameless life. Detesting idleness, I pass my vacant time in business (he was a shoemaker at Horncastle, in Lincolnshire) and work in my shoeshop near the church day after day until such time as I am required elsewhere. It would have been better for those I executed if they had preferred industry to idleness."

Marwood had not the almost patriarchal air of benevolent respectability which his predecessor Calcraft had acquired during a short experience as a family butler; but as an executioner that kindly old gentleman had been a sad bungler in his time compared with the scientific and expeditious Marwood. The Horncastle shoemaker was saving, businesslike, pious and thoughtful. Like Peace, he had interests outside his ordinary profession. He had at one time propounded a scheme for the abolition of the National Debt, a man clearly determined to benefit his fellowmen in some way or other. A predilection for gin would seem to have been his only concession to the ordinary weakness of humanity. And now he had arrived in Armley Jail to exercise his happy dispatch on the greatest of the many criminals who passed through his hands, one who, in his own words, "met death with greater firmness" than any man on whom he had officiated during seven years of Crown employment.

The day of February the 25th broke bitterly cold. Like Charles I. before him, Peace feared lest the extreme cold should make him appear to tremble on the scaffold. He had slept calmly till six o'clock in the morning. A great part of the two hours before the coming of the hangman Peace spent in letter-writing. He wrote two letters to his wife, in one of which he copied out some verses he had written in Woking Prison on the death of their little boy John. In the second he expressed his satisfaction that he was to die now and not linger twenty years in prison. To his daughter, step-son and son-in-law he wrote letters of fervent, religious exhortation and sent them tracts and pictures which he had secured from well-intentioned persons anxious about his salvation. To an old friend, George Goodlad, a pianist, who had apparently lived up to his name, he wrote: "You chose an honest industrious way through life, but I chose the one of dishonesty, villainy and sin"; let his fate, he said, be a warning.

Peace ate a hearty breakfast and awaited the coming of the executioner with calm. He had been troubled with an inconvenient cough the night before. "I wonder," he said to one of his warders, "if Marwood could cure this cough of mine." He had got an idea into his head that Marwood would "punish" him when he came to deal with him on the scaffold, and asked to see the hangman a few minutes before the appointed hour. "I hope you will not punish me. I hope you will do your work quickly," he said to Marwood. "You shall not suffer pain from my hand," replied that worthy. "God bless you," exclaimed Peace, "I hope to meet you all in heaven. I am thankful to say my sins are all forgiven." And so these two pious men—on the morning of an execution Marwood always knelt down and asked God's blessing on the work he had to do—shook hands together and set about their business. Firmly and fearlessly Peace submitted himself to the necessary preparations. For one moment he faltered as the gallows came in sight, but recovered himself quickly.

As Marwood was about to cover his face, Peace stopped him with some irritation of manner and said that he wished to speak to the gentlemen of the press who had been admitted to the ceremony. No one gainsaid him, and he thus addressed the reporters: "You gentlemen reporters, I wish you to notice the few words I am going to say. You know what my life has been. It has been base; but I wish you to notice, for the sake of others, how a man can die, as I am about to die, in fear of the Lord. Gentlemen, my heart says that I feel assured that my sins are forgiven me, that I am going to the Kingdom of Heaven, or else to the place prepared for those who rest until the great Judgment day. I do not think I have any enemies, but if there are any who would be so, I wish them well. Gentlemen, all and all, I wish them to come to the Kingdom of Heaven when they die, as I am going to die." He asked a blessing on the officials of the prison and, in conclusion, sent his last wishes and respects to his dear children and their mother. "I hope," he said, "no one will disgrace them by taunting them or jeering them on my account, but to have mercy upon them. God bless you, my dear children. Good- bye, and Heaven bless you. Amen: Oh, my Lord God, have mercy upon me!"

After the cap had been placed over his head Peace asked twice very sharply, as a man who expected to be obeyed, for a drink of water. But this time his request was not compiled with. He died instantaneously and was buried in Armley Jail.

Had Peace flourished in 1914 instead of 1874, his end might have been honourable instead of dishonourable. The war of to-day has no doubt saved many a man from a criminal career by turning to worthy account qualities which, dangerous in crime, are useful in war. Absolute fearlessness, agility, resource, cunning and determination; all these are admirable qualities in the soldier; and all these Charles Peace possessed in a signal degree. But fate denied him opportunity, he became a burglar and died on the scaffold. Years of prison life failed, as they did in those days, to make any impression for good on one resolute in whatever way he chose to go. Peace was a born fighter. A detective who knew him and had on one occasion come near capturing him in London, said that he was a fair fighter, that he always gave fair warning to those on whom he fired, and that, being a dead shot, the many wide shots which he fired are to be reckoned proofs of this. Peace maintained to the last that he had never intended to kill Dyson. This statement ex-detective Parrock believed, and that the fatal shot was fired over Peace's shoulder as he was making off. Though habitually sober, Peace was made intoxicated now and then by the drink, stood him by those whom he used to amuse with his musical tricks and antics in public- houses. At such times he would get fuddled and quarrelsome. He was in such a frame of mind on the evening of Dyson's murder. His visit to the Vicar of Ecclesall brought him little comfort or consolation. It was in this unsatisfactory frame of mind that he went to Dyson's house. This much the ex-detective would urge in his favour. To his neighbours he was an awe-inspiring but kind and sympathetic man. "If you want my true opinion of him," says Detective Parrock, "he was a burglar to the backbone but not a murderer at heart. He deserved the fate that came to him as little as any who in modern times have met with a like one." Those who are in the fighting line are always the most generous about their adversaries. Parrock as a potential target for Peace's revolver, may have erred on the side of generosity, but there is some truth in what he says.

As Peace himself admitted, his life had been base. He was well aware that he had misused such gifts as nature had bestowed on him. One must go back to mediaeval times to find the counterpart of this daring ruffian who, believing in personal God and devil, refuses until the end to allow either to interfere with his business in life. In this respect Charles Peace reminds us irresistibly of our Angevin kings.

There is only one criminal who vies with Charley Peace in that genial popular regard which makes Charles "Charley" and John "Jack," and that is Jack Sheppard. What Jack was to the eighteenth century, that Charley was to the nineteenth. And each one is in a sense typical of his period. Lecky has said that the eighteenth century is richer than any other in the romance of crime. I think it may fairly be said that in the nineteenth century the romance of crime ceased to be. In the eighteenth century the scenery and dresses, all the stage setting of crime make for romance; its literature is quaint and picturesque; there is something gay and debonair about the whole business.

Sheppard is typical of all this. There is a certain charm about the rascal; his humour is undeniable; he is a philosopher, taking all that comes with easy grace, even his betrayal by his brother and others who should have been loyal to him. Jack Sheppard has the good-humoured carelessness of that most engaging of all eighteenth century malefactors, Deacon Brodie. It is quite otherwise with Charley Peace. There is little enough gay or debonair about him. Compared with Sheppard, Peace is as drab as the surroundings of mid-Victorian crime are drab compared with the picturesqueness of eighteenth century England.

Crime in the nineteenth century becomes more scientific in its methods and in its detection also. The revolver places a more hasty, less decorous weapon than the old-fashioned pistol in the hands of the determined burglar. The literature of crime, such as it is, becomes vulgar and prosaic. Peace has no charm about him, no gaiety, but he has the virtues of his defects. He, unlike Sheppard, shuns company; he works alone, never depending on accomplices; a "tight cock," as Sheppard would have phrased it, and not relying on a like quality of tightness in his fellows. Sheppard is a slave to his women, Edgeworth Bess and Mrs. Maggot; Mrs. Peace and Sue Thompson are the slaves of Peace. Sheppard loves to stroll openly about the London streets in his fine suit of black, his ruffled shirt and his silver- hilted sword. Peace lies concealed at Peckham beneath the homely disguise of old Mr. Thompson. Sheppard is an imp, Peace a goblin. But both have that gift of personality which, in their own peculiar line, lifts them out from the ruck, and makes them Jack and Charley to those who like to know famous people by cheery nicknames.

And so we must accept Charles Peace as a remarkable character, whose unquestioned gifts as a man of action were squandered on a criminal career; neither better nor worse than a great number of other persons, whose good fortune it has been to develop similar qualities under happier surroundings. There are many more complete villains than the ordinary criminal, who contrive to go through life without offending against the law. Close and scientific investigation has shown that the average convicted criminal differs intellectually from the normal person only in a slightly lower level of intelligence, a condition that may well be explained by the fact that the convicted criminal has been found out. Crime has been happily defined by a recent and most able investigator into the character of the criminal[12] as "an unusual act committed by a perfectly normal person." At the same time, according to the same authority, there is a type of normal person who tends to be convicted of crime, and he is differentiated from his fellows by defective physique and mental capacity and an increased possession of antisocial qualities.[13]

[12] "The English Convict," a statistical study, by Charles Goring, M.D. His Majesty's Stationery Office, 1913.

[13] Murderers—at least those executed for their crimes—have not for obvious reasons been made the subject of close scientific observation. Their mental capacity would in all probability be found to be rather higher than that of less ambitious criminals.

How does Peace answer to the definition? Though short in stature, his physical development left little to be desired: he was active, agile, and enjoyed excellent health at all times. For a man of forty-seven he had aged remarkably in appearance. That is probably to be accounted for by mental worry. With two murders on his conscience we know from Sue Thompson that all she learnt of his secrets was what escaped from him in his troubled dreams—Peace may well have shown traces of mental anxiety. But in all other respects Charles Peace would seem to have been physically fit. In intellectual capacity he was undoubtedly above the average of the ordinary criminal. The facts of his career, his natural gifts, speak for themselves. Of anti-social proclivities he no doubt possessed his share at the beginning, and these were aggravated, as in most cases they were in his day, by prison life and discipline.

Judged as scientifically as is possible where the human being is concerned, Peace stands out physically and intellectually well above the average of his class, perhaps the most naturally gifted of all those who, without advantages of rank or education, have tried their hands at crime. Ordinary crime for the most part would appear to be little better than the last resort of the intellectually defective, and a poor game at that. The only interesting criminals are those worthy of something better. Peace was one of these. If his life may be said to point a moral, it is the very simple one that crime is no career for a man of brains.

THE CAREER OF ROBERT BUTLER

There is a report of Butler's trial published in Dunedin. It gives in full the speeches and the cross-examination of the witnesses, but not in all cases the evidence-in-chief. By the kindness of a friend in New Zealand I obtained a copy of the depositions taken before the magistrate; with this I have been able to supplement the report of the trial. A collection of newspaper cuttings furnished me with the details of the rest of Butler's career.

I

THE DUNEDIN MURDERS

On the evening of March 23, 1905, Mr. William Munday, a highly respected citizen of the town of Tooringa, in Queensland, was walking to the neighbouring town of Toowong to attend a masonic gathering. It was about eight o'clock, the moon shining brightly. Nearing Toowong, Mr. Munday saw a middle-aged man, bearded and wearing a white overcoat, step out into the moonlight from under the shadow of a tree. As Mr. Munday advanced, the man in the white coat stood directly in his way. "Out with all you have, and quick about it," he said. Instead of complying with this peremptory summons, Mr. Munday attempted to close with him. The man drew back quickly, whipped out a revolver, fired, and made off as fast as he could. The bullet, after passing through Mr. Munday's left arm, had lodged in the stomach. The unfortunate gentleman was taken to a neighbouring hospital where, within a few hours, he was dead.

In the meantime a vigorous search was made for his assailant. Late the same night Constable Hennessy, riding a bicycle, saw a man in a white coat who seemed to answer to the description of the assassin. He dismounted, walked up to him and asked him for a match. The man put his hand inside his coat. "What have you got there?" asked the constable. "I'll—soon show you," replied the man in the white coat, producing suddenly a large revolver. But Hennessy was too quick for him. Landing him one under the jaw, he sent him to the ground and, after a sharp struggle, secured him. Constable Hennessy little knew at the time that his capture in Queensland of the man in the white coat was almost as notable in the annals of crime as the affray at Blackheath on an autumn night in 1878, when Constable Robinson grappled successfully, wounded as he was, with Charles Peace.

The man taken by Hennessy gave the name of James Wharton, and as James Wharton he was hanged at Brisbane. But before his death it was ascertained beyond doubt, though he never admitted it himself, that Wharton was none other than one Robert Butler, whose career as a criminal and natural wickedness may well rank him with Charles Peace in the hierarchy of scoundrels. Like Peace, Butler was, in the jargon of crime, a "hatter," a "lone hand," a solitary who conceived and executed his nefarious designs alone; like Peace, he supplemented an insignificant physique by a liberal employment of the revolver; like Peace, he was something of a musician, the day before his execution he played hymns for half an hour on the prison organ; like Peace, he knew when to whine when it suited his purpose; and like Peace, though not with the same intensity, he could be an uncomfortably persistent lover, when the fit was on him. Both men were cynics in their way and viewed their fellow-men with a measure of contempt. But here parallel ends. Butler was an intellectual, inferior as a craftsman to Peace, the essentially practical, unread, naturally gifted artist. Butler was a man of books. He had been schoolmaster, journalist. He had studied the lives of great men, and as a criminal, had devoted especial attention to those of Frederick the Great and Napoleon. Butler's defence in the Dunedin murder trial was a feat of skill quite beyond the power of Peace. Peace was a religious man after the fashion of the mediaeval tyrant, Butler an infidel. Peace, dragged into the light of a court of justice, cut a sorry figure; here Butler shone. Peace escaped a conviction for murder by letting another suffer in his place; Butler escaped a similar experience by the sheer ingenuity of his defence. Peace had the modesty and reticence of the sincere artist; Butler the loquacious vanity of the literary or forensic coxcomb. Lastly, and it is the supreme difference, Butler was a murderer by instinct and conviction, as Lacenaire or Ruloff; "a man's life," he said, "was of no more importance than a dog's; nature respects the one no more than the other, a volcanic eruption kills mice and men with the one hand. The divine command, `kill, kill and spare not,' was intended not only for Joshua, but for men of all time; it is the example of our rulers, our Fredericks and Napoleons."

Butler was of the true Prussian mould. "In crime," he would say, "as in war, no half measures. Let us follow the example of our rulers whose orders in war run, `Kill, burn and sink,' and what you cannot carry away, destroy.'" Here is the gospel of frightfulness applied almost prophetically to crime. To Butler murder is a principle of warfare; to Peace it was never more than a desperate resort or an act the outcome of ungovernable passion.

Ireland can claim the honour of Butler's birth. It took place at Kilkenny about 1845. At an early age he left his native land for Australia, and commenced his professional career by being sentenced under the name of James Wilson—the same initials as those of James Wharton of Queensland—to twelve months' imprisonment for vagrancy. Of the sixteen years he passed in Victoria he spent thirteen in prison, first for stealing, then in steady progression for highway robbery and burglary. Side by side with the practical and efficient education in crime furnished by the Victorian prisons of that day, Butler availed himself of the opportunity to educate his mind. It was during this period that he found inspiration and encouragement in the study of the lives of Frederick and Napoleon, besides acquiring a knowledge of music and shorthand.

When in 1876 Butler quitted Australia for New Zealand, he was sufficiently accomplished to obtain employment as a schoolmaster.

At Cromwell, Otago, under the name of "C. J. Donelly, Esq.," Butler opened a "Commercial and Preparatory Academy," and in a prospectus that recalls Mr. Squeers' famous advertisement of Dotheboys Hall, announced that the programme of the Academy would include "reading, taught as an art and upon the most approved principles of elocution, writing, arithmetic, euclid, algebra, mensuration, trigonometry, book-keeping, geography, grammar, spelling and dictation) composition, logic and debate, French, Latin, shorthand, history, music, and general lectures on astronomy, natural philosophy, geology, and other subjects." The simpler principles of these branches of learning were to be "rendered intelligible, and a firm foundation laid for the acquirement of future knowledge." Unfortunately a suspicion of theft on Butler's part cut short the fulfilment of this really splendid programme, and Butler left Cromwell hurriedly for the ampler field of Dunedin. There, less than a fortnight after his arrivel{sic}, he was sentenced to four years' hard labour for several burglaries committed in and about that city.

On the 18th of February, 1880, Butler was released from prison. With that consummate hypocrisy which was part of the man, he had contrived to enlist the sympathies of the Governor of the Dunedin Jail, who gave him, on his departure, a suit of clothes and a small sum of money. A detective of the name of Bain tried to find him employment. Butler wished to adopt a literary career. He acted as a reporter on the Dunedin Evening Star, and gave satisfaction to the editor of that newspaper. An attempt to do some original work, in the shape of "Prison Sketches," for another newspaper, was less successful. Bain had arranged for the publication of the articles in the Sunday Advertiser, but when the time came to deliver his manuscript, Butler failed to appear. Bain, whose duty it was to keep an eye on Butler, found him in the street looking wild and haggard. He said that he had found the work "too much for his head," that he had torn up what he had written, that he had nowhere to go, and had been to the end of the jetty with the intention of drowning himself. Bain replied somewhat caustically that he thought it a pity he had not done so, as nothing would have given him greater joy than going to the end of the jetty and identifying his body. "You speak very plainly," said Butler. "Yes, and what is more, I mean what I say," replied Bain. Butler justified Bain's candour by saying that if he broke out again, he would be worse than the most savage tiger ever let loose on the community. As a means of obviating such an outbreak, Butler suggested that, intellectual employment having failed, some form of manual labour should be found him. Bain complied with Butler's request, and got him a job at levelling reclaimed ground in the neighbourhood of Dunedin. On Wednesday, March 10, Butler started work, but after three hours of it relinquished the effort. Bain saw Butler again in Dunedin on the evening of Saturday, March 13, and made an appointment to meet him at half-past eight that night. Butler did not keep the appointment. Bain searched the town for him, but he was nowhere to be found.

About the same time Butler had some talk with another member of the Dunedin police force, Inspector Mallard. They discussed the crimes of Charles Peace and other notable artists of that kind. Butler remarked to Mallard how easy it would be to destroy all traces of a murder by fire, and asked the inspector whether if he woke up one morning to find some brutal murder had been committed, he would not put it down to him. "No, Butler," replied the inspector, "the first thing I should do would be to look for suspicious circumstances, and most undoubtedly, if they pointed to you, you would be looked after."

In the early morning of this Saturday, March 13, the house of a Mr. Stamper, a solicitor of Dunedin, had been broken into, and some articles of value, among them a pair of opera glasses, stolen. The house had been set on fire, and burned to the ground. On the morning of the following day, Sunday, the 14th, Dunedin was horrified by the discovery of a far more terrible crime, tigerish certainly in its apparent ferocity. In a house in Cumberland Street, a young married couple and their little baby were cruelly murdered and un{sic}{an??} unsuccessful attempt made to fire the scene of the crime.

About half-past six on Sunday morning a man of the name of Robb, a carpenter, on getting out of bed, noticed smoke coming from the house of a neighbor of his, Mr. J. M. Dewar, who occupied a small one-floored cottage standing by itself in Cumberland Street, a large and broad thoroughfare on the outskirts of the town. Dewar was a butcher by trade, a young man, some eighteen months married, and father of a baby girl. Robb, on seeing smoke coming from Dewar's house, woke his son, who was a member of the fire brigade. The latter got up, crossed the street, and going round to the back door, which he found wide open, entered the house. As he went along the passage that separated the two front rooms, a bedroom and sitting-room, he called to the inmates to get up. He received no answer, but as he neared the bedroom he heard a "gurgling" sound. Crawling on his hands and knees he reached the bedroom door, and two feet inside it his right hand touched something. It was the body of a woman; she was still alive, but in a dying condition. Robb dragged her across the passage into the sitting-room. He got some water, and extinguished the fire in the bedroom. On the bed lay the body of Dewar. To all appearances he had been killed in his sleep. By his side was the body of the baby, suffocated by the smoke. Near the bed was an axe belonging to Dewar, stained with blood. It was with this weapon, apparently, that Mr. and Mrs. Dewar had been attacked. Under the bed was a candlestick belonging also to the Dewars, which had been used by the murderer in setting fire to the bed. The front window of the sitting-room was open, there were marks of boot nails on the sill, and on the grass in front of the window a knife was found. An attempt had been made to ransack a chest of drawers in the bedroom, but some articles of jewellery lying in one of the drawers, and a ring on the dressing-table had been left untouched. As far as was known, Mr. and Mrs. Dewar were a perfectly happy and united couple. Dewar had been last seen alive about ten o'clock on the Saturday night getting off a car near his home. At eleven a neighbour had noticed a light in the Dewars' house. About five o'clock on the Sunday morning another neighbour had been aroused from his sleep by the sound as of something falling heavily. It was a wild and boisterous night. Thinking the noise might be the slamming of his stable door, he got up and went out to see that it was secure. He then noticed that a light was burning in the bedroom window of the Dewars' cottage.

Nothing more was known of what had occurred that morning until at half-past six Robb saw the smoke coming from Dewars' house. Mrs. Dewar, who alone could have told something, never recovered consciousness and died on the day following the crime. Three considerable wounds sufficient to cause death had been inflicted on the unfortunate woman's head, and five of a similar character on that of her husband. At the head of the bed, which stood in the corner of the room, there was a large smear of blood on the wall just above the door; there were spots of blood all over the top of the bed, and some smaller ones that had to all appearances spurted on to the panel of the door nearest to the bed.

The investigation of this shocking crime was placed in the hands of Detective Bain, whose duty it had been to keep an eye on Robert Butler, but he did not at first associate his interesting charge with the commission of the murder. About half-past six on Sunday evening Bain happened to go to a place called the Scotia Hotel, where the landlord informed him that one of his servants, a girl named Sarah Gillespie, was very anxious to see him. Her story was this: On the morning of Thursday, March 11, Robert Butler had come to the hotel; he was wearing a dark lavender check suit and carried a top coat and parcel. Butler had stayed in the hotel all Thursday and slept there that night. He had not slept in the hotel on the Friday night, and Sarah Gillespie had not seen him again until he came into the house about five and twenty minutes to seven on Sunday morning. The girl noticed that he was pale and excited, seemed afraid and worried, as if someone were coming after him. After giving her some money for the landlord, he went upstairs, fetched his top coat, a muffler, and his parcel. Before leaving he said he would have a pint of beer, as he had not breakfasted. He then left, presumably to catch an early train.

Butler was next seen a few minutes later at a shop near the hotel, where he bought five tins of salmon, and about the same time a milk-boy saw him standing on the kerb in Cumberland Street in a stooping position, his head turned in the direction of Dewars' house. A little after ten the same night Butler entered a hotel at a place called Blueskin, some twelve miles distant from Dunedin. He was wearing an overcoat and a light muffler. He sat down at a table in the dining-room and seemed weary and sleepy. Someone standing at the bar said "What a shocking murder that was in Cumberland Street!" Butler started up, looked steadily from one to the other of the two men who happened to be in the room, then sat down again and, taking up a book, appeared to be reading. More than once he put down the book and kept shifting uneasily in his chair. After having some supper he got up, paid his reckoning, and left the hotel.

At half-past three the following morning, about fifteen miles from Dunedin, on the road to Waikouaiti, two constables met a man whom they recognised as Butler from a description that had been circulated by the police. The constables arrested and searched him. They found on him a pair of opera glasses, the property of Mr. Stamper, whose house had been burgled and burned down on the morning of the 13th. Of this crime Butler acknowledged himself to be the perpetrator. Besides the opera glasses the constables took from Butler two tins of salmon, a purse containing four shillings and sixpence, a pocket knife, a box of matches, a piece of candle, and a revolver and cartridges. The prisoner was carrying a top coat, and was dressed in a dark coat and grey trousers, underneath which he was wearing a white shirt, an under flannel and a Rob Roy Crimean shirt. One of the constables noticed that there were marks of blood on his shirt. Another singular feature in Butler's attire was the fact that the outer soles of his boots had been recently removed. When last seen in Dunedin Butler had been wearing a moustache; he was now clean shaven.

The same evening a remarkable interview took place in the lock-up at Waikouaiti between Butler and Inspector Mallard. Mallard, who had some reason for suspecting Butler, bearing in mind their recent conversation, told the prisoner that he would be charged with the murder in Cumberland Street. For a few seconds, according to Mallard, the prisoner seemed terribly agitated and appeared to be choking. Recovering himself somewhat, he said, "If for that, you can get no evidence against me; and if I am hanged for it, I shall be an innocent man, whatever other crimes I may have committed." Mallard replied, "There is evidence to convict you—the fire was put out." Butler than{sic} said that he would ask Mallard a question, but, after a pause, decided not to do so. Mallard, after examining Butler's clothes, told him that those were not the clothes in which he had left the Scotia Hotel. Butler admitted it, and said he had thrown those away in the North East Valley. Mallard alluded to the disappearance of the prisoner's moustache. Butler replied that he had cut it off on the road. Mallard noticed then the backs of Butler's hands were scratched, as if by contact with bushes. Butler seemed often on the point of asking questions, but would then stop and say "No, I won't ask you anything." To the constables who had arrested him Butler remarked, "You ought to remember me, because I could have shot you if I had wished." When Mallard later in the evening visited Butler again, the prisoner who was then lying down said, "I want to speak to you. I want to ask the press not to publish my career. Give me fair play. I suppose I shall be convicted and you will see I can die like a man."

A few days after Butler's arrest a ranger on the Town Belt, a hill overlooking Dunedin, found a coat, a hat and silk striped cravat, and a few days later a pair of trousers folded up and placed under a bush. These articles of clothing were identified as those which Butler had been seen wearing on the Saturday and Sunday morning. They were examined. There were a number of bloodstains on them, not one of them larger in size than a pea, some almost invisible. On the front of the trousers about the level of the groin there were blood spots on both sides. There was blood on the fold of the left breast of the coat and on the lining of the cuff of the right arm. The shirt Butler was wearing at the time of his arrest was examined also. There were small spots of blood, about fourteen altogether, on the neck and shoulder bands, the right armpit, the left sleeve, and on both wristbands. Besides the clothes, a salmon tin was found on the Town Belt, and behind a seat in the Botanical Gardens, from which a partial view of the Dewars' house in Cumberland Street could be obtained, two more salmon tins were found, all three similar to the five purchased by Butler on the Sunday morning, two of which had been in his possession at the time of his arrest.

Such were the main facts of the case which Butler had to answer when, a few weeks later, he was put on his trial before the Supreme Court at Dunedin. The presiding judge was Mr. Justice Williams, afterwards Sir Joshua Williams and a member of the Privy Council. The Crown Prosecutor, Mr. Haggitt, conducted the case for the Crown, and Butler defended himself.

II

THE TRIAL OF BUTLER

To a man of Butler's egregious vanity his trial was a glorious opportunity for displaying his intellectual gifts, such as they were. One who had known him in prison about this time describes him as a strange compound of vanity and envy, blind to his own faults and envious of the material advantages enjoyed by others. Self-willed and arrogant, he could bully or whine with equal effect. Despising men, he believed that if a man did not possess some requisite quality, he had only to ape it, as few would distinguish between the real and the sham.

But with all these advantages in the struggle for life, it is certain that Butler's defence would have been far less effective had be{sic} been denied all professional aid. As a matter of fact, throughout his trial Butler was being advised by three distinguished members of the New Zealand bar, now judges of the Supreme Court, who though not appearing for him in court, gave him the full benefit of their assistance outside it. At the same time Butler carried off the thing well. Where imagination was required, Butler broke down; he could not write sketches of life in prison; that was too much for his pedestrian intellect. But given the facts of a case, dealing with a transaction of which he alone knew the real truth, and aided by the advice and guidance of trained intellects, Butler was unquestionably clever and shrewd enough to make the best use of such advantages in meeting the case against him.

Thus equipped for the coming struggle, this high-browed ruffian, with his semi-intellectual cast of countenance, his jerky restless posturing, his splay-footed waddle, "like a lame Muscovy duck," in the graphic words of his gaol companion, stood up to plead for his life before the Supreme Court at Dunedin.

It may be said at the outset that Butler profited greatly by the scrupulous fairness shown by the Crown Prosecutor. Mr. Haggitt extended to the prisoner a degree of consideration and forbearance, justified undoubtedly towards an undefended prisoner. But, as we have seen, Butler was not in reality undefended. At every moment of the trial he was in communication with his legal advisers, and being instructed by them how to meet the evidence given against him. Under these circumstances the unfailing consideration shown him by the Crown Prosecutor seems almost excessive. From the first moment of the trial Butler was fully alive to the necessities of his situation. He refrained from including in his challenges of the jury the gentleman who was afterwards foreman; he knew he was all right, he said, because he parted his hair in the middle, a "softy," in fact. He did not know in all probability that one gentleman on the jury had a rooted conviction that the murder of the Dewars was the work of a criminal lunatic. There was certainly nothing in Butler's demeanour or behaviour to suggest homicidal mania.

The case against Butler rested on purely circumstantial evidence.

No new facts of importance were adduced at the trial. The stealing of Dewar's wages, which had been paid to him on the Saturday, was the motive for the murder suggested by the Crown. The chief facts pointing to Butler's guilt were: his conversation with Mallard and Bain previous to the crime; his demeanour after it; his departure from Dunedin; the removal of his moustache and the soles of his boots; his change of clothes and the bloodstains found upon them, added to which was his apparent inability to account for his movements on the night in question.

Such as the evidence was, Butler did little to shake it in cross- examination. His questions were many of them skilful and pointed, but on more than one occasion the judge intervened to save him from the danger common to all amateur cross-examiners, of not knowing when to stop. He was most successful in dealing with the medical witnesses. Butler had explained the bloodstains on his clothes as smears that had come from scratches on his hands, caused by contact with bushes. This explanation the medical gentlemen with good reason rejected. But they went further, and said that these stains might well have been caused by the spurting and spraying of blood on to the murderer as he struck his victims. Butler was able to show by the position of the bloodstains on the clothes that such an explanation was open to considerable doubt.

Butler's speech in his defence lasted six hours, and was a creditable performance. Its arrangement is somewhat confused and repetitious, some points are over-elaborated, but on the whole he deals very successfully with most of the evidence given against him and exposes the unquestionable weakness of the Crown case. At the outset he declared that he had taken his innocence for his defence. "I was not willing," he said, "to leave my life in the hands of a stranger. I was willing to incur all the disadvantages which the knowledge of the law might bring upon me.

I was willing, also, to enter on this case without any experience whatever of that peculiarly acquired art of cross-examination. I fear I have done wrong. If I had had the assistance of able counsel, much more light would have been thrown on this case than has been." As we have seen, Butler enjoyed throughout his trial the informal assistance of three of the most able counsel in New Zealand, so that this heroic attitude of conscious innocence braving all dangers loses most of its force. Without such assistance his danger might have been very real.

A great deal of the evidence as to his conduct and demeanour at the time of the murder Butler met by acknowledging that it was he who had broken into Mr.

Stamper's house on the Saturday morning, burgled it and set it on fire. His consciousness of guilt in this respect was, he said, quite sufficient to account for anything strange or furtive in his manner at that time. He was already known to the police; meeting Bain on the Saturday night, he felt more than ever sure that he was susspected{sic} of the robbery at Mr. Stamper's; he therefore decided to leave Dunedin as soon as possible. That night, he said, he spent wandering about the streets half drunk, taking occasional shelter from the pouring rain, until six o'clock on the Sunday morning, when he went to the Scotia Hotel. A more detailed account of his movements on the night of the Dewars' murder he did not, or would not, give.

When he comes to the facts of the murder and his theories as to the nature and motive of the crime—theories which he developed at rather unnecessary length for the purpose of his own defence— his speech is interesting. It will be recollected that on the discovery of the murder, a knife was found on the grass outside the house. This knife was not the property of the Dewars. In Butler's speech he emphasised the opinion that this knife had been brought there by the murderer: "Horrible though it may be, my conclusion is that he brought it with the intention of cutting the throats of his victims, and that, finding they lay in rather an untoward position, he changed his mind, and, having carried out the object with which he entered the house, left the knife and, going back, brought the axe with which he effected his purpose. What was the purpose of the murderer? Was it the robbery of Dewar's paltry wages? Was it the act of a tiger broken loose on the community? An act of pure wanton devilry? or was there some more reasonable explanation of this most atrocious crime?"

Butler rejected altogether the theory of ordinary theft. No thief of ambitious views, he said, would pitch upon the house of a poor journeyman butcher. The killing of the family appeared to him to be the motive: "an enemy hath done this." The murderer seems to have had a knowledge of the premises; he enters the house and does his work swiftly and promptly, and is gone. "We cannot know," Butler continues, "all the passages in the lives of the murdered man or woman. What can we know of the hundred spites and jealousies or other causes of malice which might have caused the crime? If you say some obscure quarrel, some spite or jealousy is not likely to have been the cause of so dreadful a murder, you cannot revert to the robbery theory without admitting a motive much weaker in all its utter needlessness and vagueness.

The prominent feature of the murder, indeed the only feature, is its ruthless, unrelenting, determined vindictiveness. Every blow seemed to say, `You shall die you shall not live.'"

Whether Butler were the murderer of the Dewars or not, the theory that represented them as having been killed for the purpose of robbery has its weak side all the weaker if Butler, a practical and ambitious criminal, were the guilty man.

In 1882, two years after Butler's trial, there appeared in a New Zealand newspaper, Society, published in Christchurch, a series of Prison "Portraits," written evidently by one who had himself undergone a term of imprisonment.

One of the "Portraits" was devoted to an account of Butler. The writer had known Butler in prison. According to the story told him by Butler, the latter had arrived in Dunedin with a quantity of jewellery he had stolen in Australia. This jewellery he entrusted to a young woman for safe keeping. After serving his first term of two years' imprisonment in Dunedin, Butler found on his release that the young woman had married a man of the name of Dewar. Butler went to Mrs. Dewar and asked for the return of his jewellery; she refused to give it up. On the night of the murder he called at the house in Cumberland Street and made a last appeal to her, but in vain. He determined on revenge. During his visit to Mrs. Dewar he had had an opportunity of seeing the axe and observing the best way to break into the house. He watched the husband's return, and decided to kill him as well as his wife on the chance of obtaining his week's wages. With the help of the knife which he had found in the backyard of a hotel he opened the window. The husband he killed in his sleep, the woman waked with the first blow he struck her. He found the jewellery in a drawer rolled up in a pair of stockings. He afterwards hid it in a well-marked spot some half-hour before his arrest.

A few years after its appearance in Society, this account of Butler was reproduced in an Auckland newspaper. Bain, the detective, wrote a letter questioning the truth of the writer's statements. He pointed out that when Butler first came to Dunedin he had been at liberty only a fortnight before serving his first term of imprisonment, very little time in which to make the acquaintance of a woman and dispose of the stolen jewellery. He asked why, if Butler had hidden the jewellery just before his arrest, he had not also hidden the opera-glasses which he had stolen from Mr. Stamper's house. Neither of these comments is very convincing. A fortnight seems time enough in which a man of Butler's character might get to know a woman and dispose of some jewellery; while, if Butler were the murderer of Mr. Dewar as well as the burglar who had broken into Stamper's house, it was part of his plan to acknowledge himself guilty of the latter crime and use it to justify his movements before and after the murder. Bain is more convincing when he states at the conclusion of his letter that he had known Mrs. Dewar from childhood as a "thoroughly good and true woman," who, as far as he knew, had never in her life had any acquaintance with Butler.

At the same time, the account given by Butler's fellow-prisoner, in which the conduct of the murdered woman is represented as constituting the provocation for the subsequent crime, explains one peculiar circumstance in connection with the tragedy, the selection of this journeyman butcher and his wife as the victims of the murderer. It explains the theory, urged so persistently by Butler in his speech to the jury, that the crime was the work of an enemy of the Dewars, the outcome of some hidden spite, or obscure quarrel; it explains the apparent ferocity of the murder, and the improbability of a practical thief selecting such an unprofitable couple as his prey. The rummaged chest of drawers and the fact that some trifling articles of jewellery were left untouched on the top of them, are consistent with an eager search by the murderer for some particular object.

Against this theory of revenge is the fact that Butler was a malignant ruffian and liar in any case, that, having realised very little in cash by the burglary at Stamper's house, he would not be particular as to where he might get a few shillings more, that he had threatened to do a tigerish deed, and that it is characteristic of his vanity to try to impute to his crime a higher motive than mere greed or necessity.

Butler showed himself not averse to speaking of the murder in Cumberland Street to at least one of those, with whom he came in contact in his later years. After he had left New Zealand and returned to Australia, he was walking in a street in Melbourne with a friend when they passed a lady dressed in black, carrying a baby in her arms. The baby looked at the two men and laughed. Butler frowned and walked rapidly away. His companion chaffed him, and asked whether it was the widow or the baby that he was afraid of. Butler was silent, but after a time asked his companion to come into some gardens and sit down on one of the seats, as he had something serious to say to him. For a while Butler sat silent. Then he asked the other if he had ever been in Dunedin. "Yes," was the reply. "Look here," said Butler, "you are the only man I ever made any kind of confidant of. You are a good scholar, though I could teach you a lot." After this gracious compliment he went on: "I was once tried in Dunedin on the charge of killing a man, woman and child, and although innocent, the crime was nearly brought home to me. It was my own ability that pulled me through. Had I employed a professional advocate, I should not have been here to-day talking to you." After describing the murder, Butler said: "Trying to fire the house was unnecessary, and killing the baby was unnecessary and cruel. I respect no man's life, for no man respects mine. A lot of men I have never injured have tried to put a rope round my neck more than once. I hate society in general, and one or two individuals in particular. The man who did that murder in Dunedin has, if anything, my sympathy, but it seems to me he need not have killed that child." His companion was about to speak. Butler stopped him. "Now, don't ever ask me such a silly question as that," he said. "What?" asked his friend. "You were about to ask me if I did that deed," replied Butler, "and you know perfectly well that, guilty or innocent, that question would only be answered in one way." "I was about to ask nothing of the kind," said the other, "for you have already told me that you were innocent." "Good!" said Butler, "then let that be the end of the subject, and never refer to it again, except, perhaps, in your own mind, when you can, if you like, remember that I said the killing of the child was unnecessary and cruel."

Having developed to the jury his theory of why the crime was committed, Butler told them that, as far as he was concerned, there were four points against him on which the Crown relied to prove his guilt. Firstly, there was the fact of his being in the neighbourhood of the crime on the Sunday morning; that, he said, applied to scores of other people besides himself. Then there was his alleged disturbed appearance and guilty demeanour. The evidence of that was, he contended, doubtful in any case, and referable to another cause; as also his leaving Dunedin in the way and at the time he did. He scouted the idea that murderers are compelled by some invisible force to betray their guilt. "The doings of men," he urged, "and their success are regulated by the amount of judgment that they possess, and, without impugning or denying the existence of Providence, I say this is a law that holds good in all cases, whether for evil or good. Murderers, if they have the sense and ability and discretion to cover up their crime, will escape, do escape, and have escaped. Many people, when they have gravely shaken their heads and said 'Murder will out,' consider they have done a great deal and gone a long way towards settling the question. Well, this, like many other stock formulas of Old World wisdom, is not true. How many murders are there that the world has never heard of, and never will? How many a murdered man, for instance, lies among the gum-trees of Victoria, or in the old abandoned mining-shafts on the diggings, who is missed by nobody, perhaps, but a pining wife at home, or helpless children, or an old mother? But who were their murderers? Where are they? God knows, perhaps, but nobody else, and nobody ever will." The fact, he said, that he was alleged to have walked up Cumberland Street on the Sunday morning and looked in the direction of the Dewars' house was, unless the causes of superstition and a vague and incomplete reasoning were to be accepted as proof, evidence rather of his innocence than his guilt. He had removed the soles of his boots, he said, in order to ease his feet in walking; the outer soles had become worn and ragged, and in lumps under his feet. He denied that he had told Bain, the detective, that he would break out as a desperate tiger let loose on the community; what he had said was that he was tired of living the life of a prairie dog or a tiger in the jungle.

Butler was more successful when he came to deal with the bloodstains on his clothes. These, he said, were caused by the blood from the scratches on his hands, which had been observed at the time of his arrest. The doctors had rejected this theory, and said that the spots of blood had been impelled from the axe or from the heads of the victims as the murderer struck the fatal blow. Butler put on the clothes in court, and was successful in showing that the position and appearance of certain of the blood spots was not compatible with such a theory. "I think," he said, "I am fairly warranted in saying that the evidence of these gentlemen is, not to put too fine a point on it, worth just nothing at all."

Butler's concluding words to the jury were brief but emphatic: "I stand in a terrible position. So do you. See that in your way of disposing of me you deliver yourselves of your responsibilities."

In the exercise of his forbearance towards an undefended prisoner, Mr. Haggitt did not address the jury for the Crown. At four o'clock the judge commenced his summingDup. Mr. Justice Williams impressed on the jury that they must be satisfied, before they could convict the prisoner, that the circumstances of the crime and the prisoner's conduct were inconsistent with any other reasonable hypothesis than his guilt. There was little or no evidence that robbery was the motive of the crime. The circumstance of the prisoner being out all Saturday night and in the neighbourhood of the crime on Sunday morning only amounted to the fact that he had an opportunity shared by a great number of other persons of committing the murder. The evidence of his agitation and demeanour at the time of his arrest must be accepted with caution. The evidence of the blood spots was of crucial importance; there was nothing save this to connect him directly with the crime. The jury must be satisfied that the blood on the clothes corresponded with the blood marks which, in all probability, would be found on the person who committed the murder. In regard to the medical testimony some caution must be exercised. Where medical gentlemen had made observations, seen with their own eyes, the direct inference might be highly trustworthy, but, when they proceeded to draw further inferences, they might be in danger of looking at facts through the spectacles of theory; "we know that people do that in other things besides science—politics, religion, and so forth." Taking the Crown evidence, at its strongest, there was a missing link; did the evidence of the bloodstains supply it? These bloodstains were almost invisible. Could a person be reasonably asked to explain how they came where they did? Could they be accounted for in no other reasonable way than that the clothes had been worn by the murderer of the Dewars?

In spite of a summing-up distinctly favourable to the prisoner, the jury were out three hours. According to one account of their proceedings, told to the writer, there was at first a majority of the jurymen in favour of conviction. But it was Saturday night; if they could not come to a decision they were in danger of being locked up over Sunday. For this reason the gentleman who held an obstinate and unshaken belief that the crime was the work of a homicidal maniac found an unexpected ally in a prominent member of a church choir who was down to sing a solo in his church on Sunday, and was anxious not to lose such an opportunity for distinction. Whatever the cause, after three hours' deliberation the jury returned a verdict of "Not Guilty." Later in the Session Butler pleaded guilty to the burglary at Mr. Stamper's house, and was sentenced to eighteen years' imprisonment. The severity of this sentence was not, the judge said, intended to mark the strong suspicion under which Butler laboured of being a murderer as well as a burglar.

The ends of justice had been served by Butler's acquittal. But in the light of after events, it is perhaps unfortunate that the jury did not stretch a point and so save the life of Mr. Munday of Toowong. Butler underwent his term of imprisonment in Littleton Jail. There his reputation was most unenviable. He is described by a fellow prisoner as ill-tempered, malicious, destructive, but cowardly and treacherous. He seems to have done little or no work; he looked after the choir and the library, but was not above breaking up the one and smashing the other, if the fit seized him.

III

HIS DECLINE AND FALL

In 1896 Butler was released from prison. The news of his release was described as falling like a bomb-shell among the peaceful inhabitants of Dunedin. In the colony of Victoria, where Butler had commenced his career, it was received with an apprehension that was justified by subsequent events. It was believed that on his release the New Zealand authorities had shipped Butler off to Rio. But it was not long before he made his way once more to Australia. From the moment of his arrival in Melbourne he was shadowed by the police. One or two mysterious occurrences soon led to his arrest. On June 5 he was sentenced to twelve months' imprisonment under the Criminal Influx Act, which makes it a penal offence for any convict to enter Victoria for three years after his release from prison. Not content with this, the authorities determined to put Butler on trial on two charges of burglary and one of highway robbery, committed since his return to the colony. To one charge of burglary, that of breaking into a hairdresser's shop and stealing a wig, some razors and a little money, Butler pleaded guilty.

But the charge of highway robbery, which bore a singular resemblance to the final catastrophe in Queensland, he resisted to the utmost, and showed that his experience in the Supreme Court at Dunedin had not been lost on him. At half-past six one evening in a suburb of Melbourne an elderly gentleman found himself confronted by a bearded man, wearing a long overcoat and a boxer hat and flourishing a revolver, who told him abruptly to "turn out his pockets." The old man did ashe was told. The robber then asked for his watch and chain, saying "Business must be done." The old gentleman mildly urged that this was a dangerous business. On being assured that the watch was a gold one, the robber appeared willing to risk the danger, and departed thoroughly satisfied. The old gentleman afterwards identified Butler as the man who had taken his watch. Another elderly man swore that he had seen Butler at the time of the robbery in the possession of a fine gold watch, which he said had been sent him from home. But the watch had not been found in Butler's possession.

On June 18 Butler was put on his trial in the Melbourne Criminal Court before Mr. Justice Holroyd, charged with robbery under arms. His appearance in the dock aroused very considerable interest. "It was the general verdict," wrote one newspaper, "that his intellectual head and forehead compared not unfavourably with those of the judge." He was decently dressed and wore pince-nez, which he used in the best professional manner as he referred to the various documents that lay in front of him. He went into the witness-box and stated that the evening of the crime he had spent according to his custom in the Public Library.

For an hour and a half he addressed the jury. He disputed the possibility of his identification by his alleged victim. He was "an old gentleman of sedentary pursuits and not cast in the heroic mould." Such a man would be naturally alarmed and confused at meeting suddenly an armed robber. Now, under these circumstances, could his recognition of a man whose face was hidden by a beard, his head by a boxer hat, and his body by a long overcoat, be considered trustworthy? And such recognition occurring in the course of a chance encounter in the darkness, that fruitful mother of error? The elderly gentleman had described his moustache as a slight one, but the jury could see that it was full and overhanging. He complained that he had been put up for identification singly, not with other men, according to the usual custom; the police had said to the prosecutor: "We have here a man that we think robbed you, and, if he is not the man, we shall be disappointed," to which the prosecutor had replied: "Yes, and if he is not the man, I shall be disappointed too." For the elderly person who had stated that he had seen a gold watch in Butler's possession the latter had nothing but scorn. He was a "lean and slippered pantaloon in Shakespeare's last stage"; and he, Butler, would have been a lunatic to have confided in such a man.

The jury acquitted Butler, adding as a rider to their verdict that there was not sufficient evidence of identification. The third charge against Butler was not proceeded with. He was put up to receive sentence for the burglary at the hairdresser's shop. Butler handed to the judge a written statement which Mr. Justice Holroyd described as a narrative that might have been taken from those sensational newspapers written for nursery- maids, and from which, he said, he could not find that Butler had ever done one good thing in the whole course of his life. Of that life of fifty years Butler had spent thirty-five in prison. The judge expressed his regret that a man of Butler's knowledge, information, vanity, and utter recklessness of what evil will do, could not be put away somewhere for the rest of his life, and sentenced him to fifteen years' imprisonment with hard labour. "An iniquitous and brutal sentence!" exclaimed the prisoner. After a brief altercation with the judge, who said that he could hardly express the scorn he felt for such a man, Butler was removed. The judge subsequently reduced the sentence to one of ten years. Chance or destiny would seem implacable in their pursuit of Mr. William Munday of Toowong.

Butler after his trial admitted that it was he who had robbed the old gentleman of his watch, and described to the police the house in which it was hidden. When the police went there to search they found that the house had been pulled down, but among the debris they discovered a brown paper parcel containing the old gentleman's gold watch and chain, a five-chambered revolver, a keen-edged butcher's knife, and a mask.

Butler served his term of imprisonment in Victoria, "an unmitigated nuisance" to his custodians. On his release in 1904, he made, as in Dunedin, an attempt to earn a living by his pen. He contributed some articles to a Melbourne evening paper on the inconveniences of prison discipline, but he was quite unfitted for any sustained effort as a journalist. According to his own account, with the little money he had left he made his way to Sydney, thence to Brisbane. He was half-starved, bewildered, despairing; in his own words, "if a psychological camera could have been turned on me it would have shown me like a bird fascinated by a serpent, fascinated and bewildered by the fate in front, behind, and around me." Months of suffering and privation passed, months of tramping hundreds of miles with occasional breakdowns, months of hunger and sickness; "my actions had become those of a fool; my mind and will had become a remnant guided or misguided by unreasoning impulse."

It was under the influence of such an impulse that on March 23 Butler had met and shot Mr. Munday at Toowong. On May 24 he was arraigned at Brisbane before the Supreme Court of Queensland. But the Butler who stood in the dock of the Brisbane Criminal Court was very different from the Butler who had successfully defended himself at Dunedin and Melbourne. The spirit had gone out of him; it was rather as a suppliant, represented by counsel, that he faced the charge of murder. His attitude was one of humble and appropriate penitence. In a weak and nervous voice he told the story of his hardships since his release from his Victorian prison; he would only urge that the shooting of Mr. Munday was accidental, caused by Munday picking up a stone and attacking him. When about to be sentenced to death he expressed great sorrow and contrition for his crime, for the poor wife and children of his unfortunate victim. His life, he said, was a poor thing, but he would gladly give it fifty times over.

The sentence of death was confirmed by the Executive on June 30. To a Freethought advocate who visited him shortly before his execution, Butler wrote a final confession of faith: "I shall have to find my way across the harbour bar without the aid of any pilot. In these matters I have for many years carried an exempt flag, and, as it has not been carried through caprice or igno-rance, I am compelled to carry it to the last. There is an impassable bar of what I honestly believe to be the inexorable logic of philosophy and facts, history and experience of the nature of the world, the human race and myself, between me and the views of the communion of any religious organisation. So instead of the `depart Christian soul' of the priest, I only hope for the comfort and satisfaction of the last friendly good-bye of any who cares to give it."

From this positive affirmation of unbelief Butler wilted somewhat at the approach of death. The day before his execution he spent half an hour playing hymns on the church organ in the prison; and on the scaffold, where his agitation rendered him almost speechless, he expressed his sorrow for what he had done, and the hope that, if there were a heaven, mercy would be shown him.

M. DERUES

The last word on Derues has been said by M. Georges Claretie in his excellent monograph, "Derues L'Empoisonneur," Paris. 1907. There is a full account of the case in Vol. V. of Fouquier, "Causes Celebres."

I

THE CLIMBING LITTLE GROCER

M. Etienne Saint-Faust de Lamotte, a provincial nobleman of ancient lineage and moderate health, ex-equerry to the King, de-

sired in the year 1774 to dispose of a property in the country, the estate of Buisson-Souef near Villeneuve-le-Roi, which he had purchased some ten years before out of money acquired by a prudent marriage.

With an eye to the main chance M. de Lamotte had in 1760 ran away with the daughter of a wealthy citizen of Rheims, who was then staying with her sister in Paris. They lived together in the country for some time, and a son was born to them, whom the father legitimised by subsequently marrying the mother. For a few years M. and Mme. de Lamotte dwelt happily together at Buisson-Souef. But as their boy grew up they became anxious to leave the country and return to Paris, where M. de Lamotte hoped to be able to obtain for his son some position about the Court of Louis XVI. And so it was that in May, 1775, M. de Lamotte gave a power of attorney to his wife in order that she might go to Paris and negotiate for the sale of Buisson-Souef. The legal side of the transaction was placed in the hands of one Jolly, a proctor at the Chatelet in Paris.

Now the proctor Jolly had a client with a great desire to acquire a place in the country, M. Derues de Cyrano de Bury, lord of Candeville, Herchies, and other places. Here was the very man to comply with the requirements of the de Lamottes, and such a pleasing, ready, accommodating gentleman into the bargain! Very delicate to all appearances, strangely pale, slight, fragile in build, with his beardless chin and feminine cast of feature, there was something cat-like in the soft insinuating smile of this seemingly most amiable, candid and pious of men. Always cheerful and optimistic, it was quite a pleasure to do business with M. Derues de Cyrano de Bury. The de Lamottes after one or two interviews were delighted with their prospective purchaser. Everything was speedily settled. M. Derues and his wife, a lady belonging to the distinguished family of Nicolai, visited Buisson-Souef. They were enchanted with what they saw, and their hosts were hardly less enchanted with their visitors. By the end of December, 1775, the purchase was concluded. M. Derues was to give 130,000 livres (about L20,000) for the estate, the payments to be made by instalments, the first of 12,000 livres to be paid on the actual signing of the contract of sale, which, it was agreed, was to be concluded not later than the first of June, 1776. In the meantime, as an earnest of good faith, M. Derues gave Mme. de Lamotte a bill for 4,200 livres to fall due on April 1, 1776.

What could be more satisfactory? That M. Derues was a substantial person there could be no doubt. Through his wife he was entitled to a sum of 250,000 livres as her share of the property of a wealthy kinsman, one Despeignes-Duplessis, a country gentleman, who some four years before had been found murdered in his house under mysterious circumstances. The liquidation of the Duplessis inheritance, as soon as the law's delay could be overcome, would place the Derues in a position of affluence fitting a Cyrano de Bury and a Nicolai.

At this time M. Derues was in reality far from affluent. In point of fact he was insolvent. Nor was his lineage, nor that of his wife, in any way distinguished. He had no right to call himself de Cyrano de Bury or Lord of Candeville. His wife's name was Nicolais, not Nicolai—a very important difference from the genealogical point of view. The Duplessis inheritance, though certainly existent, would seem to have had little more chance of realisation than the mythical Crawford millions of Madame Humbert. And yet, crippled with debt, without a penny in the world, this daring grocer of the Rue Beaubourg, for such was M. Derues' present condition in life, could cheerfully and confidently engage in a transaction as considerable as the purchase of a large estate for 130,000 livres! The origin of so enterprising a gentleman is worthy of attention.

Antoine Francois Derues was born at Chartres in 1744; his father was a corn merchant. His parents died when he was three years old. For some time after his birth he was assumed to be a girl; it was not until he was twelve years old that an operation determined his sex to be masculine. Apprenticed by his relatives to a grocer, Derues succeeded so well in the business that he was able in 1770 to set up on his own account in Paris, and in 1772 he married. Among the grocer's many friends and acquaintances this marriage created something of a sensation, for Derues let it be known that the lady of his choice was of noble birth and an heiress. The first statement was untrue. The lady was one Marie Louise Nicolais, daughter of a non-commissioned artillery officer, turned coachbuilder. But by suppressing the S at the end of her name, which Derues was careful also to erase in his marriage contract, the ambitious grocer was able to describe his wife as connected with the noble house of Nicolai, one of the most distinguished of the great French families.

There was more truth in the statement that Mme. Derues was an heiress. A kinsman of her mother, Beraud by name, had become the heir to a certain Marquis Desprez. Beraud was the son of a small merchant. His mother had married a second time, the hus-

band being the Marquis Desprez, and through her Beraud had inherited the Marquis' property. According to the custom of the time, Beraud, on coming into his inheritance, took a title from one of his estates and called himself thenceforth the lord of Despeignes-Duplessis. A rude, solitary, brutal man, devoted to sport, he lived alone in his castle of Candeville, hated by his neighbours, a terror to poachers. One day he was found lying dead in his bedroom; he had been shot in the chest; the assassin had escaped through an open window.

The mystery of Beraud's murder was never solved. His estate of 200,000 livres was divided among three cousins, of whom the mother of Mme. Derues was one. Mme. Derues herself was entitled to a third of his mother's share of the estate, that is, one- ninth of the whole. But in 1775 Derues acquired the rest of the mother's share on condition that he paid her an annual income of 1,200 livres. Thus on the liquidation of the Duplessis inheritance Mme. Derues would be entitled nominally to some 66,500 livres, about L11,000 in English money. But five years had passed since the death of Despeignes-Duplessis, and the estate was still in the slow process of legal settlement. If Derues were to receive the full third of the Duplessis inheritance—a very unlikely supposition after four years of liquidation—66,000 livres would not suffice to pay his ordinary debts quite apart from the purchase money of Buisson- Souef. His financial condition was in the last degree critical. Not content with the modest calling of a grocer, Derues had turned money-lender, a money-lender to spendthrift and embarrassed noblemen. Derues dearly loved a lord; he wanted to become one himself; it delighted him to receive dukes and marquises at the Rue Beaubourg, even if they came there with the avowed object of raising the wind. The smiling grocer, in his everlasting bonnet and flowered dressing-gown a la J. J. Rousseau, was ever ready to oblige the needy scion of a noble house. What he borrowed at moderate interest from his creditors he lent at enhanced interest to the quality. Duns and bailiffs jostled the dukes and marquises whose presence at the Rue Beaubourg so impressed the wondering neighbours of the facile grocer.

This aristocratic money-lending proved a hopeless trade; it only plunged Derues deeper and deeper into the mire of financial disaster. The noblemen either forgot to pay while they were alive, or on their death were found to be insolvent. Derues was driven to ordering goods and merchandise on credit, and selling them at a lower price for ready money. Victims of this treatment began to press him seriously for their money or their goods. Desperately he continued to fence them off with the long expected windfall of the Duplessis inheritance.

Paris was getting too hot for him. Gay and irrepressible as he was, the strain was severe. If he could only find some retreat in the country where he might enjoy at once refuge from his creditors and the rank and consequence of a country gentleman! Nothing—no fear, no disappointment, no disaster—could check the little grocer's ardent and overmastering desire to be a gentleman indeed, a landed proprietor, a lord or something or other. At the beginning of 1775 he had purchased a place near Rueil from a retired coffeehouse-keeper, paying 1,000 livres on account, but the non-payment of the rest of the purchase-money had resulted in the annulment of the contract. Undefeated, Derues only deter-

mined to fly the higher. Having failed to pay 9,000 livres for a modest estate near Rueil, he had no hesitation in pledging himself to pay 130,000 livres for the lordly domain of Buisson- Souef. So great were his pride and joy on the conclusion of the latter bargain that he amused himself by rehearsing on paper his future style and title: "Antoine Francois de Cyrano Derues de Bury, Seigneur de Buisson-Souef et Valle Profonde." He is worthy of Thackeray's pen, this little grocer-snob, with his grand and ruinous acquaintance with the noble and the great, his spurious titles, his unwearied climbing of the social ladder.

The confiding, if willing, dupe of aristocratic impecuniosity, Derues was a past master of the art of duping others. From the moment of the purchase of Buisson-Souef all his art was employed in cajoling the trusting and simple de Lamottes. Legally Buisson-Souef was his from the signing of the agreement in December, 1775. His first payment was due in April, 1776. Instead of making it, Derues went down to Buisson-Souef with his little girl, and stayed there as the guests of the de Lamottes for six months. His good humour and piety won all hearts. The village priest especially derived great satisfaction from the society of so devout a companion. He entertained his good friends, the merry little man, by dressing up as a woman, a role his smooth face and effeminate features well fitted him to play. If business were alluded to, the merry gentleman railed at the delay and chicanery of lawyers; it was that alone that postponed the liquidation of the Duplessis inheritance; as soon as the lawyers could be got rid of, the purchase-money of his new estate would be promptly paid up. But as time went on and no payment was forthcoming the de Lamottes began to feel a little uneasy. As soon as Derues had departed in November M. de Lamotte decided to send his wife to Paris to make further inquiries and, if possible, bring their purchaser up to the scratch. Mme. de Lamotte had developed into a stout, indolent woman, of the Mrs. Bloss type, fond of staying in bed and taking heavy meals. Her son, a fat, lethargic youth of fourteen, accompanied his mother.

On hearing of Mme. de Lamotte's contemplated visit to Paris, Derues was filled with alarm. If she were living free and independent in Paris she might find out the truth about the real state of his affairs, and then good-bye to Buisson-Souef and landed gentility! No, if Mme. de Lamotte were to come to Paris, she must come as the guest of the Derues, a pleasant return for the hospitality accorded to the grocer at Buisson-Souef. The invitation was given and readily accepted; M. de Lamotte still had enough confidence in and liking for the Derues to be glad of the opportunity of placing his wife under their roof. And so it was that on December 16, 1776, Mme. de Lamotte arrived at Paris and took up her abode at the house of the Derues in the Rue Beaubourg Her son she placed at a private school in a neighbouring street.

To Derues there was now one pressing and immediate problem to be solved—how to keep Buisson-Souef as his own without paying for it? To one less sanguine, less daring, less impudent and desperate in his need, the problem would have appeared insoluble.

But that was by no means the view of the cheery and resourceful grocer. He had a solution ready, well thought out and bearing to his mind the stamp of probability. He would make a fictitious payment of the purchase-money to Mme. de Lamotte. She would then disappear, taking her son with her. Her indiscretion in having been the mistress of de Lamotte before she became his wife, would lend colour to his story that she had gone off with a former lover, taking with her the money which Derues had paid her for Buisson-Souef. He would then produce the necessary documents proving the payment of the purchase-money, and Buisson-Souef would be his for good and all.

The prime necessity to the success of this plan was the disappearance, willing or unwilling, of Mme. de Lamotte and her son. The former had settled down quite comfortably beneath the hospitable roof of the Derues, and under the soothing influence of her host showed little vigour in pressing him for the money due to herself and her husband. She had already spent a month in quietly enjoying Paris and the society of her friends when, towards the end of January, 1770, her health and that of her son began to fail. Mme. de Lamotte was seized with sickness and internal trouble. Though Derues wrote to her husband that his wife was well and their business was on the point of conclusion, by the 30th of January Mme. de Lamotte had taken to her bed, nursed and physicked by the ready Derues. On the 31st the servant at the Rue Beaubourg was told that she could go to her home at Montrouge, whither Derues had previously sent his two children. Mme. Derues, who was in an interesting condition, was sent out for an hour by her husband to do some shopping. Derues was alone with his patient.

In the evening a friend, one Bertin, came to dine with Derues. Bertin was a short, hustling, credulous, breathless gentleman, always in a hurry, with a great belief in the abilities of M. Derues. He found the little man in excellent spirits. Bertin asked if he could see Mme. de Lamotte. Mme. Derues said that that was impossible, but that her husband had given her some medicine which was working splendidly. The young de Lamotte called to see his mother. Derues took him into her room; in the dim light the boy saw her sleeping, and crept out quietly for fear of disturbing her. The Derues and their friends sat down to dinner. Derues kept jumping up and running into the sick room, from which a horrible smell began to pervade the house. But Derues was radiant at the success of his medicine. "Was there ever such a nurse as I am?" he exclaimed. Bertin remarked that he thought it was a woman's and not a man's place to nurse a lady under such distressing circumstances. Derues protested that it was an occupation he had always liked. Next day, February 1, the servant was still at Montrouge; Mme. Derues was again sent out shopping; again Derues was alone with his patient. But she was a patient no longer; she had become a corpse. The highly successful medicine administered to the poor lady by her jolly and assiduous nurse had indeed worked wonders.

Derues had bought a large leather trunk. It is possible that to Derues belongs the distinction of being the first murderer to put that harmless and necessary article of travel to a criminal use. He was engaged in his preparations for coffining Mme. de Lamotte, when a female creditor knocked insistently at the door. She would take no denial. Clad in his bonnet and gown, Derues was compelled to admit her. She saw the large trunk, and suspected a bolt on the part of her creditor. Derues reassured her; a lady, he said, who had been stopping with them was returning to the country. The creditor departed. Later in the day Derues came out of the house and summoned some porters. With their help the heavy trunk was taken to the house of a sculptor, a friend of Derues, who agreed to keep it in his studio until Derues could take it down to his place in the country. Bertin came in to dinner again that evening, and also the young de Lamotte. Derues was gayer than ever, laughing and joking with his guests. He told the boy that his mother had quite recovered and gone to Versailles to see about finding him some post at the Court. "We'll go and see her there in a day or two," he said, "I'll let you know when."

On the following day a smartly dressed, dapper, but very pale little gentleman, giving the name of Ducoudray, hired a vacant cellar in a house in the Rue de la Mortellerie. He had, he said, some Spanish wine he wanted to store there, and three or four days later M. Ducoudray deposited in this cellar a large grey trunk. A few days after he employed a man to dig a large hole in the floor of the cellar, giving as his reason for such a proceeding that "there was no way of keeping wine like burying it." While the man worked at the job, his genial employer beguiled his labours with merry quips and tales, which he illustrated with delightful mimicry. The hole dug, the man was sent about his business. "I will bury the wine myself," said his employer, and on one or two occasions M. Ducoudray was seen by persons living in the house going in and out of his cellar, a lighted candle in his hand. One day the pale little gentleman was observed leaving the cellar, accompanied by a porter carrying a large trunk, and after that the dwellers in the Rue de la Mortellerie saw the pale little gentleman no more.

A few days later M. Derues sent down to his place at Buisson- Souef a large trunk filled with china. It was received there by M. de Lamotte. Little did the trusting gentleman guess that it was in this very trunk that the body of his dear wife had been conveyed to its last resting place in the cellar of M. Ducoudray in the Rue de la Mortellerie. Nor had M. Mesvrel- Desvergers, importunate creditor of M. Derues, guessed the contents of the large trunk that he had met his debtor one day early in February conveying through the streets of Paris. Creditors were always interrupting Derues at inconvenient moments. M. Mesvrel-Desvergers had tapped Derues on the shoulder, reminded him forcibly of his liability towards him, and spoken darkly of possible imprisonment. Derues pointed to the trunk. It contained, he said, a sample of wine; he was going to order some more of it, and he would then be in a position to pay his debt. But the creditor, still doubting, had M. Derues followed, and ascertained that he had deposited his sample of wine at a house in the Rue de la Mortellerie.

On Wednesday, February 12, a M. Beaupre of Commercy arrived at Versailles with his nephew, a fat boy, in reality some fourteen years of age, but given out as older. They hired a room at the house of a cooper named Pecquet. M. Beaupre was a very pale little gentleman, who seemed in excellent spirits, in spite of the fact that his nephew was clearly anything but well. Indeed, so sick and ailing did he appear to be that Mme. Pecquet suggested that his uncle should call in a doctor. But M. Beaupre said that that was quite unnecessary; he had no faith in doctors; he would give the boy a good purge. His illness was due, he said, to a venereal disorder and the drugs which he had been taking in order to cure it; it was a priest the boy needed rather than a doctor. On the Thursday and Friday the boy's condition showed little improvement; the vomiting continued.

But on Saturday M. Beaupre declared himself as highly delighted with the success of his medicine. The same night the boy was dead. The priest, urgently sent for by his devout uncle, arrived to find a corpse. On the following day "Louis Anotine Beaupre, aged twenty-two and a half," was buried at Versailles, his pious uncle leaving with the priest six livres to pay for masses for the repose of his erring nephew's soul.

The same evening M. Derues who, according to his own account, had left Paris with the young de Lamotte in order to take the boy to his mother in Versailles, returned home to the Rue Beaubourg. As usual, Bertin dropped in to dinner. He found his host full of merriment, singing in the lightness of his heart. Indeed, he had reason to be pleased, for at last, he told his wife and his friend, Buisson-Souef was his. He had seen Mme. de Lamotte at Versailles and paid her the full purchase-money in good, sounding gold. And, best joke of all, Mme. de Lamotte had no sooner settled the business than she had gone off with a former lover, her son and her money, and would in all probability never be heard of again. The gay gentleman laughingly reminded his hearers that such an escapade on the part of Mme. de Lamotte was hardly to be wondered at, when they recollected that her son had been born out of wedlock

To all appearances Mme. de Lamotte had undoubtedly concluded the sale of Buisson-Souef to Derues and received the price of it before disappearing with her lover. Derues had in his possession a deed of sale signed by Mme. de Lamotte and acknowledging the payment to her by Derues of 100,000 livres, which he had borrowed for that purpose from an advocate of the name of Duclos. As a fact the loan from Duclos to Derues was fictitious. A legal document proving the loan had been drawn up, but the cash which the notary had demanded to see before executing the document had been borrowed for a few hours. Duclos, a provincial advocate, had acted in good faith, in having been represented to him that such fictitious transactions were frequently used in Paris for the purpose of getting over some temporary financial difficulty. On the 15th of February the deed of the sale of Buisson-Souef had been brought by a woman to the office of a scrivener employed by Derues; it was already signed, but the woman asked that certain blanks should be filled in and that the document should be dated. She was told that the date should be that of the day on which the parties had signed it. She gave it as February 12. A few days later Derues called at the office and was told of the lady's visit. "Ah!" he said, "it was Mme. de Lamotte herself, the lady who sold me the estate."

In the meantime Derues, through his bustling and ubiquitous friend Bertin, took good care that the story of Mme. de Lamotte's sale of Buisson-Souef and subsequent elopement should be spread sedulously abroad. By Bertin it was told to M. Jolly, the proctor in whose hands the de Lamottes had placed the sale of Buisson-Souef. It was M. Jolly who had in the first instance recommended to them his client Derues as a possible purchaser. The proctor, who knew Mme. de Lamotte to be a woman devoted to her husband and her home, was astonished to hear of her infidelity, more especially as the story told by Derues represented her as saying in very coarse terms how little she cared for her husband's honour.

He was surprised, too, that she should not have consulted him about the conclusion of the business with Derues, and that Derues himself should have been able to find so considerable a sum of money as 100,000 livres. But, said M. Jolly, if he were satisfied that Mme. de Lamotte had taken away the money with her, then he would deliver up to Derues the power of attorney which M. de Lamotte had left with him in 1775, giving his wife authority to carry out the sale of Buisson- Souef. Mme. de Lamotte, being a married woman, the sale of the property to Derues would be legally invalid if the husband's power of attorney were not in the hands of the purchaser.

II

THE GAME OF BLUFF

To Derues, on the eve of victory, the statement of Jolly in regard to the power of attorney was a serious reverse. He had never thought of such an instrument, or he would have persuaded Mme. de Lamotte to have gotten permission of it before her disappearance. Now he must try to get it from Jolly himself. On the 26th of February he once again raised from a friendly notary a few thousand livres on the Duplessis inheritance, and deposited the deed of sale of Buisson-Souef as further security. His pocket full of gold, he went straight to the office of Jolly. To the surprise of the proctor Derues announced that he had come to pay him 200 livres which he owed him, and apologised for the delay. Taking the gold coins from his pockets he filled his three-cornered hat with considerably more than the sum due, and held it out invitingly to M. Jolly. Then he proceeded to tell him of his dealings with Mme. de Lamotte. She had offered, he said, to get the power of attorney for him, but he, trusting in her good faith, had said that there was no occasion for hurry; and then, faithless, ungrateful woman that she was, she had gone off with his money and left him in the lurch. "But," he added, "I trust you absolutely, M. Jolly, you have all my business in your hands, and I shall be a good client in the future. You have the power of attorney—you will give it to me?" and he rattled the coins in his hat. "I must have it," he went on, "I must have it at any price at any price," and again the coins danced in his hat, while his eyes looked knowingly at the proctor. M. Jolly saw his meaning, and his surprise turned to indignation. He told Derues bluntly that he did not believe his story, that until he was convinced of its truth he would not part with the power of attorney, and showed the confounded grocer the door.

Derues hastened home filled with wrath, and took counsel with his friend Bertin. Bertin knew something of legal process; they would try whether the law could not be invoked to compel Jolly to surrender the power of attorney. Bertin went off to the Civil Lieutenant and applied for an order to oblige M. Jolly to give up the document in question. An order was made that Jolly must either surrender it into the hands of Derues or appear before a referee and show cause why he should not comply with the order. Jolly refused still to give it up or allow a copy of it to be made, and agreed to appear before the referee to justify his action. In the meantime Derues, greatly daring, had started for Buisson-Souef to try what "bluff" could do in this serious crisis in his adventure.

At Buisson-Souef poor M. de Lamotte waited, puzzled and distressed, for news from his wife. On Saturday, 17th, the day after the return of Derues from Versailles, he heard from Mme. Derues that his wife had left Paris and gone with her son to Versailles. A second letter told him that she had completed the sale of Buisson-Souef to Derues, and was still at Versailles trying to obtain some post for the boy. On February 19 Mme. Derues wrote again expressing surprise that M. de Lamotte had not had any letter from his wife and asking if he had received some oysters which the Derues had sent him. The distracted husband was in no mood for oysters. "Do not send me oysters," he writes, "I am too ill with worry. I thank you for all your kindness to my son. I love him better than myself, and God grant he will be good and grateful." The only reply he received from the Derues was an assurance that he would see his wife again in a few days.

The days passed, but Mme. de Lamotte made no sign. About four o'clock on the afternoon of February 28, Derues, accompanied by the parish priest of Villeneuvele-Roi, presented himself before M. de Lamotte at Buisson-Souef. For the moment M. de Lamotte was rejoiced to see the little man; at last he would get news of his wife. But he was disappointed. Derues could tell him only what he had been told already, that his wife had sold their estate and gone away with the money.

M. de Lamotte was hardly convinced. How, he asked Derues, had he found the 100,000 livres to buy Buisson-Souef, he who had not a halfpenny a short time ago? Derues replied that he had borrowed it from a friend; that there was no use in talking about it; the place was his now, his alone, and M. de Lamotte had no longer a right to be there; he was very sorry, poor dear gentleman, that his wife had gone off and left him without a shilling, but personally he would always be a friend to him and would allow him 3,000 livres a year for the rest of his life. In the meantime, he said, he had already sold forty casks of the last year's vintage, and would be obliged if M. de Lamotte would see to their being sent off at once.

By this time the anger and indignation of M. de Lamotte blazed forth. He told Derues that his story was a pack of lies, that he was still master at Buisson-Souef, and not a bottle of wine should leave it. "You are torturing me," he exclaimed, "I know something has happened to my wife and child. I am coming to Paris myself, and if it is as I fear, you shall answer for it with your head!" Derues, undismayed by this outburst, re-

asserted his ownership and departed in defiant mood, leaving on the premises a butcher of the neighbourhood to look after his property.

But things were going ill with Derues. M. de Lamotte meant to show fight; he would have powerful friends to back him; class against class, the little grocer would be no match for him. It was immediate possession of Buisson-Souef that Derues wanted, not lawsuits; they were expensive and the results uncertain. He spoke freely to his friends of the difficulties of the situation.

What could he do? The general opinion seemed to be that some fresh news of Mme. de Lamotte—her reappearance, perhaps—would be the only effective settlement of the dispute. He had made Mme. de Lamotte disappear, why should he not make her reappear? He was not the man to stick at trifles. His powers of female impersonation, with which he had amused his good friends at Buisson-Souef, could now be turned to practical account. On March 5 he left Paris again.

On the evening of March 7 a gentleman, M. Desportes of Paris, hired a room at the Hotel Blanc in Lyons. On the following day he went out early in the morning, leaving word that, should a lady whom he was expecting, call to see him, she was to be shown up to his room. The same morning a gentleman, resembling M. Desportes of Paris, bought two lady's dresses at a shop in Lyons.

The same afternoon a lady dressed in black silk, with a hood well drawn over her eyes, called at the office of M. Pourra, a notary.

The latter was not greatly attracted by his visitor, whose nose struck him as large for a woman. She said that she had spent her youth in Lyons, but her accent was distinctly Parisian. The lady gave her name as Madame de Lamotte, and asked for a power of attorney by which she could give her husband the interest due to her on a sum of 30,000 livres, part of the purchase-money of the estate of Buisson-Souef, which she had recently sold. As Mme. de Lamotte represented herself as having been sent to M. Pourra by a respectable merchant for whom he was in the habit of doing business, he agreed to draw up the necessary document, accepting her statement that she and her husband had separate estates. Mme. de Lamotte said that she would not have time to wait until the power of attorney was ready, and therefore asked M. Pourra to send it to the parish priest at Villeneuvele-Roi; this he promised to do. Mme. de-Lamotte had called twice during the day at the Hotel Blanc and asked for M. Desportes of Paris, but he was not at home. While Derues, alias Desportes, alias Mme. de Lamotte, was masquerading in Lyons, events had been moving swiftly and unfavourably in Paris. Sick with misgiving and anxiety, M. de Lamotte had come there to find, if possible, his wife and child. By a strange coincidence he alighted at an inn in the Rue de la Mortellerie, only a few yards from the wine-cellar in which the corpse of his ill-fated wife lay buried. He lost no time in putting his case before the Lieutenant of Police, who placed the affair in the hands of one of the magistrates of the Chatelet, then the criminal court of Paris. At first the magistrate believed that the case was one of fraud and that Mme. de Lamotte and her son were being kept somewhere in concealment by Derues. But as he investigated the circumstances further, the evidence of the illness of the mother and son, the date of the disappearance of Mme. de Lamotte, and her reputed signature to the deed of sale on February 12, led him to suspect that he was dealing with a case of murder.

When Derues returned to Paris from Lyons, on March 11, he found that the police had already visited the house and questioned his wife, and that he himself was under close surveillance. A day or two later the advocate, Duclos, revealed to the magistrate the fictitious character of the loan of 100,000 livres, which Derues alleged that he had paid to Mme. de Lamotte as the price of Buisson-Souef. When the new power of attorney purporting to be signed by Mme. de Lamotte arrived from Lyons, and the signature was compared with that on the deed of sale of Buisson- Souef to Derues, both were pronounced to be forgeries. Derues was arrested and lodged in the Prison of For l'Eveque.

The approach of danger had not dashed the spirits of the little man, nor was he without partisans in Paris. Opinion in the city was divided as to the truth of his account of Mme. de Lamotte's elopement. The nobility were on the side of the injured de Lamotte, but the bourgeoisie accepted the grocer's story and made merry over the deceived husband. Interrogated, however, by the magistrate of the Chatelet, Derues' position became more difficult. Under the stress of close questioning the flimsy fabric of his financial statements fell to pieces like a house of cards. He had to admit that he had never paid Mme. de Lamotte 100,000 livres; he had paid her only 25,000 livres in gold; further pressed he said that the 25,000 livres had been made up partly in gold, partly in bills; but where the gold had come from, or on whom he had drawn the bills, he could not explain. Still his position was not desperate; and he knew it. In the absence of Mme. de Lamotte he could not be charged with fraud or forgery; and until her body was discovered, it would be impossible to charge him with murder.

A month passed; Mme. Derues, who had made a belated attempt to follow her husband's example by impersonating Mme. de Lamotte in Paris, had been arrested and imprisoned in the Grand Chatelet; when, on April 18, information was received by the authorities which determined them to explore the wine-cellar in the Rue de la Mortellerie. Whether the woman who had let the cellar to Derues, or the creditor who had met him taking his cask of wine there, had informed the investigating magistrate, seems uncertain. In any case, the corpse of the unhappy lady was soon brought to light and Derues confronted with it. At first he said that he failed to recognise it as the remains of Mme. de Lamotte, but he soon abandoned that rather impossible attitude. He admitted that he had given some harmless medicine to Mme. de Lamotte during her illness, and then, to his horror, one morning had awakened to find her dead. A fear lest her husband would accuse him of having caused her death had led him to conceal the body, and also that of her son who, he now confessed, had died and been buried by him at Versailles. On April 23 the body of the young de Lamotte was exhumed. Both bodies were examined by doctors, and they declared themselves satisfied that mother and son had died "from a bitter and corrosive poison administered in some kind of drink." What the poison was they did not venture to state, but one of their number, in the light of subsequent investigation, arrived at the conclusion that Derues had used in both cases corrosive sublimate. How or where he had obtained the poison was never discovered.

Justice moved swiftly in Paris in those days. The preliminary investigation in Derues' case was ended on April 28. Two days later his trial commenced before the tribunal of the Chatelet.

It lasted one day. The judges had before them the depositions taken by the examining magistrate. Both Derues and his wife were interrogated. He maintained that he had not poisoned either Mme. de Lamotte or her son; his only crime, he said, lay in having concealed their deaths. Mme; Derues said: "It is Buisson-Souef that has ruined us! I always told my husband that he was mad to buy these properties—I am sure my husband is not a poisoner—I trusted my husband and believed every word he said." The court condemned Derues to death, but deferred judgment in his wife's case on the ground of her pregnancy.

And now the frail, cat-like little man had to brace himself to meet a cruel and protracted execution. But sanguine to the last, he still hoped. An appeal lay from the Chatelet to the Parliament of Paris. It was heard on March 5. Derues was brought to the Palais de Justice. The room in which he waited was filled with curious spectators, who marvelled at his coolness and impudence. He recognised among them a Benedictine monk of his acquaintance. "My case," he called out to him, "will soon be over; we'll meet again yet and have a good time together." One visitor, wishing not to appear too curious, pretended to be looking at a picture. "Come, sir," said Derues, "you haven't come here to see the pictures, but to see me. Have a good look at me. Why study copies of nature when you can look at such a remarkable original as I?" But there were to be no more days of mirth and gaiety for the jesting grocer. His appeal was rejected, and he was ordered for execution on the morrow.

At six o'clock on the morning of May 6 Derues returned to the Palais de Justice, there to submit to the superfluous torments of the question ordinary and extraordinary. Though condemned to death, torture was to be applied in the hope of wringing from the prisoner some sort of confession. The doctors declared him too delicate to undergo the torture of pouring cold water into him, which his illustrious predecessor, Mme. de Brinvilliers, had suffered; he was to endure the less severe torture of the "boot."

His legs were tightly encased in wood, and wedges were then hammered in until the flesh was crushed and the bones broken. But never a word of confession was wrung from the suffering creature. Four wedges constituting the ordinary torture he endured; at the third of the extraordinary he fainted away. Put in the front of a fire the warmth restored him. Again he was questioned, again he asserted his wife's innocence and his own.

At two o'clock in the afternoon Derues was recovered sufficiently to be taken to Notre Dame. There, in front of the Cathedral, candle in hand and rope round his neck, he made the amende honorable. But as the sentence was read aloud to the people Derues reiterated the assertion of his innocence. From Notre Dame he was taken to the Hotel de Ville. A condemned man had the right to stop there on his way to execution, to make his will and last dying declarations. Derues availed himself of this opportunity to protest solemnly and emphatically his wife's absolute innocence of any complicity in whatever he had done. "I want above all," he said, "to state that my wife is entirely innocent. She knew nothing. I used fifty cunning devices to hide everything from her. I am speaking nothing but the truth, she is wholly innocent—as for me, I am about to die." His wife was allowed to see him; he enjoined her to bring up their children in the fear of God and love of duty, and to let them know how he had died. Once again, as he took up the pen to sign the record of his last words, he re-asserted her innocence.

Of the last dreadful punishment the offending grocer was to be spared nothing. For an aristocrat like Mme. de Brinvilliers beheading was considered indignity enough. But Derues must go through with it all; he must be broken on the wheel and burnt alive and his ashes scattered to the four winds of heaven; there was to be no retentum for him, a clause sometimes inserted in the sentence permitting the executioner to strangle the broken victim before casting him on to the fire. He must endure all to the utmost agony the law could inflict.

It was six o'clock when Derues arrived at the Place de Greve, crowded to its capacity, the square itself, the windows of the houses; places had been bought at high prices, stools, ladders, anything that would give a good view of the end of the now famous poisoner.

Pale but calm, Derues faced his audience. He was stripped of all but his shirt; lying flat on the scaffold, his face looking up to the sky, his head resting on a stone, his limbs were fastened to the wheel. Then with a heavy bar of iron the executioner broke them one after another, and each time he struck a fearful cry came from the culprit. The customary three final blows on the stomach were inflicted, but still the little man lived. Alive and broken, he was thrown on to the fire. His burnt ashes, scattered to the winds, were picked up eagerly by the mob, reputed, as in England the pieces of the hangman's rope, talismans.

Some two months after the execution of her husband Mme. Derues was delivered in the Conciergerie of a male child; it is hardly surprising, in face of her experiences during her pregnancy, that it was born an idiot. In January, 1778, the judges of the Parliament, by a majority of one, decided that she should remain a prisoner in the Conciergerie for another year, while judgment in her case was reserved. In the following August she was charged with having forged the signature of Mme. de Lamotte on the deeds of sale. In February, 1779, the two experts in handwriting to whom the question had been submitted decided in her favour, and the charge was abandoned.

But Mme. Derues had a far sterner, more implacable and, be it added, more unscrupulous adversary than the law in M. de Lamotte.

Not content with her husband's death, M. de Lamotte believed the wife to have been his partner in guilt, and thirsted for revenge.

- To accomplish it he even stooped to suborn witnesses, but the conspiracy was exposed, and so strong became the sympathy with the accused woman that a young proctor of the Parliament published a pamphlet in her defence, asking for an immediate inquiry into the charges made against her, charges that had in no instance been proved.

At last, in March, 1779, the Parliament decided to finish with the affair. In secret session the judges met, examined once more all the documents in the case, listened to a report on it from one of their number, interrogated the now weary, hopeless prisoner, and, by a large majority, condemned her to a punishment that fell only just short of the supreme penalty. On the grounds that she had wilfully and knowingly participated with her husband in the fraudulent attempt to become possessed of the estate of Buisson-Souef, and was strongly suspected of having participated with him in his greater crime, she was sentenced to be publicly flogged, branded on both shoulders with the letter V (Voleuse) and imprisoned for life in the Salpetriere Prison. On March 13, in front of the Conciergerie Mme. Derues underwent the first part of her punishment. The same day her hair was cut short, and she was dressed in the uniform of the prison in which she was to pass the remainder of her days.

Paris had just begun to forget Mme. Derues when a temporary interest was-excited in her fortunes by the astonishing intelligence that, two months after her condemnation, she had been delivered of a child in her new prison. Its fatherhood was never determined, and, taken from her mother, the child died in fifteen days. Was its birth the result of some passing love affair, or some act of drunken violence on the part of her jailors, or had the wretched woman, fearing a sentence of death, made an effort to avert once again the supreme penalty? History does not relate.

Ten years passed. A fellow prisoner in the Salpetriere described Mme. Derues as "scheming, malicious, capable of anything." She was accused of being violent, and of wishing to revenge herself by setting fire to Paris. At length the Revolution broke on France, the Bastille fell, and in that same year an old uncle of Mme. Derues, an ex-soldier of Louis XV., living in Brittany, petitioned for his niece's release. He protested her innocence, and begged that he might take her to his home and restore her to her children. For three years he persisted vainly in his efforts. At last, in the year 1792, it seemed as if they might be crowned with success. He was told that the case would be re-examined; that it was possible that the Parliament had judged unjustly. This good news came to him in March. But in September of that year there took place those shocking massacres in the Paris prisons, which rank high among the atrocities of the Revolution. At four o'clock on the afternoon of September 4, the slaughterers visited the Salpetriere Prison, and fifth among their victims fell the widow of Derues.

DR. CASTAING

There are two reports of the trial of Castaing: "Proces Complet d'Edme Samuel Castaing," Paris, 1823; "Affaire Castaing," Paris, 1823.

I

AN UNHAPPY COINCIDENCE

Edme Castaing, born at Alencon in 1796, was the youngest of the three sons of an Inspector-General in the department of Woods and Forests. His elder brother had entered the same service as his father, the other brother was a staff-captain of engineers. Without being wealthy, the family, consisting of M. and Mme. Castaing and four children, was in comfortable circumstances. The young Edme was educated at the College of Angers—the Alma Mater of Barre and Lebiez—where, intelligent and hard working, he carried off many prizes. He decided to enter the medical profession, and at the age of nineteen commenced his studies at the School of Medicine in Paris. For two years he worked hard and well, living within the modest allowance made him by his father. At the end of that time this young man of two or three- and-twenty formed a passionate attachment for a lady, the widow of a judge, and the mother of three children. Of the genuine depth and sincerity of this passion for a woman who must have been considerably older than himself, there can be no doubt. Henceforth the one object in life to Castaing was to make money enough to relieve the comparative poverty of his adored mistress, and place her and her children beyond the reach of want. In 1821 Castaing became a duly qualified doctor, and by that time had added to the responsibilities of his mistress and himself by becoming the father of two children, whom she had brought into the world. The lady was exigent, and Castaing found it difficult to combine his work with a due regard to her claims on his society. Nor was work plentiful or lucrative. To add to his embarrassments Castaing, in 1818, had backed a bill for a friend for 600 francs. To meet it when it fell due two years later was impossible, and desperate were the efforts made by Castaing and his mother to put off the day of reckoning. His father, displeased with his son's conduct, would do nothing to help him. But his mother spared no effort to extricate him from his difficulties. She begged a highly placed official to plead with the insistent creditor, but all in vain. There seemed no hope of a further delay when suddenly, in the October of 1822, Castaing became the possessor of 100,000 francs. How he became possessed of this considerable sum of money forms part of a strange and mysterious story.

Among the friends of Castaing were two young men of about his own age, Auguste and Hippolyte Ballet. Auguste, the elder, had the misfortune a few days after his birth to incur his mother's lasting dislike. The nurse had let the child fall from her arms in the mother's presence, and the shock had endangered Mme. Ballet's life. From that moment the mother took a strong aversion to her son; he was left to the charge of servants; his meals were taken in the kitchen. As soon as he was five years old he was put out to board elsewhere, while his brother Hippolyte and his sister were well cared for at home. The effect of this unjust neglect on the character of Auguste Ballet was, as may be imagined, bad; he became indolent and dissipated. His brother Hippolyte, on the other hand, had justified the affectionate care bestowed on his upbringing; he had grown into a studious, intelligent youth of a refined and attractive temperament. Unhappily, early in his life he had developed consumption, a disease he inherited from his mother. As he grew older his health grew steadily worse until, in 1822, his friends were seriously alarmed at his condition. It became so much graver that, in the August of that year, the doctors recommended him to take the waters at Enghien. In September he returned to Paris apparently much better, but on October 2 he was seized with sudden illness, and three days later he was dead.

A few years before the death of Hippolyte his father and mother had died almost at the same time. M. Ballet had left to each of his sons a fortune of some 260,000 francs. Though called to the bar, both Auguste and Hippolyte Ballet were now men of independent means. After the death of their parents, whatever jealousy Auguste may have felt at the unfair preference which his mother had shown for her younger son, had died down. At the time of Hippolyte's death the brothers were on good terms, though the more prudent Hippolyte disapproved of his elder brother's extravagance.

Of Hippolyte Ballet Dr. Castaing had become the fast friend. Apart from his personal liking for Castaing, it was a source of comfort to Hippolyte, in his critical state of health, to have as his friend one whose medical knowledge was always at his service.

About the middle of August, 1822, Hippolyte, on the advice of his doctors, went to Enghien to take the waters. There Castaing paid him frequent visits. He returned to Paris on September 22, and seemed to have benefited greatly by the cure. On Tuesday, October 1, he saw his sister, Mme. Martignon, and her husband; he seemed well, but said that he was having leeches applied to him by his friend Castaing. On the Wednesday evening his sister saw him again, and found him well and with a good appetite. On the Thursday, after a night disturbed by severe attacks of vomiting, his condition seemed serious. His brother-in-law, who visited him, found that he had taken to his bed, his face was swollen, his eyes were red. His sister called in the evening, but could not see him. The servants told her that her brother was a little better but resting, and that he did not wish to be disturbed; they said that Dr. Castaing had been with him all day.

On Friday Castaing himself called on the Martignons, and told them that Hippolyte had passed a shockingly bad night. Madame Martignon insisted on going to nurse her brother herself, but Castaing refused positively to let her see him; the sight of her, he said, would be too agitating to the patient. Later in the day Mme. Martignon went to her brother's house. In order to obey Dr. Castaing's injunctions, she dressed herself in some of the clothes of the servant

Victoire, in the hope that if she went into his bedroom thus disguised, Hippolyte would not recognise her. But even this subterfuge was forbidden by Castaing, and Mme. Martignon had to content herself with listening in an adjoining room for the sound of her brother's voice. At eight o'clock that evening the Martignons learnt that Hippolyte was better, but at ten o'clock they received a message that he was dying, and that his brother Auguste had been sent for. Mme. Martignon was prostrated with grief, but her husband hastened to his brother-in-law's house. There he found Castaing, who said that the death agony of his friend was so dreadful that he had not the strength to remain in the room with the dying man. Another doctor was sent for, but at ten o'clock the following morning, after protracted suffering, Hippolyte Ballet passed away.

A post-mortem was held on his body. It was made by Drs. Segalas and Castaing. They stated that death was due to pleurisy aggravated by the consumptive condition of the deceased, which, however serious, was not of itself likely to have been so rapidly fatal in its consequences.

Hippolyte had died, leaving a fortune of some 240,000 francs. In the previous September he had spoken to the notary Lebret, a former clerk of his father's, of his intention of making a will. He had seen that his brother Auguste was squandering his share of their inheritance; he told Lebret that whatever he might leave to Auguste should not be placed at his absolute disposal. To his servant Victoire, during his last illness, Hippolyte had spoken of a will he had made which he wished to destroy. If Hippolyte had made such a will, did he destroy it before his death? In any case, no trace of it was ever found after his death. He was presumed to have died intestate, and his fortune was divided, three-quarters of it going to his brother Auguste, the remaining quarter to his sister, Mme. Martignon.

On the day of Hippolyte's death Auguste Ballet wrote from his brother's house to one Prignon: "With great grief I have to tell you that I have just lost my brother; I write at the same time to say that I must have 100,000 francs to-day if possible. I have the greatest need of it. Destroy my letter, and reply at once. M. Sandrie will, I am sure, accommodate me. I am at my poor brother's house, from which I am writing." Prignon did as he was asked, but it was two days before the stockbroker, Sandrie, could raise the necessary sum. On October 7 he sold out sufficient of Auguste's stock to realise 100,000 francs, and the following day gave Prignon an order on the Bank of France for that amount. The same day Prignon took the order to Auguste. Accompanied by Castaing and Jean, Auguste's black servant, Auguste and Prignon drove to the bank. There the order was cashed. Prignon's part of the business was at an end. He said good-bye to Auguste outside the bank. As the latter got into his cabriolet, carrying the bundle of notes, Prignon heard him say to Castaing: "There are the 100,000 francs."

Why had Auguste Ballet, after his brother's death, such urgent need of 100,000 francs? If the statements of Auguste made to other persons are to be believed, he had paid the 100,000 francs which he had raised through Prignon to Lebret, his father's former clerk, who would seem to have acted as legal and financial adviser to his old master's children. According to Auguste's story, his sister, Mme. Martignon, had offered Lebret 80,000 francs to preserve a copy of a will made by Hippolyte, leaving her the bulk of his fortune. Castaing, however, had ascertained that Lebret would be willing, if Auguste would outbid his sister and pay 100,000 francs, to destroy the will so that, Hippolyte dying intestate, Auguste would take the greater part of his brother's fortune. Auguste agreed to accept Lebret's terms, raised the necessary sum, and handed over the money to Castaing, who, in turn, gave it to Lebret, who had thereupon destroyed the copy of the will. Castaing, according to the evidence of Auguste's mistress, an actress of the name of Percillie, had spoken in her presence of having himself destroyed one copy of Hippolyte's will before his death, and admitted having arranged with Lebret after Hippolyte's death for the destruction of the other copy.

How far was the story told by Auguste, and repeated in somewhat different shape by Castaing to other persons, true? There is no doubt that after the visit to the Bank of France with Prignon on October 8, Auguste and Castaing drove together to Lebret's office. The negro servant said that on arriving there one of them got out of the cab and went up to Lebret's house, but which of the two he would not at first say positively. Later he swore that it was Auguste Ballet. Whatever happened on that visit to Lebret's—and it was the theory of the prosecution that Castaing and not Auguste had gone up to the office—the same afternoon Auguste Ballet showed his mistress the seals of the copy of his brother's will which Lebret had destroyed, and told her that Lebret, all through the business, had refused to deal directly with him, and would only act through the intermediary of Castaing.

Did Lebret, as a fact, receive the 100,000 francs? A close examination of his finances showed no trace of such a sum. Castaing, on the other hand, on October 10, 1822, had given a stockbroker a sum of 66,000 francs to invest in securities; on the 11th of the same month he had lent his mother 30,000 francs; and on the 14th had given his mistress 4,000 francs. Of how this large sum of money had come to Castaing at a time when he was practically insolvent he gave various accounts. His final version was that in the will destroyed by Auguste, Hippolyte Ballet had left him an income for life equivalent to a capital of 100,000 francs, and that Auguste had given him that sum out of respect for his brother's wishes. If that explanation were true, it was certainly strange that shortly after his brother's death Auguste Ballet should have expressed surprise and suspicion to a friend on hearing that Castaing had been buying stock to the value of 8,000 francs. If he had given Castaing 100,000 francs for himself, there was no occasion for surprise or suspicion at his investing 8,000. That Auguste had paid out 100,000 francs to some one in October the state of his finances at his death clearly proved. According to the theory of the prosecution, Auguste believed that he had paid that money to Lebret through the intermediary of Castaing, and not to Castaing himself. Hence his surprise at hearing that Castaing, whom he knew to be impecunious, was investing such a sum as 8,000 francs.

No money had ever reached Lebret. His honesty and good faith were demonstrated beyond any shadow of a doubt; no copy of any will of Hippolyte Ballet had ever been in his possession. But Castaing had shown Auguste Ballet a copy of his brother's will, the seals of which Auguste had shown to his mistress. In all probability, and possibly at the instigation of Castaing, Hip-
polyte Ballet had made a will, leaving the greater part of his property to his sister. Somehow or other Castaing had got possession of this will. On his death Castaing had invented the story of Mme. Martignon's bribe to Lebret, and so persuaded Auguste to outbid her. He had ingeniously kept Auguste and Lebret apart by representing Lebret as refusing to deal direct with Auguste, and by these means had secured to his own use the sum of 100,000 francs, which Auguste believed was being paid to Lebret as the price of his alleged destruction of his brother's will. The plot was ingenious and successful. To Lebret and the Martignons Castaing said that Hippolyte had made a will in Mme. Martignon's favour, but had destroyed it himself some days before his death. The Martignons expressed themselves as glad that Hippolyte had done so, for they feared lest such a will should have provoked resentment against them on the part of Auguste. By keeping Auguste and Lebret apart, Castaing prevented awkward explanations. The only possible danger of discovery lay in Auguste's incautious admissions to his mistress and friends; but even had the fact of the destruction of the will come to the ears of the Martignons, it is unlikely that they would have taken any steps involving the disgrace of Auguste.

Castaing had enriched himself considerably by the opportune death of his friend Hippolyte. It might be made a matter of unfriendly comment that, on the first day of May preceding that sad event, Castaing had purchased ten grains of acetate of morphia from a chemist in Paris, and on September 18, less than a month before Hippolyte's death, he had purchased another ten grains of acetate of morphia from the same chemist. The subject of poisons had always been a favourite branch of Castaing's medical studies, especially vegetable poisons; morphia is a vegetable poison.

Castaing's position relative to Auguste Ballet was now a strong one. They were accomplices in the unlawful destruction of Hippolyte's will. Auguste believed it to be in his friend's power to ruin him at any time by revealing his dealings with Lebret. But, more than that, to Auguste, who believed that his 100,000 francs had gone into Lebret's pocket, Castaing could represent himself as so far unrewarded for his share in the business; Lebret had taken all the money, while he had received no recompense of any kind for the trouble he had taken and the risk he was encountering on his friend's behalf. Whatever the motive, from fear or gratitude, Auguste Ballet was persuaded to make a will leaving Dr. Edme Samuel Castaing the whole of his fortune, subject to a few trifling legacies. But Auguste's feelings towards his sole legatee were no longer cordial. To one or two of his friends he expressed his growing distaste for Castaing's society.

Dr. Castaing can hardly have failed to observe this change. He knew Auguste to be reckless and extravagant with his money; he learnt that he had realised another 100,000 francs out of his securities, and that he kept the money locked up in a drawer in his desk. If Auguste's fortune were dissipated by extravagance, or he revoked his will, Castaing stood to lose heavily. As time went on Castaing felt less and less sure that he could place much reliance on the favourable disposition or thrift of Auguste. The latter had fallen in love with a new mistress; he began to entertain expensively; even if he should not change his mind and leave his money away from Castaing, there might very soon be no money to leave. At the end of May, 1823, Castaing consulted a cousin of his, Malassis, a notary's clerk, as to the validity of a will made by a sick man in favour of his medical attendant. He said that he had a patient gravely ill who, not wishing to leave his money to his sister, whom he disliked, intended to leave it to him. Malassis reassured him as to the validity of such a will, and gave him the necessary instructions for preparing it. On May 29 Castaing sent Malassis the will of Auguste Ballet with the following note, "I send you the will of M. Ballets examine it and keep it as his representative." The will was dated December 1, 1822, and made Castaing sole legatee. On the same day that the will was deposited with Malassis, Castaing and Auguste Ballet started to-

gether on a little two days' trip into the country. To his friends Auguste seemed in the best of health and spirits; so much so that his housekeeper remarked as he left how well he was looking, and Castaing echoed her remark, saying that he looked like a prince!

During the afternoon the two friends visited Saint Germain, then returned to Paris, and at seven o'clock in the evening arrived at the Tete Noire Hotel at Saint Cloud, where they took a double- bedded room, Castaing paying five francs in advance. They spent the following day, Friday, May 30, in walking about the neighbourhood, dined at the hotel at seven, went out again and returned about nine o'clock. Soon after their return Castaing ordered some warmed wine to be sent up to the bedroom. It was taken up by one of the maid-servants. Two glasses were mixed with lemon and sugar which Castaing had brought with him. Both the young men drank of the beverage. Auguste complained that it was sour, and thought that he had put too much lemon in it. He gave his glass to the servant to taste, who also found the drink sour. Shortly after she left the room and went upstairs to the bedside of one of her fellow-servants who was ill. Castaing, for no apparent reason, followed her up and stayed in the room for about five minutes. Auguste spent a bad night, suffering from internal pains, and in the morning his legs were so swollen that he could not put on his boots.

Castaing got up at four o'clock that morning and asked one of the servants to let him out. Two hours later he drove up in a cabriolet to the door of a chemist in Paris, and asked for twelve grains of tartar emetic, which he wanted to mix in a wash according to a prescription of Dr. Castaing. But he did not tell the chemist that he was Dr. Castaing himself. An hour later Cas- taing arrived at the shop of another chemist, Chevalier, with whom he had already some acquaintance; he had bought acetate of morphia from him some months before, and had discussed with him then the effects of vegetable poisons. On this particular morning he bought of his assistant thirty-six grains of acetate of morphia, paying, as a medical man, three francs fifty centimes for it instead of the usual price of four francs. Later in the morning Castaing returned to Saint Cloud, a distance of ten miles from Paris, and said that he had been out for a long walk. He found Auguste ill in bed. Castaing asked for some cold milk, which was taken up to the bedroom by one of the servants. Shortly after this Castaing went out again. During his absence Auguste was seized with violent pains and sickness. When Castaing returned he found his friend in the care of the people of the hotel. He told them to throw away the matter that had been vomited, as the smell was offensive, and Auguste told them to do as his friend directed. Castaing proposed to send for a doctor from Paris, but Auguste insisted that a local doctor should be called in at once.

Accordingly Dr. Pigache of Saint Cloud was summoned. He arrived at the hotel about eleven o'clock. Before seeing the patient Castaing told the doctor that he believed him to be suffering from cholera. Pigache asked to see the matter vomited but was told that it had been thrown away. He prescribed a careful diet, lemonade and a soothing draught.

Dr. Pigache returned at three o'clock, when he found that the patient had taken some lemonade, but, according to Castaing, had refused to take the draught. He called again that afternoon. Ballet was much better; he said that he would be quite well if he could get some sleep, and expressed a wish to return to Paris. Dr. Pigache dissuaded him from this and left, saying that he would come again in the evening. Castaing said that that would be unnecessary, and it was agreed that Pigache should see the patient again at eight o'clock the next morning. During the afternoon Castaing sent a letter to Paris to Jean, Auguste's negro servant, telling him to take the two keys of his master's desk to his cousin Malassis. But the negro distrusted Castaing. He knew of the will which his master had made in the doctor's favour. Rather than compromise himself by any injudicious act, he brought the keys to Saint Cloud and there handed them over to Castaing.

When Jean arrived his master complained to him of feeling very ill. Jean said that he hoped he would be well enough to go back to Paris the following day, to which Auguste replied, "I don't think so. But if I am lucky enough to get away to-morrow, I shall leave fifty francs for the poor here." About eleven o'clock that night Castaing, in Jean's presence, gave the sick man a spoonful of the draught prescribed by Dr. Pigache. Four or five minutes later Auguste was seized with terrible convulsions, followed by unconsciousness. Dr. Pigache was sent for. He found Ballet lying on his back unconscious, his throat strained, his mouth shut and his eyes fixed; the pulse was weak, his body covered with cold sweat; and every now and then he was seized with strong convulsions. The doctor asked Castaing the cause of the sudden change in Ballet's condition. Castaing replied that it had commenced shortly after he had taken a spoonful of the draught which the doctor had prescribed for him. Dr. Pigache bled the patient and applied twenty leeches. He returned about six; Ballet was sinking, and Castaing appeared to be greatly upset. He told the doctor what an unhappy coincidence it was that he should have been present at the deathbeds of both Hippolyte and his brother Auguste; and that the position was the more distressing for him as he was the sole heir to Auguste's fortune. To M. Pelletan, a professor of medicine, who had been sent for to St. Cloud in the early hours of Sunday morning, Castaing appeared to be in a state of great grief and agitation; he was shedding tears. Pelletan was from the first impressed by the suspicious nature of the case, and pointed out to Castaing the awkwardness of his situation as heir to the dying man. "You're right," replied Castaing, "my position is dreadful, horrible. In my great grief I had never thought of it till now, but now you make me see it clearly. Do you think there will be an investigation?" Pelletan answered that he should be compelled to ask for a post-mortem. "Ah! You will be doing me the greatest service," said Castaing, "I beg you to insist on a post-mortem. You will be acting as a second father to me in doing so." The parish priest was sent for to administer extreme unction to the dying man. To the parish clerk who accompanied the priest Castaing said, "I am losing a friend of my childhood," and both priest and clerk went away greatly edified by the sincere sorrow and pious demeanour of the young doctor. About mid-day on Sunday, June 1, Auguste Ballet died.

During the afternoon Castaing left the hotel for some hours, and that same afternoon a young man about twenty-five years of age, short and fair, left a letter at the house of Malassis. The letter was from Castaing and said, "My dear friend, Ballet has just died, but do nothing before to-morrow, Monday. I will see you and tell you, yes or no, whether it is time to act. I expect that his brother-in-law, M. Martignon, whose face is pock-marked and who carries a decoration, will call and see you. I have said that I did not know what dispositions Ballet may have made, but that before his death he had told me to give you two little keys which I am going to deliver to you myself to-morrow, Monday. I have not said that we are cousins, but only that I had seen you once or twice at Ballet's, with whom you were friendly. So say nothing till I have seen you, but whatever you do, don't say you are a relative of mine." When he returned to the hotel Castaing found Martignon, Lebret, and one or two friends of Auguste already assembled. It was only that morning that Martignon had received from Castaing any intimation of his brother-in-law's critical condition. From the first Castaing was regarded with suspicion; the nature of the illness, the secrecy maintained about it by Castaing, the coincidence of some of the circumstances with those of the death of Hippolyte, all combined to excite suspicion. Asked if Auguste had left a will Castaing said no; but the next day he admitted its existence, and said that it was in the hands of Malassis.

Monday, June 2, was the day fixed for the post-mortem; it was performed in the hotel at Saint Cloud. Castaing was still in the hotel under provisional arrest. While the post-mortem was going on his agitation was extreme; he kept opening the door of the room in which he was confined, to hear if possible some news of the result. At last M. Pelletan obtained permission to inform him of the verdict of the doctors. It was favourable to Castaing; no trace of death by violence or poison had been discovered.

The medical men declared death to be due to an inflammation of the stomach, which could be attributed to natural causes; that the inflammation had subsided; that it had been succeeded by cerebral inflammation, which frequently follows inflammation of the stomach, and may have been aggravated in this case by exposure to the sun or by over-indulgence of any kind.

II

THE TRIAL OF DR. CASTAING

Castaing expected, as a result of the doctors' report, immediate release. In this he was disappointed; he was placed under stricter arrest and taken to Paris, where a preliminary investigation commenced, lasting five months. During the early part of his imprisonment Castaing feigned insanity, going to disgusting lengths in the hope of convincing those about him of the reality of his madness. But after three days of futile effort he gave up the attempt, and turned his attention to more practical means of defence. In the prison at Versailles, whither he had been removed from Paris, he got on friendly terms with a prisoner, one Goupil, who was awaiting trial for some unimportant offence. To Goupil Castaing described the cruelty of his position and the causes that had led to his wrongful arrest. He admitted his unfortunate possession of the poison, and said that the 100,000 francs which he had invested he had inherited from an uncle. Through Goupil he succeeded in communicating with his mother in the hope that she would use her influence to stifle some of the more serious evidence against him. Through other prisoners he tried to get at the chemists from whom he had bought acetate of morphia, and persuade them to say that the preparation of morphia which he had purchased was harmless.

The trial of Castaing commenced before the Paris Assize Court on November 10, 1823. He was charged with the murder of Hippolyte Ballet, the destruction of a document containing the final dispositions of Hippolyte's property, and with the murder of Auguste Ballet. The three charges were to be tried simultaneously. The Act of Accusation in Castaing's case is a remarkable document, covering a hundred closely-printed pages. It is a well-reasoned, graphic and unfair statement of the case for the prosecution. It tells the whole story of the crime, and inserts everything that can possibly prejudice the prisoner in the eyes of the jury. As an example, it quotes against Castaing a letter of his mistress in which, in the course of some quarrel, she had written to him saying that his mother had said some "horrible things" (des horreurs) of him; but what those "horrible things" were was not revealed, nor were they ever alluded to again in the course of the trial, nor was his mistress called as a witness, though payments of money by Castaing to her formed an important part of the evidence against him. Again, the evidence of Goupil, his fellow prisoner, as to the incriminating statements made to him by Castaing is given in the Act of Accusation, but Goupil himself was not called at the trial.

During the reading of the Act of Accusation by the Clerk of the Court Castaing listened calmly. Only when some allusion was made to his mistress and their children did he betray any sign of emotion. As soon as the actual facts of the case were set out he was all attention, making notes busily. He is described as rather attractive in appearance, his face long, his features regular, his forehead high, his hair, fair in colour, brushed back from the brows; he wore rather large side-whiskers. One of the witnesses at Saint Cloud said that Castaing looked more like a priest than a doctor; his downcast eyes, gentle voice, quiet and unassuming demeanour, lent him an air of patience and humility.

The interrogatory of Castaing by the presiding judge lasted all the afternoon of the first day of the trial and the morning of the second. The opening part of it dealt with the murder of Hippolyte Ballet, and elicited little or nothing that was fresh. Beyond the purchase of acetate of morphia previous to Hippolyte's death, which Castaing reluctantly admitted, there was no serious evidence against him, and before the end of the trial the prosecution abandoned that part of the charge.

Questioned by the President as to the destruction of Hippolyte Ballet's will, Castaing admitted that he had seen a draft of a will executed by Hippolyte in favour of his sister, but he denied having told Auguste that Lebret had in his possession a copy which he was prepared to destroy for 100,000 francs. Asked to explain the assertion of Mlle. Percillie, Auguste's mistress, that statements to this effect had been made in her presence by both Auguste Ballet and himself, he said that it was not true; that he had never been to her house. "What motive," he was asked, "could Mlle. Percillie have for accusing you?" "She hated me," was the reply, "because I had tried to separate Auguste from her." Castaing denied that he had driven with Auguste to Lebret's office on October 8. Asked to explain his sudden possession of 100,000 francs at a moment when he was apparently without a penny, he repeated his statement that Auguste had given him the capital sum as an equivalent for an income of 4,000 francs which his brother had intended to leave him. "Why, when first asked if you had received anything from Auguste, did you say you had received nothing?" was the question.

"It was a thoughtless statement," was the answer. "Why," pursued the President, "should you not have admitted at once a fact that went to prove your own good faith? If, however, this fact be true, it does not explain the mysterious way in which Auguste asked Prignon to raise for him 100,000 francs; and unless those 100,000 francs were given to you, it is impossible to account for them. It is important to your case that you should give the jury a satisfactory explanation on this point." Castaing could only repeat his previous explanations.

The interrogatory was then directed to the death of Auguste Ballet. Castaing said that Auguste Ballet had left him all his fortune on account of a disagreement with his sister. Asked why, after Auguste's death, he had at first denied all knowledge of the will made in his favour and deposited by him with

Malassis, he could give no satisfactory reason. Coming to the facts of the alleged poisoning of Auguste Ballet, the President asked Castaing why, shortly after the warm wine was brought up on the night of May 30, he went up to the room where one of the servants of the hotel was lying sick. Castaing replied that he was sent for by the wife of the hotel-keeper. This the woman denied; she said that she did not even know that he was a doctor. "According to the prosecution," said the judge, "you left the room in order to avoid drinking your share of the wine." Castaing said that he had drunk half a cupful of it. The judge reminded him that to one of the witnesses Castaing had said that he had drunk only a little.

A ridiculous statement made by Castaing to explain the purchase of morphia and antimony in Paris on May 31 was brought up against him. Shortly after his arrest Castaing had said that the cats and dogs about the hotel had made such a noise on the night of May 30 that they had disturbed the rest of Auguste, who, in the early morning, had asked Castaing to get some poison to kill them. He had accordingly gone all the way, about ten miles, to Paris at four in the morning to purchase antimony and morphia to kill cats and dogs. All the people of the hotel denied that there had been any such disturbance on the night in question. Castaing now said that he had bought the poisons at Auguste's request, partly to kill the noisy cats and dogs, and partly for the purpose of their making experiments on animals. Asked why he had not given this second reason before, he said that as Auguste was not a medical man it would have been damaging to his reputation to divulge the fact of his wishing to make unauthorised experiments on animals. "Why go to Paris for the poison?" asked the judge, "there was a chemist a few yards from the hotel. And when in Paris, why go to two chemists?" To all these questions Castaing's answers were such as to lead the President to express a doubt as to whether they were likely to convince the jury. Castaing was obliged to admit that he had allowed, if not ordered, the evacuations of the sick man to be thrown away. He stated that he had thrown away the morphia and antimony, which he had bought in Paris, in the closets of the hotel, because, owing to the concatenation of circumstances, he thought that he would be suspected of murder. In reply to a question from one of the jury, Castaing said that he had mixed the acetate of morphia and tartar emetic together before reaching Saint Cloud, but why he had done so he could not explain.

The medical evidence at the trial was favourable to the accused. Orfila, the famous chemist of that day, said that, though the symptoms in Auguste Ballet's case might be attributed to poisoning by acetate of morphia or some other vegetable poison, at the same time they could be equally well attributed to sudden illness of a natural kind. The liquids, taken from the stomach of Ballet, had yielded on analysis no trace of poison of any sort. The convulsive symptoms present in Ballet's case were un-

doubtedly a characteristic result of a severe dose of acetate of morphia.[14] Castaing said that he had mixed the acetate of morphia and tartar emetic together, but in any case no trace of either poison was found in Auguste's body, and his illness might, from all appearances, have been occasioned by natural causes. Some attempt was made by the prosecution to prove that the apoplexy to which Hippolyte Ballet had finally succumbed, might be attributed to a vegetable poison; one of the doctors expressed an opinion favourable to that conclusion "as a man but not as a physician." But the evidence did not go further.

[14] It was asserted some years later by one medical authority in Palmer's case that it might have been morphia and not strychnine that had caused the tetanic symptoms which preceded Cook's death.

To the young priest-like doctor the ordeal of his trial was a severe one. It lasted eight days. It was only at midday on the sixth day that the evidence was concluded. Not only was Castaing compelled to submit to a long interrogatory by the President, but, after each witness had given his or her evidence, the prisoner was called on to refute or explain any points unfavourable to him. This he did briefly, with varying success; as the trial went on, with increasing embarrassment. A great deal of the evidence given against Castaing was hearsay, and would have been inadmissible in an English court of justice. Statements made by Auguste to other persons about Castaing were freely admitted. But more serious was the evidence of Mlle. Percillie, Auguste's mistress. She swore that on one occasion in her presence Castaing had reproached Auguste with ingratitude; he had complained that he had destroyed one copy of Hippolyte Ballet's will, and for Auguste's sake had procured the destruction of the other, and that yet, in spite of all this, Auguste hesitated to entrust him with 100,000 francs. Asked what he had to say to this statement Castaing denied its truth. He had, he said, only been in Mlle. Percillie's house once, and then not with Auguste Ballet. Mlle. Percillie adhered to the truth of her evidence, and the President left it to the jury to decide between them.

A Mme. Durand, a patient of Castaing, gave some curious evidence as to a story told her by the young doctor. He said that a friend of his, suffering from lung disease, had been persuaded into making a will in his sister's favour. The sister had offered a bribe of 80,000 francs to her brother's lawyer to persuade him to make such a will, and paid one of his clerks 3,000 francs for drawing it up. Castaing, in his friend's interest, and in order to expose the fraud, invited the clerk to come and see him. His friend, hidden in an alcove in the room, overheard the conversation between Castaing and the clerk, and so learnt the details of his sister's intrigue. He at once destroyed the will and became reconciled with his brother, whom he had been about to disinherit. After his death the brother, out of gratitude, had given Castaing 100,000 francs.

President: Castaing, did you tell this story to Mme. Durand?

Castaing: I don't recollect.

Avocat-General: But Mme. Durand says that you did.

Castaing: I don't recollect.

President: You always say that you don't recollect; that is no answer. Have you, yes or no, made such a statement to Mme. Durand?

Castaing: I don't recollect; if I had said it, I should recollect it.

Another lady whom Castaing had attended free of charge swore, with a good deal of reluctance, that Castaing had told her a somewhat similar story as accounting for his possession of 100,000 francs.

Witnesses were called for the defence who spoke to the diligence and good conduct of Castaing as a medical student; and eighteen, whom he had treated free of expense, testified to his kindness and generosity. "All these witnesses," said the President, "speak to your generosity; but, for that very reason, you must have made little profit out of your profession, and had little opportunity for saving anything," to which Castaing replied: "These are not the only patients I attended; I have not called those who paid me for my services." At the same time Castaing found it impossible to prove that he had ever made a substantial living by the exercise of his profession.

One of the medical witnesses called for the defence, M. Chaussier, had volunteered the remark that the absence of any trace of poison in the portions of Auguste Ballet's body submitted to analysis, constituted an absence of the corpus delicti. To this the President replied that that was a question of criminal law, and no concern of his. But in his speech for the prosecution the Avocat-General dealt with the point raised at some length—a point which, if it had held good as a principle of English law, would have secured the acquittal of so wicked a poisoner as Palmer. He quoted from the famous French lawyer d'Aguesseau: "The corpus delicti is no other thing than the delictum itself; but the proofs of the delictum are infinitely variable according to the nature of things; they may be general or special, principal or accessory, direct or indirect; in a word, they form that general effect (ensemble) which goes to determine the conviction of an honest man." If such a contention as M. Chaussier's were correct, said the Avocat-General, then it would be impossible in a case of poisoning to convict a prisoner after his victim's death, or, if his victim survived, to convict him of the attempt to poison. He reminded the jury of that paragraph in the Code of Criminal Procedure which instructed them as to their duties: "The Law does not ask you to give the reasons that have convinced you; it lays down no rules by which you are to decide as to the fullness or sufficiency of proof . . . it only asks you one question: `Have you an inward conviction?'" "If," he said, "the actual traces of poison are a material proof of murder by poison, then a new paragraph must be added to the Criminal Code—`Since, however, vegetable poisons leave no trace, poisoning by such means may be committed with impunity.'" To poisoners he would say in future: "Bunglers that you are, don't use arsenic or any mineral poison; they leave traces; you will be found out. Use vegetable poisons; poison your fathers, poison your mothers, poison all your families, and their inheritance will be yours— fear nothing; you will go unpunished! You have committed murder by poisoning, it is true; but the corpus delicti will not be there because it can't be there!" This was a case, he urged, of circumstantial evidence. "We have," he said, "gone through a large number of facts. Of these there is not one that does not go directly to the proof of poisoning, and that can only be explained on the supposition of poisoning; whereas, if the theory of the defence be admitted, all these facts, from the first to the last, become meaningless and absurd. They can only be refuted by arguments or explanations that are childish and ridiculous."

Castaing was defended by two advocates—Roussel, a schoolfellow of his, and the famous Berryer, reckoned by some the greatest French orator since Mirabeau. Both advocates were allowed to address the jury. Roussel insisted on the importance of the corpus delicti. "The delictum," he said, "is the effect, the guilty man merely the cause; it is useless to deal with the cause if the effect is uncertain," and he cited a case in which a woman had been sent for trial, charged with murdering her husband; the moral proof of her guilt seemed conclusive, when suddenly her husband appeared in court alive and well. The advocate made a good deal of the fact that the remains of the draught prescribed by Dr. Pigache, a spoonful of which Castaing had given to Auguste Ballet, had been analysed and showed no trace of poison. Against this the prosecution set the evidence of the chemist at Saint Cloud, who had made up the prescription. He said that the same day he had made up a second prescription similar to that of Dr. Pigache, but not made out for Auguste Ballet, which contained, in addition to the other ingredients, acetate of morphia. The original of this prescription he had given to a friend of Castaing, who had come to his shop and asked him for it a few days after Ballet's death. It would seem therefore that there had been two bottles of medicine, one of which containing morphia had disappeared.

M. Roussel combatted the suggestion that the family of Castaing were in a state of indigence. He showed that his father had an income of 10,000 francs, while his two brothers were holding good positions, one as an officer in the army, the other as a government official. The mistress of Castaing he represented as enjoying an income of 5,000 francs. He protested against the quantity of hearsay evidence that had been admitted into the case. "In England," he said, "when a witness is called, he is asked `What have you seen?' If he can only testify to mere talk, and hearsay, he is not heard." He quoted the concluding paragraph of the will of Auguste Ballet as showing his friendly feeling towards Castaing: "It is only after careful reflection that I have made this final disposition of my property, in order to mark the sincere friendship which I have never for one moment ceased to feel for MM. Castaing, Briant and Leuchere, in order to recognise the faithful loyalty of my servants, and deprive M. and Mme. Martignon, my brother-in-law and sister, of all rights to which they might be legally entitled on my death, fully persuaded in soul and conscience that, in doing so, I am giving to each their just and proper due." "Is this," asked M. Roussel, "a document wrested by surprise from a weak man, extorted by trickery? Is he not acting in the full exercise of his faculties? He forgets no one, and justifies his conduct."

When M. Roussel came to the incident of the noisy cats and dogs at Saint Cloud, he was as ingenious as the circumstances permitted: "A serious charge engrosses public attention; men's minds are concentrated on the large, broad aspects of the case; they are in a state of unnatural excitement. They see only the greatness, the solemnity of the accusation, and then, suddenly, in the midst of all that is of such tragic and surpassing interest, comes this trivial fact about cats and dogs.

It makes an unfavourable impression, because it is dramatically out of keeping with the tragedy of the story. But we are not here to construct a drama. No, gentlemen, look at it merely as a trivial incident of ordinary, everyday life, and you will see it in its proper light." M. Roussel concluded by saying that Castaing's most eloquent advocate, if he could have been present, would have been Auguste Ballet. "If Providence had permitted him to enter this court, he would cry out to you, 'Save my friend's life! His heart is undefiled! He is innocent!'"

M. Roussel concluded his speech at ten o'clock on Sunday night, November 16. The next morning Berryer addressed the jury. His speech in defence of Castaing is not considered one of his most successful efforts. He gave personal testimony as to the taste of acetate of morphia. He said that with the help of his own chemist he had put a quarter of a grain of the acetate into a large spoonful of milk, and had found it so insupportably bitter to the taste that he could not keep it in his mouth. If, he contended, Ballet had been poisoned by tartar emetic, then twelve grains given in milk would have given it an insipid taste, and vomiting immediately after would have got rid of the poison. Later investigations have shown that, in cases of antimonial poisoning, vomiting does not necessarily get rid of all the poison, and the convulsions in which Auguste Ballet died are symptomatic of poisoning either by morphia or antimony. In conclusion, Berryer quoted the words addressed by one of the Kings of France to his judges: "When God has not vouchsafed clear proof of a crime, it is a sign that He does not wish that man should determine it, but leaves its judgment to a higher tribunal."

The Avocat-General, in reply, made a telling answer to M. Roussel's attempt to minimise the importance of the cats and dogs: "He has spoken of the drama of life, and of its ordinary everyday incidents. If there is drama in this case, it is of Castaing's making. As to the ordinary incidents of everyday life, a man buys poison, brings it to the bedside of his sick friend, saying it is for experiments on cats and dogs, the friend dies, the other, his sole heir, after foretelling his death, takes possession of his keys, and proceeds to gather up the spoils—are these ordinary incidents of every-day life?"

It was nine o'clock at night when the jury retired to consider their verdict. They returned into court after two hours' deliberation. They found the prisoner "Not Guilty" of the murder of Hippolyte Ballet, "Guilty" of destroying his will, and "Guilty" by seven votes to five of the murder of Auguste Ballet. Asked if he had anything to say before judgment was given, Castaing, in a very loud voice, said "No; but I shall know how to die, though I am the victim of ill-fortune, of fatal circum-

stance. I shall go to meet my two friends. I am accused of having treacherously murdered them. There is a Providence above us! If there is such a thing as an immortal soul, I shall see Hippolyte and Auguste Ballet again. This is no empty declamation; I don't ask for human pity" (raising his hands to heaven),

"I look to God's mercy, and shall go joyfully to the scaffold. My conscience is clear. It will not reproach me even when I feel" (putting his hands to his neck). "Alas! It is easier to feel what I am feeling than to express what I dare not express." (In a feeble voice): "You have desired my death; you have it!" The judges retired to consider the sentence. The candles were guttering, the light of the lamps was beginning to fade; the aspect of the court grim and terrible. M. Roussel broke down and burst into tears. Castaing leant over to his old schoolfellow: "Courage, Roussel," he said; "you have always believed me innocent, and I am innocent. Embrace for me my father, my mother, my brothers, my child." He turned to a group of young advocates standing near: "And you, young people, who have listened to my trial, attend also my execution; I shall be as firm then as I am now. All I ask is to die soon. I should be ashamed to plead for mercy." The judges returned. Castaing was condemned to death, and ordered to pay 100,000 francs damages to the family of Auguste Ballet.

Castaing was not ashamed to appeal to the Court of Cassation for a revision of his trial, but on December 4 his appeal was rejected. Two days later he was executed. He had attempted suicide by means of poison, which one of his friends had brought to him in prison, concealed inside a watch. His courage failed him at the last, and he met his death in a state of collapse.

It is not often, happily, that a young man of gentle birth and good education is a double murderer at twenty-six. And such a soft, humble, insinuating young man too!—good to his mother, good to his mistress, fond of his children, kind to his patients.

Yet this gentle creature can deliberately poison his two friends.

Was ever such a contradictory fellow?

PROFESSOR WEBSTER

The best report of Webster's trial is that edited by Bemis. The following tracts in the British Museum have been consulted by the writer: "Appendix to the Webster Trial," Boston, 1850: "Thoughts on the Conviction of Webster"; "The Boston Tragedy," by W. E. Bigelow.

It is not often that the gaunt spectre of murder invades the cloistered calm of academic life. Yet such a strange and unwonted tragedy befell Harvard University in the year 1849, when John W. Webster, Professor of Chemistry, took the life of Dr. George Parkman, a distinguished citizen of Boston. The scene of the crime, the old Medical School, now a Dental Hospital, is still standing, or was when the present writer visited Boston in 1907. It is a large and rather dreary red-brick, three-storied building, situated in the lower part of the city, flanked on its west side by the mud flats leading down to the Charles River. The first floor consists of two large rooms, separated from each other by the main entrance hall, which is approached by a flight of steps leading up from the street level. Of these two rooms, the left, as you face the building, is fitted up as a lecture- room. In the year 1849 it was the lecture-room of Professor Webster. Behind the lecture-room is a laboratory, known as the upper laboratory, communicating by a private staircase with the lower laboratory, which occupies the left wing of the ground floor. A small passage, entered by a door on the left-hand side of the front of the building, separated this lower laboratory from the dissecting-room, an out-house built on to the west wall of the college, but now demolished. From this description it will be seen that any person, provided with the necessary keys, could enter the college by the side-door near the dissecting room on the ground floor, and pass up through the lower and upper laboratory into Professor Webster's lecture-room without entering any other part of the building. The Professor of Chemistry, by locking the doors of his lecture-rooms and the lower laboratory, could, if he wished, make himself perfectly secure against intrusion, and come and go by the side-door without attracting much attention. These rooms are little altered at the present time from their arrangement in 1849. The lecture-room and laboratory are used for the same purposes to- day; the lower laboratory, a dismal chamber, now disused and somewhat rearranged, is still recognisable as the scene of the Professor's chemical experiments.

On the second floor of the hospital is a museum, once anatomical, now dental. One of the principal objects of interest in this museum is a plaster cast of the jaws of Dr. George Parkman, made by a well-known dentist of Boston, Dr. Keep, in the year 1846. In that year the new medical college was formally opened. Dr. Parkman, a wealthy and public-spirited citizen of Boston, had given the piece of land, on which the college had been erected. He had been invited to be present at the opening ceremony. In anticipation of being asked to make a speech on this occasion Dr. Parkman, whose teeth were few and far between, had himself fitted by Dr. Keep with a complete set of false teeth. Oliver Wendell Holmes, then Professor of Anatomy at Harvard, who was present at the opening of the college, noticed how very nice and white the doctor's teeth appeared to be. It was the discovery of the remains of these same admirable teeth three years later in the furnace in Professor Webster's lower laboratory that led to the conviction of Dr. Parkman's murderer. By a strange coincidence the doctor met his death in the very college which his generosity had helped to build. Though to-day the state of the college has declined from the medical to the dental, his memory still lives within its walls by the cast of his jaws preserved in the dental museum as a relic of a case, in which the art of dentistry did signal service to the cause of justice.

In his lifetime Dr. Parkman was a well-known figure in the streets of Boston. His peculiar personal appearance and eccentric habits combined to make him something of a character. As he walked through the streets he presented a remarkable appearance. He was exceptionally tall, longer in the body than the legs; his lower jaw protruded some half an inch beyond the upper; he carried his body bent forward from the small of his back. He seemed to be always in a hurry; so impetuous was he that, if his horse did not travel fast enough to please him, he would get off its back, and, leaving the steed in the middle of the street, hasten on his way on foot. A just and generous man, he was extremely punctilious in matters of business, and uncom-

promising in his resentment of any form of falsehood or deceit. It was the force of his resentment in such a case that cost him his life.

The doctor was unfailingly punctual in taking his meals. Dr. Kingsley, during the fourteen years he had acted as his agent, had always been able to make sure of finding him at home at his dinner hour, half-past two o'clock. But on Friday, November 23, 1849, to his surprise and that of his family, Dr. Parkman did not come home to dinner; and their anxiety was increased when the day passed, and there was still no sign of the doctor's return. Inquiries were made. From these it appeared that Dr. Parkman had been last seen alive between one and two o'clock on the Friday afternoon. About half-past one he had visited a grocer's shop in Bridge Street, made some purchases, and left behind him a paper bag containing a lettuce, which, he said, he would call for on his way home. Shortly before two o'clock he was seen by a workman, at a distance of forty or fifty feet from the Medical College, going in that direction. From that moment all certain trace of him was lost. His family knew that he had made an appointment for half-past one that day, but where and with whom they did not know. As a matter of fact, Professor John W. Webster had appointed that hour to receive Dr. Parkman in his lecture-room in the Medical College.

John W. Webster was at this time Professor of Chemistry and Mineralogy in Harvard University, a Doctor of Medicine and a Member of the American Academy of Arts and Sciences, the London Geological Society and the St. Petersburg Mineralogical Society. He was the author of several works on geology and chemistry, a man now close on sixty years of age. His countenance was genial, his manner mild and unassuming; he was clean shaven, wore spectacles, and looked younger than his years.

Professor Webster was popular with a large circle of friends. To those who liked him he was a man of pleasing and attractive manners, artistic in his tastes—he was especially fond of music—not a very profound or remarkable chemist, but a pleasant social companion. His temper was hasty and irritable. Spoilt in his boyhood as an only child, he was self-willed and self- indulgent. His wife and daughters were better liked than he. By unfriendly criticics{sic} the Professor was thought to be selfish, fonder of the good things of the table and a good cigar than was consistent with his duty to his family or the smallness of his income. His father, a successful apothecary at Boston, had died in 1833, leaving John, his only son, a fortune of some L10,000. In rather less than ten years Webster had run through the whole of his inheritance. He had built himself a costly mansion in Cambridge, spent a large sum of money in collecting minerals, and delighted to exercise lavish hospitality. By living consistently beyond his means he found himself at length entirely dependent on his professional earnings. These were small. His salary as Professor was fixed at L240 a year;[15] the rest of his income he derived from the sale of tickets for his lectures at the Medical College. That income was insufficient to meet his wants.

[15] I have given these sums of money in their English equivalents in order to give the reader an idea of the smallness of the sum which brought about the tragedy.

As early as 1842 he had borrowed L80 from his friend Dr. Parkman. It was to Parkman's good offices that he owed his appointment as a Professor at Harvard; they had entered the University as under-graduates in the same year. Up to 1847 Webster had repaid Parkman twenty pounds of his debt; but, in that year he found it necessary to raise a further loan of L490, which was subscribed by a few friends, among them Parkman himself. As a security for the repayment of this loan, the professor executed a mortgage on his valuable collection of minerals in favour of Parkman. In the April of 1848 the Professor's financial difficulties became so serious that he was threatened with an execution in his house. In this predicament he went to a Mr. Shaw, Dr. Parkman's brother-in-law, and begged a loan of L240, offering him as security a bill of sale on the collection of minerals, which he had already mortgaged to Parkman. Shaw accepted the security, and lent the money. Shaw would seem to have had a good deal of sympathy with Webster's embarrassments; he considered the Professor's income very inadequate to his position, and showed himself quite ready at a later period to waive his debt altogether.

Dr. Parkman was a less easy-going creditor. Forbearing and patient as long as he was dealt with fairly, he was merciless where he thought he detected trickery or evasion. His forbearance and his patience were utterly exhausted, his anger and indignation strongly aroused, when he learnt from Shaw that Webster had given him as security for his debt a bill of sale on the collection of minerals, already mortgaged to himself. From the moment of the discovery of this act of dishonesty on the part of Webster, Parkman pursued his debtor with unrelenting severity.

He threatened him with an action at law; he said openly that he was neither an honourable, honest, nor upright man; he tried to appropriate to the payment of his debt the fees for lectures which Mr. Pettee, Webster's agent, collected on the Professor's behalf. He even visited Webster in his lecture-room and sat glaring at him in the front row of seats, while the Professor was striving under these somewhat unfavourable conditions to impart instruction to his pupils—a proceeding which the Doctor's odd cast of features must have aggravated in no small degree.

It was early in November that Parkman adopted these aggressive tactics. On the 19th of that month Webster and the janitor of the College, Ephraim Littlefield, were working in the upper laboratory. It was dark; they had lit candles. Webster was reading a chemical book. As he looked up from the book he saw Parkman standing in the doorway leading from the lecture-room. "Dr. Webster, are you ready for me to-night?" asked Parkman. "No," replied the other, "I am not ready to-night." After a little further conversation in regard to the mortgage, Parkman departed with the ominous remark, "Doctor, something must be done to-morrow."

Unfortunately the Professor was not in a position to do anything.

He had no means sufficient to meet his creditor's demands; and that creditor was unrelenting. On the 22nd Parkman rode into Cambridge, where Webster lived, to press him further, but failed to find him. Webster's patience, none too great at any time, was being sorely tried. To whom could he turn? What further resource was open to him? There was none. He determined to see his creditor once more. At 8 o'clock on the morning of Friday the 23rd, Webster called at Dr. Parkman's house and made the appointment for their meeting at the Medical College at half-past one, to which the Doctor had been seen hastening just before his disappearance. At nine o'clock the same morning Pettee, the agent, had called on the Professor at the College and paid him by cheque a balance of L28 due on his lecture tickets, informing him at the same time that, owing to the trouble with Dr. Parkman, he must decline to receive any further sums of money on his behalf. Webster replied that Parkman was a nervous, excitable man, subject to mental aberrations, but he added, "You will have no further trouble with Dr. Parkman, for I have settled with him." It is difficult to see how the Professor could have settled, or proposed to settle, with his creditor on that day. A balance of L28 at his bank, and the L18 which Mr. Pettee had paid to him that morning, represented the sum of Professor Webster's fortune on Friday, November 23, 1849.

Since the afternoon of that day the search for the missing Parkman had been unremitting. On the Saturday his friends communicated with the police. On Sunday hand-bills were issued stating the fact of the Doctor's disappearance, and on Monday, the 26th, a description and the offer of a considerable reward for the discovery of his body were circulated both in and out of the city. Two days later a further reward was offered. But these efforts were fruitless. The only person who gave any information beyond that afforded by those who had seen the Doctor in the streets on the morning of his disappearance, was Professor

Webster. About four o'clock on the Sunday afternoon the Professor called at the house of the Revd. Francis Parkman, the Doctor's brother. They were intimate friends. Webster had for a time attended Parkman's chapel; and Mr. Parkman had baptised the Professor's grand-daughter. On this Sunday afternoon Mr. Parkman could not help remarking Webster's peculiar manner. With a bare greeting and no expression of condolence with the family's distress, his visitor entered abruptly and nervously on the object of his errand. He had called, he said, to tell Mr. Parkman that he had seen his brother at the Medical College on Friday afternoon, that he had paid him L90 which he owed him, and that the Doctor had in the course of their interview taken out a paper and dashed his pen through it, presumably as an acknowledgment of the liquidation of the Professor's debt. Having communicated this intelligence to the somewhat astonished gentleman, Webster left him as abruptly as he had come.

Another relative of Dr. Parkman, his nephew, Mr. Parkman Blake, in the course of inquiries as to his uncle's fate, thought it right to see Webster. Accordingly he went to the college on Monday, the 26th, about eleven o'clock in the morning. Though not one of his lecture days, the janitor Littlefield informed him that the Professor was in his room. The door of the lecture—

room, however, was found to be locked, and it was only after considerable delay that Mr. Blake gained admittance. As he descended the steps to the floor of the lecture-room Webster, dressed in a working suit of blue overalls and wearing on his head a smoking cap, came in from the back door. Instead of advancing to greet his visitor, he stood fixed to the spot, and waited, as if defensively, for Mr. Blake to speak. In answer to Mr. Blake's questions Webster described his interview with Dr. Parkman on the Friday afternoon. He gave a very similar account of it to that he had already given to Mr. Francis Parkman. He added that at the end of their interview he had asked the Doctor for the return of the mortgage, to which the latter had replied, "I haven't it with me, but I will see it is properly cancelled." Mr. Blake asked Webster if he could recollect in what form of money it was that he had paid Dr. Parkman. Webster answered that he could only recollect a bill of L20 on the New Zealand Bank: pressed on this point, he seemed to rather avoid any further inquiries. Mr. Blake left him, dissatisfied with the result of his visit.

One particular in Webster's statement was unquestionably strange, if not incredible. He had, he said, paid Parkman a sum of L90, which he had given him personally, and represented the Doctor as having at their interview promised to cancel the mortgage on the collection of minerals which Webster had given as security for the loan of L490 that had been subscribed by Parkman and four of his friends. Now L120 of this loan was still owing. If Webster's statement were true, Parkman had a perfect right to cancel Webster's personal debt to himself; but he had no right to cancel entirely the mortgage on the minerals, so long as money due to others on that mortgage was yet unpaid. Was it conceivable that one so strict and scrupulous in all monetary transactions as Parkman would have settled his own personal claim, and then sacrificed in so discreditable a manner the claims of others, for the satisfaction of which he had made himself responsible?

There was yet another singular circumstance. On Saturday, the 24th, the day after his settlement with Parkman, Webster paid into his own account at the Charles River Bank the cheque for L18, lecture fees, handed over to him by the agent Pettee just before Dr. Parkman's visit on the Friday. This sum had not apparently gone towards the making up of the L90, which Webster said that he had paid to Parkman that day. The means by which Webster had been enabled to settle this debt became more mysterious than ever.

On Tuesday, November 27, the Professor received three other visitors in his lecture-room. These were police officers who, in the course of their search for the missing man, felt it their duty to examine, however perfunctorily, the Medical College. With apologies to the Professor, they passed through his lecture room to the laboratory at the back, and from thence, down the private stairs, past a privy, into the lower laboratory. As they passed the privy one of the officers asked what place it was. "Dr. Webster's private lavatory," replied the janitor, who was conducting them. At that moment Webster's voice called them away to examine the store-room in the lower laboratory, and after a cursory examination the officers departed.

The janitor, Ephraim Littlefield, did not take the opportunity afforded him by the visit of the police officers to impart to them the feelings of uneasiness; which the conduct of Professor Webster during the last three days had excited in his breast. There were circumstances in the Professor's behaviour which could not fail to attract the attention of a man, whose business throughout the day was to dust and sweep the College, light the fires and overlook generally the order and cleanliness of the building.

Littlefield, it will be remembered, had seen Dr. Parkman on the Monday before his disappearance, when he visited Webster at the College, and been present at the interview, in the course of which the Doctor told Webster that "something must be done." That Monday morning Webster asked Littlefield a number of questions about the dissecting-room vault, which was situated just outside the door of the lower laboratory. He asked how it was built, whether a light could be put into it, and how it was reached for the purpose of repair. On the following Thursday, the day before Parkman's disappearance, the Professor told Littlefield to get him a pint of blood from the Massachusetts Hospital; he said that he wanted it for an experiment. On the morning of Friday, the day of Parkman's disappearance, Littlefield informed the Professor that he had been unsuccessful in his efforts to get the blood, as they had not been bleeding anyone lately at the hospital. The same morning Littlefield found to his surprise a sledge-hammer behind the door of the Professor's back room; he presumed that it had been left there by masons, and took it down to the lower laboratory. This sledge-hammer Littlefield never saw again. About a quarter to two that afternoon Littlefield, standing at the front door, after his dinner, saw Dr. Parkman coming towards the College. At two o'clock Littlefield went up to Dr. Oliver Wendell Holmes' room, immediately above Professor Webster's, to help the Doctor to clear his table after his lecture, which was the last delivered that day. About a quarter of an hour later he let Dr. Holmes out, locked the front door and began to clear out the stoves in the other lecture-rooms. When he reached Webster's he was surprised to find that both doors, that of the lecture room and that of the lower laboratory, were either locked or bolted. He could hear nothing but the running of water in one of the sinks. About half-past five Littlefield saw the Professor coming down the back stairs with a lighted candle in his hand. Webster blew out the candle and left the building. Late that night Littlefield again tried the Professor's doors; they were still fastened. The janitor was surprised at this, as he had never known such a thing to happen before.

On Saturday, the 24th, though not lecturing that day, the Professor came to the College in the morning. He told Littlefield to light the stove in the lower laboratory. When Littlefield made to pass from the lecture-room into the Professor's private room at the back, and so down by the private stairs to the lower laboratory, the Professor stopped him and told him to go round by the door in front of the building. The whole of that day and Sunday, the Professor's doors remained fast. On Sunday evening at sunset Littlefield, who was talking with a friend in North Grove Street, the street that faces the College, was accosted by Webster. The Professor asked him if he recollected Parkman's visit to the College on Friday, the 23rd, and, on his replying in the affirmative, the Professor described to him their interview and the repayment of his debt. Littlefield was struck during their conversation by the uneasiness of the Professor's bearing; contrary to his habit he seemed unable to look him in the face, his manner was confused, his face pale.

During the whole of Monday, except for a visit from Mr. Parkman Blake, Professor Webster was again locked alone in his laboratory. Neither that night, nor early Tuesday morning, could Littlefield get into the Professor's rooms to perform his customary duties. On Tuesday the Professor lectured at twelve o'clock, and later received the visit of the police officers that has been described already. At four o'clock that afternoon, the Professor's bell rang. Littlefield answered it. The Pro-

fessor asked the janitor whether he had bought his turkey for Thanksgiving Day, which was on the following Thursday. Littlefield said that he had not done so yet. Webster then handed him an order on his provision dealer. "Take that," he said, "and get a nice turkey; perhaps I shall want you to do some odd jobs for me." Littlefield thanked him, and said that he would be glad to do anything for him that he could. The janitor was the more surprised at Webster's generosity on this occasion, as this turkey was the first present he had received at the Professor's hands during the seven years he had worked in the College. Littlefield saw the Professor again about half-past six that evening as the latter was leaving the College. The janitor asked him if he wanted any more fires lighted in his rooms, because owing to the holidays there were to be no further lectures that week. Webster said that he did not, and asked Lit-

tlefield whether he were a freemason. The janitor said "Yes," and with that they parted.

Littlefield was curious. The mysterious activity of the Professor of Chemistry seemed to him more than unusual. His perplexity was increased on the following day. Though on account of the holidays all work had been suspended at the College for the remainder of the week, Webster was again busy in his room early Wednesday morning. Littlefield could hear him moving about. In vain did the janitor look through the keyhole, bore a hole in the door, peep under it; all he could get was a sight of the Professor's feet moving about the laboratory. Perplexity gave way to apprehension when in the course of the afternoon Littlefield discovered that the outer wall of the lower laboratory was so hot that he could hardly bear to place his hand on it. On the outer side of this wall was a furnace sometimes used by the Professor in his chemical experiments. How came it to be so heated? The Professor had told Littlefield on Tuesday that he should not be requiring any fires during the remainder of the week.

The janitor determined to resolve his suspicions. He climbed up to the back windows of the lower laboratory, found one of them unfastened, and let himself in. But, beyond evidences of the considerable fires that had been kept burning during the last few days, Littlefield saw nothing to excite peculiar attention. Still he was uneasy. Those he met in the street kept on telling him that Dr. Parkman would be found in the Medical College. He felt that he himself was beginning to be suspected of having some share in the mystery, whilst in his own mind he became more certain every day that the real solution lay within the walls of Professor Webster's laboratory. His attention had fixed itself particularly on the lavatory at the foot of the stairs connecting the upper and lower laboratories. This room he found to be locked and the key, a large one, had disappeared. He recollected that when the police officers had paid their visit to the col-lege, the Professor had diverted their attention as they were about to inspect this room. The only method by which, unknown to the Professor and without breaking open the door, Littlefield could examine the vault of this retiring room was by going down to the basement floor of the college and digging a hole through the wall into the vault itself. This he determined to do.

On Thursday, Thanksgiving Day, Littlefield commenced operations with a hatchet and a chisel. Progress was slow, as that evening he had been invited to attend a festal gathering. On Friday the janitor, before resuming work, acquainted two of the Professors of the college with his proposed investigation, and received their sanction. As Webster, however, was going constantly in and out of his rooms, he could make little further progress that day. The Professor had come into town early in the morning.

Before going to the college he purchased some fish-hooks and gave orders for the making of a strong tin box with firm handles, a foot and a half square and a little more than a foot in depth; during the rest of the day he had been busy in his rooms until he left the college about four o'clock. Not till then was the watchful janitor able to resume his labours. Armed with a crow-bar, he worked vigorously until he succeeded in penetrating the wall sufficiently to admit a light into the vault of the lavatory. The first objects which the light revealed to his eyes, were the pelvis of a man and two parts of a human leg.

Leaving his wife in charge of the remains, Littlefield went immediately to the house of Professor Bigelow, and informed him of the result of his search. They returned to the college some twenty minutes later, accompanied by the City Marshal. The human remains—a pelvis, a thigh and a leg—were taken out of the vault, and on a further search some pieces of bone were removed from one of the furnaces in the lower laboratory. The City Marshal at once dispatched three of his officers to Cambridge, to the house of Professor Webster.

To his immediate circle of friends and relations the conduct of the Professor during this eventful week had betrayed no unwonted discomposure or disturbance of mind. His evenings had been spent either at the house of friends, or at his own, playing whist, or reading Milton's "Allegro" and "Penseroso" to his wife and daugh-

ters. On Friday evening, about eight o'clock, as the Professor was saying good-bye to a friend on the steps of his house at Cambridge, the three police officers drove up to the door and asked him to accompany them to the Medical College. It was proposed, they said, to make a further search there that evening, and his presence was considered advisable. Webster assented immediately, put on his boots, his hat and coat, and got into the hired coach. As they drove towards the city, Webster spoke to the officers of Parkman's disappearance, and suggested that they should stop at the house of a lady who, he said, could give them some peculiar information on that subject. As they entered Boston, he remarked that they were taking the wrong direction for reaching the college. One of the officers replied that the driver might be "green," but that he would find his way to the college in time. At length the coach stopped. One of the offi-

cers alighted, and invited his companions to follow him into the office of the Leverett Street Jail. They obeyed. The Professor asked what it all meant; he was informed that he must consider himself in custody, charged with the murder of Dr. George Parkman. Webster, somewhat taken aback, desired that word should be sent to his family, but was dissuaded from his purpose for the time being. He was searched, and among other articles taken from him was a key some four or five inches long; it was the missing lavatory key. Whilst one of the officers withdrew to make out a mittimus, the Professor asked one of the others if they had found Dr. Parkman. The officer begged him not to question him. "You might tell me something about it," pleaded Webster. "Where did they find him? Did they find the whole body? Oh, my children! What will they do? What will they think of me? Where did you get the information?" The officers asked him if anybody had access to his apartments but himself. "Nobody," he replied, "but the porter who makes the fire." Then, after a pause, he ex-

claimed: "That villain! I am a ruined man." He was walking up and down wringing his hands, when one of the officers saw him put one hand into his waistcoat pocket, and raise it to his lips. A few moments later the unhappy man was seized with violent spasms. He was unable to stand, and was laid down in one of the cells. From this distressing state he was roused shortly before eleven, to be taken to the college. He was quite incapable of walking, and had to be supported by two of the officers. He was present there while his rooms were searched; but his state was painful in the extreme. He asked for water, but trembled so convulsively that he could only snap at the tumbler like a dog; his limbs were rigid; tears and sweat poured down his cheeks. On the way back to the jail, one of the officers, moved by his condition, expressed his pity for him. "Do you pity me? Are you sorry for me? What for?" asked Webster. "To see you so excited," replied the officer. "Oh! that's it," said the Professor.

The whole night through the prisoner lay without moving, and not until the following afternoon were his limbs relaxed sufficiently to allow of his sitting up. As his condition improved, he grew more confident. "That is no more Dr. Parkman's body," he said, "than mine. How in the world it came there I don't know," and he added: "I never liked the looks of Littlefield the janitor; I opposed his coming there all I could."

In the meantime a further examination of the Professor's rooms on Saturday had resulted in the discovery, in a tea-chest in the lower laboratory, of a thorax, the left thigh of a leg, and a hunting knife embedded in tan and covered over with minerals; some portions of bone and teeth were found mixed with the slag and cinders of one of the furnaces; also some fish-hooks and a quantity of twine, the latter identical with a piece of twine that had been tied round the thigh found in the chest.

Two days later the Professor furnished unwittingly some additional evidence against himself. On the Monday evening after his arrest he wrote from prison to one of his daughters the following letter:

"MY DEAREST MARIANNE,—I wrote Mama yesterday; I had a good sleep last night, and dreamt of you all. I got my clothes off, for the first time, and awoke in the morning quite hungry. It was a long time before my first breakfast from Parker's came; and it was relished, I can assure you. At one o'clock I was notified that I must appear at the court room. All was arranged with great regard to my comfort, and went off better than I had anticipated.

On my return I had a bit of turkey and rice from Parker's. They send much more than I can eat, and I have directed the steward to distribute the surplus to any poor ones here.

"If you will send me a small canister of tea, I can make my own. A little pepper I may want some day. I would send the dirty clothes, but they were taken to dry. Tell Mama NOT TO OPEN the little bundle I gave her the other day, but to keep it just as she received it. With many kisses to you all. Good night!— From your affectionate

"FATHER."

"P.S.—My tongue troubles me yet very much, and I must have bitten it in my distress the other night; it is painful and swollen, affecting my speech. Had Mama better send for Nancy? I think so; or Aunt Amelia."

"Couple of coloured neck handkerchiefs, one Madras."

This letter, which shows an anxiety about his personal comfort singular in one so tragically situated, passed through the hands of the keeper of the jail. He was struck by the words underlined," NOT TO OPEN," in regard to the small bundle confided to Mrs. Webster. He called the attention of the police to this phrase. They sent immediately an officer armed with a search warrant to the Professor's house. He received from Mrs. Webster among other papers a package which, on being opened, was found to contain the two notes given by Webster to Parkman as acknowledgments of his indebtedness to him in 1842 and 1847, and a paper showing the amount of his debts to Parkman in 1847. There were daubs and erasures made across these documents, and across one was written twice over the word "paid." All these evidences of payments and cancellations appeared on examination to be in the handwriting of the Professor.

After an inquest lasting nine days the coroner's jury declared the remains found in the college to be those of Dr. George Parkman, and that the deceased had met his death at the hands of Professor J. W. Webster. The prisoner waived his right to a magisterial investigation, and on January 26, 1850, the Grand Jury returned a true bill. But it was not until March 17 that the Professor's trial opened before the Supreme Court of Massachusetts. The proceedings were conducted with that dignity and propriety which we look for in the courts of that State. The principal features in the defence were an attempt to impugn the testimony of the janitor Littlefield, and to question the possibility of the identification of the remains of Parkman's teeth. There was a further attempt to prove that the deceased had been seen by a number of persons in the streets of Boston on the Friday afternoon, after his visit to the Medical College. The witness Littlefield was unshaken by a severe cross- examination. The very reluctance with which Dr. Keep gave his fatal evidence, and the support given to his conclusions by distinguished testimony told strongly in favour of the absolute trustworthiness of his statements. The evidence called to prove that the murdered man had been seen alive late on Friday afternoon was highly inconclusive.

Contrary to the advice of his counsel, Webster addressed the jury himself. He complained of the conduct of his case, and enumerated various points that his counsel had omitted to make, which he conceived to be in his favour. The value of his statements may be judged by the fact that he called God to witness that he had not written any one of the anonymous letters, purporting to give a true account of the doctor's fate, which had been received by the police at the time of Parkman's disap-

pearance. After his condemnation Webster confessed to the authorship of at least one of them.

The jury retired at eight o'clock on the eleventh day of the trial. They would seem to have approached their duty in a most solemn and devout spirit, and it was with the greatest reluctance and after some searching of heart that they brought themselves to find the prisoner guilty of wilful murder. On hearing their verdict, the Professor sank into a seat, and, dropping his head, rubbed his eyes behind his spectacles as if wiping away tears. On the following morning the Chief Justice sentenced him to death after a well-meaning speech of quite unnecessary length and elaboration, at the conclusion of which the condemned man wept freely.

A petition for a writ of error having been dismissed, the Professor in July addressed a petition for clemency to the Council of the State. Dr. Putnam, who had been attending Webster in the jail, read to the Council a confession which he had persuaded the prisoner to make. According to this statement Webster had, on the Friday afternoon, struck Parkman on the head with a heavy wooden stick in a wild moment of rage, induced by the violent taunts and threats of his creditor. Appalled by his deed, he had in panic locked himself in his room, and proceeded with desperate haste to dismember the body; he had placed it for that purpose in the sink in his back room, through which was running a constant stream of water that carried away the blood. Some portions of the body he had burnt in the furnace; those in the lavatory and the tea-chest he had concealed there, until he should have had an opportunity of getting rid of them.

In this statement Professor Webster denied all premeditation. Dr. Putnam asked him solemnly whether he had not, immediately before the crime, meditated at any time on the advantages that would accrue to him from Parkman's death. Webster replied "Never, before God!" He had, he protested, no idea of doing Parkman an injury until the bitter tongue of the latter provoked him. "I am irritable and violent," he said, "a quickness and brief violence of temper has been the besetting sin of my life. I was an only child, much indulged, and I have never secured the control over my passions that I ought to have acquired early; and the consequence is—all this!" He denied having told Parkman that he was going to settle with him that afternoon, and said that he had asked him to come to the college with the sole object of pleading with him for further indulgence. He explained his convulsive seizure at the time of his arrest by his having taken a dose of strychnine, which he had carried in his pocket since the crime. In spite of these statements and the prayers of the unfortunate man's wife and daughters, who, until his confession to Dr. Putnam, had believed implicity in his innocence, the Council decided that the law must take its course, and fixed August 30 as the day of execution.

The Professor resigned himself to his fate. He sent for Littlefield and his wife, and expressed his regret for any injustice he had done them: "All you said was true. You have misrepresented nothing." Asked by the sheriff whether he was to understand from some of his expressions that he contemplated an attempt at suicide, "Why should I?" he replied, "all the proceedings in my case have been just . . . and it is just that I should die upon the scaffold in accordance with that sentence." "Everybody is right," he said to the keeper of the jail, "and I am wrong. And I feel that, if the yielding up of my life to the injured law will atone, even in part, for the crime I have committed, that is a consolation."

In a letter to the Reverend Francis Parkman he expressed deep contrition for his guilt. He added one sentence which may perhaps fairly express the measure of premeditation that accompanied his crime. "I had never," he wrote, "until the two or three last interviews with your brother, felt towards him anything but gratitude for his many acts of kindness and friendship."

Professor Webster met his death with fortitude and resignation. That he deserved his fate few will be inclined to deny. The attempt to procure blood, the questions about the dissecting-room vault, the appointment made with Parkman at the college, the statement to Pettee, all point to some degree of premeditation, or at least would make it appear that the murder of Parkman had been considered by him as a possible eventuality. His accusation of Littlefield deprives him of a good deal of sympathy. On the other hand, the age and position of Webster, the aggravating persistency of Parkman, his threats and denunciations, coupled with his own shortness of temper, make it conceivable that he may have killed his victim on a sudden and overmastering provocation, in which case he had better at once have acknowledged his crime instead of making a repulsive attempt to conceal it. But for the evidence of Dr. Keep he would possibly have escaped punishment altogether. Save for the portions of his false teeth, there was not sufficient evidence to identify the remains found in the college as those of Parkman. Without these teeth the proof of the corpus delicti would have been incomplete, and so afforded Webster a fair chance of acquittal.

THE MYSTERIOUS MR. HOLMES

"The Holmes-Pitezel Case," by F. B. Geyer, 1896; "Holmes' Own Story," Philadelphia, 1895; and "Celebrated Criminal Cases of America," by T. S. Duke, San Francisco, are the authorities for this account of the case.

I

HONOUR AMONGST THIEVES

In the year 1894 Mr. Smith, a carpenter, of Philadelphia, had patented a new saw-set. Wishing to make some money out of his invention, Mr. Smith was attracted by the sign:

B. F. PERRY
PATENTS BOUGHT AND SOLD

which he saw stretched across the window of a two-storied house, 1,316 Callowhill Street. He entered the house and made the acquaintance of Mr. Perry, a tall, dark, bony man, to whom he explained the merits of his invention. Perry listened with interest, and asked for a model. In the meantime he suggested that Smith should do some carpenter's work for him in the house. Smith agreed, and on August 22, while at work there saw a man enter the house and go up with Perry to a room on the second story.

A few days later Smith called at Callowhill Street to ask Perry about the sale of the patent. He waited half an hour in the shop below, called out to Perry who, he thought, might be in the rooms above, received no answer and went away. Next day, September 4, Smith returned, found the place just as he had left it the day before; called Perry again, but again got no answer. Surprised, he went upstairs, and in the back room of the second story the morning sunshine, streaming through the window, showed him the dead body of a man, his face charred beyond recognition, lying with his feet to the window and his head to the door. There was evidence of some sort of explosion: a broken bottle that had contained an inflammable substance, a broken pipe filled with tobacco, and a burnt match lay by the side of the body.

The general appearance of the dead man answered to that of B. F. Perry. A medical examination of the body showed that death had been sudden, that there had been paralysis of the involuntary muscles, and that the stomach, besides showing symptoms of alcoholic irritation, emitted a strong odour of chloroform. An inquest was held, and a verdict returned that B. F. Perry had died of congestion of the lungs caused by the inhalation of flame or chloroform. After lying in the mortuary for eleven days the body was buried.

In the meantime the Philadelphia branch of the Fidelity Mutual Life Association had received a letter from one Jephtha D. Howe, an attorney at St. Louis, stating that the deceased B. F. Perry was Benjamin F. Pitezel of that city, who had been insured in their office for a sum of ten thousand dollars. The insurance had been effected in Chicago in the November of 1893. Mr. Howe proposed to come to Philadelphia with some members of the Pitezel family to identify the remains. Referring to their Chicago branch, the insurance company found that the only person who would seem to have known Pitezel when in that city, was a certain H. H. Holmes, living at Wilmette, Illinois. They got into communication with Mr. Holmes, and forwarded to him a cutting from a newspaper, which stated erroneously that the death of B. F. Perry had taken place in Chicago.

On September 18 they received a letter from Mr. Holmes, in which he offered what assistance he could toward the identification of B. F. Perry as B. F. Pitezel. He gave the name of a dentist in Chicago who would be able to recognise teeth which he had made for Pitezel, and himself furnished a description of the man, especially of a malformation of the knee and a warty growth on the back of the neck by which he could be further identified. Mr. Holmes offered, if his expenses were paid, to come to Chicago to view the body. Two days later he wrote again saying that he had seen by other papers that Perry's death had taken place in Philadelphia and not in Chicago, and that as he had to be in Baltimore in a day or two, he would run over to Philadelphia and visit the office of the Fidelity Life Association.

On September 20 the assiduous Mr. Holmes called at the office of the Association in Philadelphia, inquired anxiously about the nature and cause of Perry's death, gave again a description of him and, on learning that Mr. Howe, the attorney from St. Louis, was about to come to Philadelphia to represent the widow, Mrs. Pitezel, and complete the identification, said that he would return to give the company any further help he could in the matter. The following day Mr. Jephtha D. Howe, attorney of St. Louis, arrived in Philadelphia, accompanied by Alice Pitezel, a daughter of the deceased. Howe explained that Pitezel had taken the name of Perry owing to financial difficulties. The company said that they accepted the fact that Perry and Pitezel were one and the same man, but were not convinced that the body was Pitezel's body. The visit of Holmes was mentioned. Howe said that he did not know Mr. Holmes, but would be willing to meet him. At this moment Holmes arrived at the office. He was introduced to Howe as a stranger, and recognised as a friend by Alice Pitezel, a shy, awkward girl of fourteen or fifteen years of age. It was then arranged that all the parties should meet again next day to identify, if possible, the body, which had been disinterred for that purpose.

The unpleasant duty of identifying the rapidly decomposing remains was greatly curtailed by the readiness of Mr. Holmes. When the party met on the 22nd at the Potter's Field, where the body had been disinterred and laid out, the doctor present was unable to find the distinctive marks which would show Perry and Pitezel to have been the same man. Holmes at once stepped into the breach, took off his coat, rolled up his sleeves, put on the rubber gloves, and taking a surgeon's knife from his pocket, cut off the wart at the back of the neck, showed the injury to the leg, and revealed also a bruised thumb-nail which had been another distinctive mark of Pitezel. The body was then covered up all but the teeth; the girl Alice was brought in, and she said that the teeth appeared to be like those of her father. The insurance company declared themselves satisfied, and handed to Mr. Howe a cheque for 9,175 dollars, and to Mr. Holmes ten dollars for his expenses. Smith, the carpenter, had been present at the proceedings at the Potter's Field. For a moment he thought he detected a likeness in Mr. Holmes to the man who had visited Perry at Callowhill Street on August 22 and gone upstairs with him, but he did not feel sure enough of the fact to make any mention of it.

In the prison at St. Louis there languished in the year 1894 one Marion Hedgspeth, serving a sentence of twenty years' imprisonment for an audacious train robbery. On the night of November 30, 1891, the "'Friscow express from St. Louis had been boarded by four ruffians, the express car blown open with dynamite, and 10,000 dollars carried off. Hedgspeth and another man were tried for the robbery, and sentenced to twenty years' imprisonment. On October 9, 1894, Hegspeth{sic} made a statement to the Governor of the St. Louis prison, which he said he wished to be communicated to the Fidelity Mutual Life Association. In the previous July Hedgspeth said that he had met in the prison a man of the name of H. M. Howard, who was charged with fraud, but had been released on bail later in the month. While in prison Howard told Hedgspeth that he had devised a scheme for swindling an insurance company of 10,000 dollars, and promised Hedgspeth that, if he would recommend him a lawyer suitable for such an enterprise, he should have 500 dollars as his share of the proceeds. Hedgspeth recommended Jephtha D. Howe. The latter entered with enthusiasm into the scheme, and told Hedgspeth that he thought Mr. Howard "one of the smoothest and slickest" men he had ever known. A corpse was to be found answering to Pitezel's description, and to be so treated as to appear to have been the victim of an accidental explosion, while Pitezel himself would disappear to Germany. From Howe Hedgspeth learnt that the swindle had been carried out successfully, but he had never received from Howard the 500 dollars promised him. Consequently, he had but little compunction in divulging the plot to the authorities.

It was realised at once that H. M. Howard and H. H. Holmes were the same person, and that Jephtha D. Howe and Mr. Holmes were not the strangers to each other that they had affected to be when they met in Philadelphia. Though somewhat doubtful of the truth of Hedgspeth's statement, the insurance company decided to set Pinkerton's detectives on the track of Mr. H. H. Holmes. After more than a month's search he was traced to his father's house at Gilmanton, N. H., and arrested in Boston on November 17.

Inquiry showed that, early in 1894, Holmes and Pitezel had acquired some real property at Fort Worth in Texas and commenced building operations, but had soon after left Texas under a cloud, arising from the theft of a horse and other dubious transactions.

Holmes had obtained the property at Fort Worth from a Miss Minnie Williams, and transferred it to Pitezel. Pitezel was a drunken "crook," of mean ~elligence, a mesmeric subject entirely under the influence of Holmes, who claimed to have considerable hypnotic powers. Pitezel had a wife living at St. Louis and five children, three girls—Dessie, Alice, and Nellie—a boy, Howard, and a baby in arms. At the time of Holmes' arrest Mrs. Pitezel, with her eldest daughter, Dessie, and her little baby, was living at a house rented by Holmes at Burlington, Vermont. She also was arrested on a charge of complicity in the insurance fraud and brought to Boston.

Two days after his arrest Holmes, who dreaded being sent back to Texas on a charge of horse-stealing, for which in that State the punishment is apt to be rough and ready, made a statement to the police, in which he acknowledged the fraud practised by him and Pitezel on the insurance company. The body substituted for Pitezel had been obtained, said Holmes, from a doctor in New York, packed in a trunk and sent to Philadelphia, but he declined for the present to give the doctor's name. Pitezel, he said, had gone with three of his children— Alice, Nellie and Howard—to South America. This fact, however, Holmes had not communicated to Mrs. Pitezel. When she arrived at Boston, the poor woman was in great distress of mind. Questioned by the officers, she attempted to deny any complicity in the fraud, but her real anxiety was to get news of her husband and her three children. Alice she had not seen since the girl had gone to Philadelphia to identify the supposed remains of her father. Shortly after this Holmes had come to Mrs. Pitezel at St. Louis, and taken away Nellie and Howard to join Alice, who, he said, was in the care of a widow lady at Ovington, Kentucky. Since then Mrs. Pitezel had seen nothing of the children or her husband. At Holmes' direction she had gone to Detroit, Toronto, Ogdensberg and, lastly, to Burlington in the hope of meeting either Pitezel or the children, but in vain. She believed that her husband had deserted her; her only desire was to recover her children.

On November 20 Holmes and Mrs. Pitezel were transferred from Boston to Philadelphia, and there, along with Benjamin Pitezel and Jephtha D. Howe, were charged with defrauding the Fidelity Life Association of 10,000 dollars. Soon after his arrival in Philadelphia Holmes, who was never averse to talking, was asked by an inspector of the insurance company who it was that had helped him to double up the body sent from New York and pack it into the trunk. He replied that he had done it alone, having learned the trick when studying medicine in Michigan. The inspector recollected that the body when removed from Callowhill Street had been straight and rigid. He asked Holmes what trick he had learnt in the course of his medical studies by which it was possible to re-stiffen a body once the rigor mortis had been broken. To this Holmes made no reply. But he realised his mistake, and a few weeks later volunteered a second statement. He now said that Pitezel, in a fit of depression, aggravated by his drinking habits, had committed suicide on the third story of the house in Callowhill Street. There Holmes had found his body,carried it down on to the floor below, and arranged it in the manner agreed upon for deceiving the insurance company. Pitezel, he said, had taken his life by lying on the floor and allowing chloroform to run slowly into his mouth through a rubber tube placed on a chair. The three children, Holmes now stated, had gone to England with a friend of his, Miss Minnie Williams.

Miss Minnie Williams was the lady, from whom Holmes was said to have acquired the property in Texas which he and Pitezel had set about developing. There was quite a tragedy, according to Holmes, connected with the life of Miss Williams. She had come to Holmes in 1893, as secretary, at a drug store which he was then keeping in Chicago. Their relations had become more intimate, and later in the year Miss Williams wrote to her sister, Nannie, saying that she was going to be married, and inviting her to the wedding. Nannie arrived, but unfortunately a violent quarrel broke out between the two sisters, and Holmes came home to find that Minnie in her rage had killed her sister. He had helped her out of the trouble by dropping Nannie's body into the Chicago lake. After such a distressing occurrence Miss Williams was only too glad of the opportunity of leaving America with the Pitezel children. In the meantime Holmes, under the name of Bond, and Pitezel, under that of Lyman, had proceeded to deal with Miss Williams' property in Texas.

For women Holmes would always appear to have possessed some power of attraction, a power of which he availed himself generously. Holmes, whose real name was Herman W. Mudgett, was thirty-four years of age at the time of his arrest. As a boy he had spent his life farming in Vermont, after which he had taken up medicine and acquired some kind of medical degree. In the course of his training Holmes and a fellow student, finding a body that bore a striking resemblance to the latter; obtained 1,000 dollars from an insurance company by a fraud similar to that in which Holmes had engaged subsequently with Pitezel. After spending some time on the staff of a lunatic asylum in Pennsylvania, Holmes set up as a druggist in Chicago. His affairs in this city prospered, and he was enabled to erect, at the corner of Wallace and Sixty-Third Streets, the four-storied building known later as "Holmes Castle." It was a singular structure. The lower part consisted of a shop and offices. Holmes occupied the second floor, and had a laboratory on the third. In his office was a vault, air proof and sound proof. In the bathroom a trap-door, covered by a rug, opened on to a secret staircase leading down to the cellar, and a similar staircase connected the cellar with the laboratory. In the cellar was a large grate. To this building Miss Minnie Williams had invited her sister to come for her wedding with Holmes, and it was in this building, according to Holmes, that the tragedy of Nannie's untimely death occurred.

In hoping to become Holmes' wife, Miss Minnie Williams was not to enjoy an exclusive privilege. At the time of his arrest Holmes had three wives, each ignorant of the others' existence. He had married the first in 1878, under the name of Mudgett, and was visiting her at Burlington, Vermont, when the Pinkerton detectives first got on his track. The second he had married at Chicago, under the name of Howard, and the third at Denver as recently as January, 1894, under the name of Holmes. The third Mrs. Holmes had been with him when he came to Philadelphia to identify Pitezel's body. The appearance of Holmes was commonplace, but he was a man of plausible and ingratiating address, apparent candour, and able in case of necessity to "let loose," as he phrased it, "the fount of emotion."

The year 1895 opened to find the much enduring Holmes still a prisoner in Philadelphia. The authorities seemed in no haste to indict him for fraud; their interest was concentrated rather in endeavouring to find the whereabouts of Miss Williams and her children, and of one Edward Hatch, whom Holmes had described as helping him in arranging for their departure. The "great humiliation" of being a prisoner was very distressing to Holmes.
"I only know the sky has lost its blue,
The days are weary and the night is drear."

These struck him as two beautiful lines very appropriate to his situation. He made a New Year's resolve to give up meat during his close confinement. The visits of his third wife brought him some comfort. He was "agreeably surprised" to find that, as an unconvicted prisoner, he could order in his own meals and receive newspapers and periodicals. But he was hurt at an unfriendly suggestion on the part of the authorities that Pitezel had not died by his own hand, and that Edward Hatch was but a figment of his rich imagination. He would like to have been released on bail, but in the same unfriendly spirit was informed that, if he were, he would be detained on a charge of murder. And so the months dragged on. Holmes, studious, patient, injured, the authorities puzzled, suspicions, baffled—still no news of Miss Williams or the three children. It was not until June 3 that Holmes was put on his trial for fraud, and the following day pleaded guilty. Sentence was postponed.

The same day Holmes was sent for to the office of the District Attorney, who thus addressed him: "It is strongly suspected, Holmes, that you have not only murdered Pitezel, but that you have killed the children. The best way to remove this suspicion is to produce the children at once. Now, where are they?" Unfriendly as was this approach, Holmes met it calmly, reiterated his previous statement that the children had gone with Miss Williams to England, and gave her address in London, 80 Veder or Vadar Street, where, he said, Miss Williams had opened a massage establishment. He offered to draw up and insert a cipher advertisement in the New York Herald, by means of which, he said, Miss Williams and he had agreed to communicate, and almost tearfully he added, "Why should I kill innocent children?"

Asked to give the name of any person who had seen Miss Williams and the children in the course of their journeyings in America, he resented the disbelief implied in such a question, and strong was his manly indignation when one of the gentlemen present expressed his opinion that the story was a lie from beginning to end. This rude estimate of Holmes' veracity was, however, in some degree confirmed when a cipher advertisement published in the New York Herald according to Holmes' directions, produced no reply from Miss Williams, and inquiry showed that no such street as Veder or Vadar Street was to be found in London.

In spite of these disappointments, Holmes' quiet confidence in his own good faith continued unshaken. When the hapless Mrs. Pitezel was released, he wrote her a long letter. "Knowing me as you do," he said, "can you imagine me killing little and innocent children, especially without any motive?" But even Mrs. Pitezel was not wholly reassured. She recollected how Holmes had taken her just before his arrest to a house he had rented at Burlington, Vermont, how he had written asking her to carry a package of nitro-glycerine from the bottom to the top of the house, and how one day she had found him busily removing the boards in the cellar.

II

THE WANDERING ASSASSIN

The District Attorney and the Insurance Company were not in agreement as to the fate of the Pitezel children. The former still inclined to the hope and belief that they were in England with Miss Williams, but the insurance company took a more sinister view. No trace of them existed except a tin box found among Holmes' effects, containing letters they had written to their mother and grandparents from Cincinnati, Indianapolis, and Detroit, which had been given to Holmes to dispatch but had never reached their destination. The box contained letters from Mrs. Pitezel to her children, which Holmes had presumably intercepted.

It was decided to make a final attempt to resolve all doubts by sending an experienced detective over the route taken by the children in America. He was to make exhaustive inquiries in each city with a view to tracing the visits of Holmes or the three children. For this purpose a detective of the name of Geyer was chosen. The record of his search is a remarkable story of patient and persistent investigation.

Alice Pitezel had not seen her mother since she had gone with Holmes to identify her father's remains in Philadelphia. From there Holmes had taken her to Indianapolis. In the meantime he had visited Mrs. Pitezel at St. Louis, and taken away with him the girl, Nellie, and the boy, Howard, alleging as his reason for doing so that they and Alice were to join their father, whose temporary effacement was necessary to carry out successfully the fraud on the insurance company, to which Mrs. Pitezel had been from the first an unwilling party. Holmes, Nellie and Howard had joined Alice at Indianapolis, and from there all four were believed to have gone to Cincinnati. It was here, accordingly, on June 27, 1895, that Geyer commenced his search.

After calling at a number of hotels, Geyer found that on Friday, September 28, 1894, a man, giving the name of Alexander E. Cook, and three children had stayed at a hotel called the Atlantic House. Geyer recollected that Holmes, when later on he had sent Mrs. Pitezel to the house in Burlington, had described her as Mrs. A. E. Cook and, though not positive, the hotel clerk thought that he recognised in the photographs of Holmes and he three children, which Geyer showed him, the four visitors to the hotel.

They had left the Atlantic House the next day, and on that same day, the 29th, Geyer found that Mr. A. E. Cook and three children had registered at the Bristol Hotel, where they had stayed until Sunday the 30th.

Knowing Holmes' habit of renting houses, Geyer did not confine his enquiries to the hotels. He visited a number of estate agents and learnt that a man and a boy, identified as Holmes and Howard Pitezel, had occupied a house No. 305 Poplar Street. The man had given the name of A. C. Hayes. He had taken the house on Friday the 28th, and on the 29th had driven up to it with the boy in a furniture wagon. A curious neighbour, interested in the advent of a newcomer, saw the wagon arrive, and was somewhat astonished to observe that the only furniture taken into the house was a large iron cylinder stove. She was still further surprised when, on the following day, Mr. Hayes told her that he was not going after all to occupy the house, and made her a present of the cylinder stove.

From Cincinnati Geyer went to Indianapolis. Here inquiry showed that on September 30 three children had been brought by a man identified as Holmes to the Hotel English, and registered in the name of Canning. This was the maiden name of Mrs. Pitezel. The children had stayed at the hotel one night. After that Geyer seemed to lose track of them until he was reminded of a hotel then closed, called the Circle House. With some difficulty he got a sight of the books of the hotel, and found that the three Canning children had arrived there on October 1 and stayed until the 10th. From the former proprietor of the hotel he learnt that Holmes had described himself as the children's uncle, and had said that Howard was a bad boy, whom he was trying to place in some institution. The children seldom went out; they would sit in their room drawing or writing, often they were found crying; they seemed homesick and unhappy.

There are letters of the children written from Indianapolis to their mothers, letters found in Holmes' possession, which had never reached her. In these letters they ask their mother why she does not write to them. She had written, but her letters were in Holmes' possession. Alice writes that she is reading "Uncle Tom's Cabin." She has read so much that her eyes hurt; they have bought a crystal pen for five cents which gives them some amusement; they had been to the Zoo in Cincinnati the Sunday before: "I expect this Sunday will pass away slower than I don't know—Howard is two (sic) dirty to be seen out on the street to-day." Sometimes they go and watch a man who paints "genuine oil paintings" in a shoe store, which are given away with every dollar purchase of shoes—"he can paint a picture in one and a half minutes, ain't that quick!" Howard was getting a little troublesome. "I don't like to tell you," writes Alice, "but you ask me, so I will have to. Howard won't mind me at all. He wanted a book and I got `Life of General Sheridan,' and it is awful nice, but now he don't read it at all hardly." Poor Howard! One morning, says Alice, Mr. Holmes told him to stay in and wait for him, as he was coming to take him out, but Howard was disobedient, and when Mr. Holmes arrived he had gone out. Better for Howard had he never returned! "We have written two or three letters to you," Alice tells her mother, "and I guess you will begin to get them now. She will not get them. Mr. Holmes is so very particular that the insurance company shall get no clue to the whereabouts of any member of the Pitezel family.

Geyer knew that from Indianapolis Holmes had gone to Detroit. He ascertained that two girls, "Etta and Nellie Canning," had registered on October 12 at the New Western Hotel in that city, and from there had moved on the 15th to a boarding-house in Congress Street. From Detroit Alice had written to her grandparents. It was cold and wet, she wrote; she and Etta had colds and chapped hands: "We have to stay in all the time. All that Nell and I can do is to draw, and I get so tired sitting that I could get up and fly almost. I wish I could see you all. I am getting so homesick that I don't know what to do. I suppose Wharton (their baby brother) walks by this time, don't he? I would like to have him here, he would pass away the time a good deal." As a fact little Wharton, his mother and sister Dessie, were at this very moment in Detroit, within ten minutes' walk of the hotel at which Holmes had registered "Etta and Nellie Canning."

On October 14 there had arrived in that city a weary, anxious- looking woman, with a girl and a little baby. They took a room at Geis's Hotel, registering as Mrs. Adams and daughter. Mrs. Adams seemed in great distress of mind, and never left her room.

The housekeeper, being shown their photographs, identified the woman and the girl as Mrs. Pitezel and her eldest daughter Dessie. As the same time there had been staying at another hotel in Detroit a Mr. and Mrs. Holmes, whose photographs showed them to be the Mr. Holmes in question and his third wife. These three parties—the two children, Mrs. Pitezel and her baby, and the third Mrs. Holmes—were all ignorant of each other's presence in Detroit; and under the secret guidance of Mr. Holmes the three parties (still unaware of their proximity to each other, left Detroit for Canada, arriving in Toronto on or about October 18, and registering at three separate hotels. The only one who had not to all appearances reached Toronto was the boy Howard.

In Toronto "Alice and Nellie Canning" stayed at the Albion Hotel.

They arrived there on October 19, and left on the 25th. During their stay a man, identified as Holmes, had called every morning for the two children, and taken them out; but they had come back alone, usually in time for supper. On the 25th he had called and taken them out, but they had not returned to supper. After that date Geyer could find no trace of them. Bearing in mind Holmes' custom of renting houses, he compiled a list of all the house agents in Toronto, and laboriously applied to each one for information. The process was a slow one, and the result seemed likely to be disappointing.

To aid his search Geyer decided to call in the assistance of the Press. The newspapers readily published long accounts of the case and portraits of Holmes and the children. At last, after eight days of patient and untiring investigation, after following up more than one false clue, Geyer received a report that there was a house—No. 16 St. Vincent Street—which had been rented in the previous October by a man answering to the description of Holmes. The information came from an old Scottish gentleman living next door. Geyer hastened to see him. The old gentleman said that the man who had occupied No. 16 in October had told him that he had taken the house for his widowed sister, and he recognised the photograph of Alice Pitezel as one of the two girls accompanying him. The only furniture the man had taken into the house was a bed, a mattress and a trunk. During his stay at No. 16 this man had called on his neighbour about four o'clock one afternoon and borrowed a spade, saying that he wanted to dig a place in the cellar where his widowed sister could keep potatoes; he had returned the spade the following morning. The lady to whom the house belonged recognised Holmes' portrait as that of the man to whom she had let No. 16.

At last Geyer seemed to be on the right track. He hurried back to St. Vincent Street, borrowed from the old gentleman at No. 18 the very spade which he had lent to Holmes in the previous October, and got the permission of the present occupier of No. 16 to make a search. In the centre of the kitchen Geyer found a trap-door leading down into a small cellar. In one corner of the cellar he saw that the earth had been recently dug up. With the help of the spade the loose earth was removed, and at a depth of some three feet, in a state of advanced decomposition, lay the remains of what appeared to be two children. A little toy wooden egg with a snake inside it, belonging to the Pitezel children, had been found by the tenant who had taken the house after Holmes; a later tenant had found stuffed into the chimney, but not burnt, some clothing that answered the description of that worn by Alice and Etta Pitezel; and by the teeth and hair of the two corpses Mrs. Pitezel was able to identify them as those of her two daughters. The very day that Alice and Etta had met their deaths at St. Vincent Street, their mother had been staying near them at a hotel in the same city, and later on the same day Holmes had persuaded her to leave Toronto for Ogdensburg. He said that they were being watched by detectives, and so it would be impossible for her husband to come to see her there.

But the problem was not yet wholly solved. What had become of Howard? So far Geyer's search had shown that Holmes had rented three houses, one in Cincinnati, one in Detroit, and one in Toronto. Howard had been with his sisters at the hotels in Indianapolis, and in Detroit the house agents had said that, when Holmes had rented a house there, he had been accompanied by a boy. Yet an exhaustive search of that house had revealed no trace of him. Geyer returned to Detroit and again questioned the house agents; on being pressed their recollection of the boy who had accompanied Holmes seemed very vague and uncertain. This served only to justify a conclusion at which Geyer had already arrived, that Howard had never reached Detroit, but had disappeared in Indianapolis. Alice's letters, written from there, had described how Holmes had wanted to take Howard out one day and how the boy had refused to stay in and wait for him. In the same way Holmes had called for the two girls at the Albion Hotel in Toronto on October 25 and taken them out with him, after which they had never been seen alive except by the old gentleman at No. 18 St. Vincent Street.

If Geyer could discover that Holmes had not departed in Indianapolis from his usual custom of renting houses, he might be on the high way to solving the mystery of Howard's fate. Accordingly he returned to Indianapolis.

In the meantime, Holmes, in his prison at Philadelphia, learnt of the discovery at Toronto. "On the morning of the 16th of July," he writes in his journal, "my newspaper was delivered to me about 8.30 a.m., and I had hardly opened it before I saw in large headlines the announcement of the finding of the children in Toronto. For the moment it seemed so impossible that I was inclined to think it was one of the frequent newspaper excitements that had attended the earlier part of the case, but, in attempting to gain some accurate comprehension of what was stated in the article, I became convinced that at least certain bodies had been found there, and upon comparing the date when the house was hired I knew it to be the same as when the children had been in Toronto; and thus being forced to realise the awfulness of what had probably happened, I gave up trying to read the article, and saw instead the two little faces as they had looked when I hurriedly left them—felt the innocent child's kiss so timidly given, and heard again their earnest words of farewell, and realised that I had received another burden to carry to my grave with me, equal, if not worse, than the horrors of Nannie Williams' death."

Questioned by the district attorney, Holmes met this fresh evidence by evoking once again the mythical Edward Hatch and suggesting that Miss Minnie Williams, in a "hellish wish for vengeance" because of Holmes' fancied desertion, and in order to make it appear probable that he, and not she, had murdered her sister, had prompted Hatch to commit the horrid deed. Holmes asked to be allowed to go to Toronto that he might collect any evidence which he could find there in his favour. The district attorney refused his request; he had determined to try Holmes in Philadelphia. "What more could, be said?" writes Holmes. Indeed, under the circumstances, and in the unaccountable absence of Edward Hatch and Minnie Williams, there was little more to be said.

Detective Geyer reopened his search in Indianapolis by obtaining a list of advertisements of houses to let in the city in 1894. Nine hundred of these were followed up in vain. He then turned his attention to the small towns lying around Indianapolis with no happier result. Geyer wrote in something of despair to his superiors: "By Monday we will have searched every outlying town except Irvington. After Irvington, I scarcely know where we shall go." Thither he went on August 27, exactly two months from the day on which his quest had begun. As he entered the town he noticed the advertisement of an estate agent. He called at the office and found a "pleasant-faced old gentleman," who greeted him amiably. Once again Geyer opened his now soiled and ragged packet of photographs, and asked the gentleman if in October, 1894, he had let a house to a man who said that he wanted one for a widowed sister. He showed him the portrait of Holmes.

The old man put on his glasses and looked at the photograph for some time. Yes, he said, he did remember that he had given the keys of a cottage in October, 1894, to a man of Holmes' appearance, and he recollected the man the more distinctly for the uncivil abruptness with which he had asked for the keys; "I felt," he said, "he should have had more respect for my grey hairs."

From the old gentleman's office Geyer hastened to the cottage, and made at once for the cellar. There he could find no sign of recent disturbance. But beneath the floor of a piazza adjoining the house he found the remains of a trunk, answering to the description of that which the Pitezel children had had with them, and in an outhouse he discovered the inevitable stove, Holmes' one indispensable piece of furniture. It was stained with blood on the top. A neighbour had seen Holmes in the same October drive up to the house in the furniture wagon accompanied by a boy, and later in the day Holmes had asked him to come over to the cottage and help him to put up a stove. The neighbour asked him why he did not use gas; Holmes replied that he did not think gas was healthy for children. While the two men were putting up the stove, the little boy stood by and watched them. After further search there were discovered in the cellar chimney some bones, teeth, a pelvis and the baked remains of a stomach, liver and spleen.

Medical examination showed them to be the remains of a child between seven and ten years of age. A spinning top, a scarf-pin, a pair of shoes and some articles of clothing that had belonged to the little Pitezels, had been found in the house at different times, and were handed over to Geyer.

His search was ended. On September 1 he returned to Philadelphia.

Holmes was put on his trial on October 28, 1895, before the Court of Oyer and Terminer in Philadelphia, charged with the murder of Benjamin Pitezel. In the course of the trial the district attorney offered to put in evidence showing that Holmes had also murdered the three children of Pitezel, contending that such evidence was admissible on the ground that the murders of the children and their father were parts of the same transaction. The judge refused to admit the evidence, though expressing a doubt as to its inadmissibility. The defence did not dispute the identity of the body found in Callowhill Street, but contended that Pitezel had committed suicide. The medical evidence negatived such a theory. The position of the body, its condition when discovered, were entirely inconsistent with self- destruction, and the absence of irritation in the stomach showed that the chloroform found there must have been poured into it after death. In all probability, Holmes had chloroformed Pitezel when he was drunk or asleep. He had taken the chloroform to Callowhill Street as a proposed ingredient in a solution for cleaning clothes, which he and Pitezel were to patent. It was no doubt with the help of the same drug that he had done to death the little children, and failing the nitro-glycerine, with that drug he had intended to put Mrs. Pitezel and her two remaining children out of the way at the house in Burlington; for after his trial there was found there, hidden away in the cellar, a bottle containing eight or ten ounces of chloroform.

Though assisted by counsel, Holmes took an active part in his defence. He betrayed no feeling at the sight of Mrs. Pitezel, the greater part of whose family he had destroyed, but the appearance of his third wife as a witness he made an opportunity for "letting loose the fount of emotion," taking care to inform his counsel beforehand that he intended to perform this touching feat. He was convicted and sentenced to death on November 2.

Previous to the trial of Holmes the police had made an exhaustive investigation of the mysterious building in Chicago known as "Holmes' Castle." The result was sufficiently sinister. In the stove in the cellar charred human bones were found, and in the middle of the room stood a large dissecting table stained with blood. On digging up the cellar floor some human ribs, sections of vertebrae and teeth were discovered buried in quicklime, and in other parts of the "castle" the police found more charred bones, some metal buttons, a trunk, and a piece of a watch chain.

The trunk and piece of watch chain were identified as having belonged to Miss Minnie Williams.

Inquiry showed that Miss Williams had entered Holmes' employment as a typist in 1893, and had lived with him at the castle. In the latter part of the year she had invited her sister, Nannie, to be present at her wedding with Holmes. Nannie had come to Chicago for that purpose, and since then the two sisters had never been seen alive. In February in the following year Pitezel, under the name of Lyman, had deposited at Fort Worth, Texas, a deed according to which a man named Bond had transferred to him property in that city which had belonged to Miss Williams, and shortly after, Holmes, under the name of Pratt, joined him at Fort Worth, whereupon the two commenced building on Miss Williams' land.

Other mysterious cases besides those of the Williams sisters revealed the Bluebeard-like character of this latterday castle of Mr. Holmes. In 1887 a man of the name of Connor entered Holmes' employment. He brought with him to the castle a handsome, intelligent wife and a little girl of eight or nine years of age.

After a short time Connor quarrelled with his wife and went away, leaving Mrs. Connor and the little girl with Holmes. After 1892 Mrs. Connor and her daughter had disappeared, but in August, 1895, the police found in the castle some clothes identified as theirs, and the janitor, Quinlan, admitted having seen the dead body of Mrs. Connor in the castle. Holmes, questioned in his prison in Philadelphia, said that Mrs. Connor had died under an operation, but that he did not know what had become of the little girl.

In the year of Mrs. Connor's disappearance, a typist named Emily Cigrand, who had been employed in a hospital in which Benjamin Pitezel had been a patient, was recommended by the latter to Holmes. She entered his employment, and she and Holmes soon became intimate, passing as "Mr. and Mrs. Gordon." Emily Cigrand had been in the habit of writing regularly to her parents in Indiana, but after December 6, 1892, they had never heard from her again, nor could any further trace of her be found.

A man who worked for Holmes as a handy man at the castle stated to the police that in 1892 Holmes had given him a skeleton of a man to mount, and in January, 1893, showed him in the laboratory another male skeleton with some flesh still on it, which also he asked him to mount. As there was a set of surgical instruments in the laboratory and also a tank filled with a fluid preparation for removing flesh, the handy man thought that Holmes was engaged in some kind of surgical work.

About a month before his execution, when Holmes' appeals from his sentence had failed and death appeared imminent, he sold to the newspapers for 7,500 dollars a confession in which he claimed to have committed twenty-seven murders in the course of his career. The day after it appeared he declared the whole confession to be a "fake." He was tired, he said, of being accused by the newspapers of having committed every mysterious murder that had occurred during the last ten years. When it was pointed out to him that the account given in his confession of the murder of the Pitezel children was clearly untrue, he replied, "Of course, it is not true, but the newspapers wanted a sensation and they have got it." The confession was certainly sensational enough to satisfy the most exacting of penny-a-liners, and a lasting tribute to Holmes' undoubted power of extravagant romancing.

According to his story, some of his twenty-seven victims had met their death by poison, some by more violent methods, some had died a lingering death in the air-tight and sound-proof vault of the castle. Most of these he mentioned by name, but some of these were proved afterwards to be alive. Holmes had actually perpetrated, in all probability, about ten murders. But, given further time and opportunity, there is no reason why this peri-patetic assassin should not have attained to the considerable figure with which he credited himself in his bogus confession.

Holmes was executed in Philadelphia on May 7, 1896. He seemed to meet his fate with indifference.

The motive of Holmes in murdering Pitezel and three of his children and in planning to murder his wife and remaining children, originated in all probability in a quarrel that occurred between Pitezel and himself in the July of 1894. Pitezel had tired apparently of Holmes and his doings, and wanted to break off the connection. But he must have known enough of Holmes' past to make him a dangerous enemy. It was Pitezel who had introduced to Holmes Emily Cigrand, the typist, who had disappeared so mysteriously in the castle; Pitezel had been his partner in the fraudulent appropriation of Miss Minnie Williams' property in Texas; it is more than likely, therefore, that Pitezel knew something of the fate of Miss Williams and her sister. By reviving, with Pitezel's help, his old plan for defrauding insurance companies, Holmes saw the opportunity of making 10,000 dollars, which he needed sorely, and at the same time removing his inconvenient and now lukewarm associate. Having killed Pitezel and received the insurance money, Holmes appropriated to his own use the greater part of the 10,000 dollars, giving Mrs. Pitezel in return for her share of the plunder a bogus bill for 5,000 dollars. Having robbed Mrs. Pitezel of both her husband and her money, to this thoroughgoing criminal there seemed only one satisfactory way of escaping detection, and that was to exterminate her and the whole of her family.

Had Holmes not confided his scheme of the insurance fraud to Hedgspeth in St. Louis prison and then broken faith with him, there is no reason why the fraud should ever have been discovered. The subsequent murders had been so cunningly contrived that, had the Insurance Company not put the Pinkerton detectives on his track, Holmes would in all probability have ended by successfully disposing of Mrs. Pitezel, Dessie, and the baby at the house in Burlington, Vermont, and the entire Pitezel family would have disappeared as completely as his other victims.

Holmes admitted afterwards that his one mistake had been his confiding to Hedgspeth his plans for defrauding an insurance company—a mistake, the unfortunate results of which might have been avoided, if he had kept faith with the train robber and given him the 500 dollars which he had promised.

The case of Holmes illustrates the practical as well as the purely ethical value of "honour among thieves," and shows how a comparatively insignificant misdeed may ruin a great and comprehensive plan of crime. To dare to attempt the extermination of a family of seven persons, and to succeed so nearly in effecting it, could be the work of no tyro, no beginner like J. B. Troppmann. It was the act of one who having already succeeded in putting out of the way a number of other persons un-

detected, might well and justifiably believe that he was born for greater and more compendious achievements in robbery and murder than any who had gone before him. One can almost subscribe to America's claim that Holmes is the "greatest criminal" of a century boasting no mean record in such persons.

In the remarkable character of his achievements as an assassin we are apt to lose sight of Holmes' singular skill and daring as a liar and a bigamist. As an instance of the former may be cited his audacious explanation to his family, when they heard of his having married a second time. He said that he had met with a serious accident to his head, and that when he left the hospital, found that he had entirely lost his memory; that, while in this state of oblivion, he had married again and then, when his memory returned, realised to his horror his unfortunate position. Plausibility would seem to have been one of Holmes' most useful gifts; men and women alike—particularly the latter— he seems to have deceived with ease. His appearance was commonplace, in no way suggesting the conventional criminal, his manner courteous, ingratiating and seemingly candid, and like so many scoundrels, he could play consummately the man of sentiment.

The weak spot in Holmes' armour as an enemy of society was a dangerous tendency to loquacity, the defect no doubt of his qualities of plausible and insinuating address and ever ready mendacity.

THE WIDOW GRAS

Report of the trial of the woman Gras and Gaudry in the Gazette des Tribunaux. The case is dealt with also by Mace in his "Femmes Criminelles."

I

THE CHARMER

Jenny Amenaide Brecourt was born in Paris in the year 1837. Her father was a printer, her mother sold vegetables. The parents neglected the child, but a lady of title took pity on her, and when she was five years old adopted her. Even as a little girl she was haughty and imperious. At the age of eight she refused to play with another child on the ground of her companion's social inferiority. "The daughter of a Baroness," she said, "cannot play with the daughter of a wine-merchant." When she was eleven years old, her parents took her away from her protectress and sent her into the streets to sell gingerbread—a dangerous experience for a child of tender years. After six years of street life, Amenaide sought out her benefactress and begged her to take her back. The Baroness consented, and found her employment in a silk manufactory. One day the girl, now eighteen years old, attended the wedding of one of her companions in the factory. She returned home after the ceremony thoughtful.

She said that she wanted to get married. The Baroness did not take her statement seriously, and on the grocer calling one day, said in jest to Amenaide, "You want a husband, there's one."

But Amenaide was in earnest. She accepted the suggestion and, to the Baroness' surprise, insisted on taking the grocer as her husband. Reluctantly the good lady gave her consent, and in 1855 Amenaide Brecourt became the wife of the grocer Gras.

A union, so hasty and ill-considered, was not likely to be of long duration. With the help of the worthy Baroness the newly married couple started a grocery business. But Amenaide was too economical for her husband and mother-in-law. Quarrels ensued, recriminations. In a spirit of unamiable prophecy husband and wife foretold each other's future. "You will die in a hospital," said the wife. "You will land your carcase in prison," retorted the husband. In both instances they were correct in their anticipations. One day the husband disappeared. For a short time Amenaide returned to her long-suffering protectress, and then she too disappeared.

When she is heard of again, Amenaide Brecourt has become Jeanne de la Cour. Jeanne de la Cour is a courtesan. She has tried commerce, acting, literature, journalism, and failed at them all. Henceforth men are to make her fortune for her. Such charms as she may possess, such allurements as she can offer, she is ready to employ without heart or feeling to accomplish her end. Without real passion, she has an almost abnormal, erotic sensibility, which serves in its stead. She cares only for one person, her sister. To her Jeanne de la

Cour unfolded her philosophy of life. While pretending to love men, she is going to make them suffer. They are to be her playthings, she knows how to snare them: "All is dust and lies. So much the worse for the men who get in my way. Men are mere stepping-stones to me. As soon as they begin to fail or are played out, I put them scornfully aside. Society is a vast chess-board, men the pawns, some white, some black; I move them as I please, and break them when they bore me."

The early years of Jeanne de la Cour's career as a Phryne were hardly more successful than her attempts at literature, acting and journalism. True to her philosophy, she had driven one lover, a German, to suicide, and brought another to his death by over-doses of cantharides. On learning of the death of the first, she reflected patriotically, "One German the less in Paris!" That of the second elicited the matter-of-fact comment, "It was bound to happen; he had no moderation." A third admirer, who died in a hospital, was dismissed as "a fool who, in spite of all, still respects women." But, in ruining her lovers, she had ruined her own health. In 1865 she was compelled to enter a private asylum. There she is described as "dark in complexion, with dark expressive eyes, very pale, and of a nervous temperament, agreeable, and pretty." She was suffering at the time of her admission from hysterical seizures, accompanied by insane exaltation, convulsions and loss of speech. In speaking of her humble parents she said, "I don't know such people"; her manner was bombastic, and she was fond of posing as a fine lady.

After a few months Jeanne de la Cour was discharged from the asylum as cured, and on the advice of her doctors went to Vittel.

There she assumed the rank of Baroness and recommenced her career, but this time in a more reasonable and businesslike manner. Her comments, written to her sister, on her fellow guests at the hotel are caustic. She mocks at some respectable married women who are trying to convert her to Catholicism. To others who refuse her recognition, she makes herself so mischievous and objectionable that in self-defence they are frightened into acknowledging her. Admirers among men she has many, ex-ministers, prefects. It was at Vittel that occurred the incident of the wounded pigeon. There had been some pigeon-shooting. One of the wounded birds flew into the room of the Baroness de la Cour. She took pity on it, tended it, taught it not to be afraid of her and to stay in her room. So touching was her conduct considered by some of those who heard it, that she was nicknamed "the Charmer." But she is well aware, she writes to her sister, that with the true ingratitude of the male, the pigeon will leave her as soon as it needs her help no longer.

However, for the moment, "disfigured as it is, beautiful or ugly," she loves it. "Don't forget," she writes, "that a woman who is practical and foreseeing, she too enjoys her pigeon shooting, but the birds are her lovers."

Shortly after she left Vittel an event occurred which afforded Jeanne de la Cour the prospect of acquiring that settled position in life which, "practical and foreseeing," she now regarded as indispensable to her future welfare. Her husband, Gras, died, as she had foretold, in the Charity Hospital. The widow was free. If she could bring down her bird, it was now in her power to make it hers for life. Henceforth all her efforts were directed to that end. She was reaching her fortieth year, her hair was turning grey, her charms were waning. Poverty, degradation, a miserable old age, a return to the wretched surroundings of her childhood, such she knew to be the fate of many of her kind. There was nothing to be hoped for from the generosity of men. Her lovers were leaving her. Blackmail, speculation on the Bourse, even the desperate expedient of a supposititious child, all these she tried as means of acquiring a competence. But for-

tune was shy of the widow. There was need for dispatch. The time was drawing near when it might be man's unkind privilege to put her scornfully aside as a thing spent and done with. She must bring down her bird, and that quickly. It was at this critical point in the widow's career, in the year 1873, that she met at a public ball for the first time Georges de Saint Pierre.[16]

[16] For obvious reasons I have suppressed the real name of the widow's lover.

Georges de Saint Pierre was twenty years of age when he made the acquaintance of the Widow Gras. He had lost his mother at an early age, and since then lived with relatives in the country. He was a young man of independent means, idle, of a simple, confiding and affectionate disposition. Four months after his first meeting with the widow they met again. The end of the year 1873 saw the commencement of an intimacy, which to all appearances was characterised by a more lasting and sincere affection than is usually associated with unions of this kind. There can be no doubt that during the three years the Widow Gras was the mistress of Georges de Saint Pierre, she had succeeded in subjugating entirely the senses and the affection of her young lover. In spite of the twenty years between them, Georges de Saint Pierre idolised his middle-aged mistress. She was astute enough to play not only the lover, but the mother to this motherless youth. After three years of intimacy he writes to her: "It is enough for me that you love me, because I don't weary you, and I, I love you with all my heart. I cannot bear to leave you. We will live happily together. You will always love me truly, and as for me, my loving care will ever protect you. I don't know what would become of me if I did not feel that your love watched over me." The confidence of Georges in the widow was absolute. When, in 1876, he spent six months in Egypt, he made her free of his rooms in Paris, she was at liberty to go there when she liked; he trusted her entirely, idolised her. Whatever her faults, he was blind to them. "Your form," he writes, "is ever before my eyes; I wish I could enshrine your pure heart in gold and crystal."

The widow's conquest, to all appearances, was complete. But Georges was very young. He had a family anxious for his future; they knew of his liaison; they would be hopeful, no doubt, of one day breaking it off and of marrying him to some desirable young person. From the widow's point of view the situation lacked finality. How was that to be secured?

One day, toward the end of the year 1876, after the return of Georges from Egypt, the widow happened to be at the house of a friend, a ballet dancer. She saw her friend lead into the room a young man; he was sightless, and her friend with tender care guided him to a seat on the sofa. The widow was touched by the spectacle. When they were alone, she inquired of her friend the reason of her solicitude for the young man. "I love this victim of nature," she replied, "and look after him with every care. He is young, rich, without family, and is going to marry me. Like you, I am just on forty; my hair is turning grey, my youth vanishing. I shall soon be cast adrift on the sea, a wreck. This boy is the providential spar to which I am going to cling that I may reach land in safety." "You mean, then," said the widow, "that you will soon be beyond the reach of want?" "Yes," answered the friend, "I needn't worry any more about the future."

"I congratulate you," said the widow, "and what is more, your lover will never see you grow old."

To be cast adrift on the sea and to have found a providential spar! The widow was greatly impressed by her friend's rare good fortune. Indeed, her experience gave the widow furiously to think, as she revolved in her brain various expedients by which Georges de Saint Pierre might become the "providential spar" in her own impending wreck. The picture of the blind young man tenderly cared for, dependent utterly on the ministrations of his devoted wife, fixed itself in the widow's mind; there was something inexpressibly pathetic in the picture, whilst its practical significance had its sinister appeal to one in her situation.

At this point in the story there appears on the scene a character as remarkable in his way as the widow herself, remarkable at least for his share in the drama that is to follow. Nathalis Gaudry, of humble parentage, rude and uncultivated, had been a playmate of the widow when she was a child in her parents' house.

They had grown up together, but, after Gaudry entered the army, had lost sight of each other. Gaudry served through the Italian war of 1859, gaining a medal for valour. In 1864 he had married.

Eleven years later his wife died, leaving him with two children. He came to Paris and obtained employment in an oil refinery at Saint Denis. His character was excellent; he was a good workman, honest, hard-working, his record unblemished. When he returned to Paris, Gaudry renewed his friendship with the companion of his youth. But Jeanne Brecourt was now Jeanne de la Cour, living in refinement and some luxury, moving in a sphere altogether remote from and unapproachable by the humble workman in an oil refinery. He could do no more than worship from afar this strange being, to him wonderfully seductive in her charm and distinction.

On her side the widow was quite friendly toward her homely admirer. She refused to marry him, as he would have wished, but she did her best without success to marry him to others of her acquaintance. Neither a sempstress nor an inferior actress could she persuade, for all her zeal, to unite themselves with a hand in an oil mill, a widower with two children. It is typical of the widow's nervous energy that she should have undertaken so hopeless a task. In the meantime she made use of her admirer. On Sundays he helped her in her apartment, carried coals, bottled wine, scrubbed the floors, and made himself generally useful. He was supposed by those about the house to be her brother. Occasionally, in the absence of a maid, the widow allowed him to attend on her personally, even to assist her in her toilette and perform for her such offices as one woman would perform for another. The man soon came to be madly in love with the woman; his passion, excited but not gratified, enslaved and consumed him. To some of his fellow-workmen who saw him moody and pre-occupied, he confessed that he ardently desired to marry a friend of his childhood, not a working woman but a lady.

Such was the situation and state of mind of Nathalis Gaudry when, in November, 1876, he received a letter from the widow, in which she wrote, "Come at once. I want you on a matter of business. Tell your employer it is a family affair; I will make up your wages." In obedience to this message Gaudry was absent from the distillery from the 17th to the 23rd of November.

The "matter of business" about which the widow wished to consult with Gaudry turned out to be a scheme of revenge. She told him that she had been basely defrauded by a man to whom she had entrusted money. She desired to be revenged on him, and could think of no better way than to strike at his dearest affections by seriously injuring his son. This she proposed to do with the help of a knuckle-duster, which she produced and gave to Gaudry. Armed with this formidable weapon, Gaudry was to strike her enemy's son so forcibly in the pit of the stomach as to disable him for life. The widow offered to point out to Gaudry the young man whom he was to attack. She took him outside the young man's club and showed him his victim. He was Georges de Saint Pierre.

The good fortune of her friend, the ballet-dancer, had proved a veritable toxin in the intellectual system of the Widow Gras. The poison of envy, disappointment, suspicion, apprehension had entered into her soul. Of what use to her was a lover, however generous and faithful, who was free to take her up and lay her aside at will? But such was her situation relative to Georges de Saint Pierre. She remembered that the wounded pigeon, as long as it was dependent on her kind offices, had been-compelled to stay by her side; recovered, it had flown away. Only a pigeon, maimed beyond hope of recovery, could she be sure of compelling to be hers for all time, tied to her by its helpless infirmity, too suffering and disfigured to be lured from its captivity. And so, in accordance with her philosophy of life, the widow, by a blow in the pit of the stomach with a knuckle-duster, was to bring down her bird which henceforth would be tended and cared for by "the Charmer" to her own satisfaction and the admiration of all beholders.

For some reason, the natural reluctance of Gaudry, or perhaps a feeling of compunction in the heart of the widow, this plan was not put into immediate execution. Possibly she hesitated before adopting a plan more cruel, more efficacious. Her hesitation did not last long.

With the dawn of the year 1877 the vigilant apprehension of the widow was roused by the tone of M. de Saint Pierre's letters. He wrote from his home in the country, "I cannot bear leaving you, and I don't mean to. We will live together." But he adds that he is depressed by difficulties with his family, "not about money or business but of a kind he can only communicate to her verbally." To the widow it was clear that these difficulties must relate to the subject of marriage. The character of Georges was not a strong one; sooner or later he might yield to the importunities of his family; her reign would be ended, a modest and insufficient pension the utmost she could hope for. She had passed the meridian of her life as a charmer of men, her health was giving way, she was greedy, ambitious, acquisitive. In January she asked her nephew, who worked as a gilder, to get her some vitriol for cleaning her copper. He complied with her request.

During Jeanne de la Cour's brief and unsuccessful appearance as an actress she had taken part in a play with the rather cumbrous title, Who Puts out the Eyes must Pay for Them. The widow may have forgotten this event; its occurrence so many years before may have been merely a sinister coincidence. But the incident of the ballet-dancer and her sightless lover was fresh in her mind.

Early in January the widow wrote to Georges, who was in the country, and asked him to take her to the masked ball at the Opera on the 13th. Her lover was rather surprised at her request, nor did he wish to appear with her at so public a gathering. "I don't understand," he writes, "why you are so anxious to go to the Opera. I can't see any real reason for your wanting to tire yourself out at such a disreputable gathering. However, if you are happy and well, and promise to be careful, I will take you. I would be the last person, my dear little wife, to deny you anything that would give you pleasure." But for some reason Georges was unhappy, depressed. Some undefined presentiment of evil seems to have oppressed him. His brother noticed his pre-occupation.

He himself alludes to it in writing to his mistress: "I am depressed this evening. For a very little I could break down altogether and give way to tears. You can't imagine what horrid thoughts possess me. If I felt your love close to me, I should be less sad." Against his better inclination Georges promised to take the widow to the ball on the 13th. He was to come to Paris on the night of the 12th.

II

THE WOUNDED PIGEON

On the afternoon of January 11, Gaudry called to see the widow. There had been an accident at the distillery that morning, and work was suspended for three days. The widow showed Gaudry the bottle containing the vitriol which her nephew had procured for her use. She was ill, suffering, she said; the only thing that could make her well again would be the execution of her revenge on the son of the man who had defrauded her so wickedly: "Make him suffer, here are the means, and I swear I will be yours." She dropped a little of the vitriol on to the floor to show its virulent effect. At first Gaudry was shocked, horrified. He protested that he was a soldier, that he could not do such a deed; he suggested that he should provoke the young man to a duel and kill him. "That is no use," said the widow, always sensitive to social distinctions; "he is not of your class, he would refuse to fight with you." Mad with desire for the woman, his senses irritated and excited, the ultimate gratification of his passion held alluringly before him, the honest soldier consented to play the cowardly ruffian. The trick was done. The widow explained to her accomplice his method of proceeding. The building in the Rue de Boulogne, in which the widow had her apartment, stood at the end of a drive some twenty-seven and a half yards long and five and a half yards wide. About half-way up the drive, on either side, there were two small houses, or pavilions, standing by themselves and occupied by single gentlemen. The whole was shut off from the street by a large gate, generally kept closed, in which a smaller gate served to admit persons going in or out. According to the widow's plan, the young man, her enemy's son, was to take her to the ball at the Opera on the night of January 13. Gaudry was to wait in her apartment until their return. When he heard the bell ring, which communicated with the outer gate, he was to come down, take his place in the shadow of one of the pavilions on either side of the drive, and from the cover of this position fling in the face of the young man the vitriol which she had given him. The widow herself, under the pretence of closing the smaller gate, would be well behind the victim, and take care to leave the gate open so that Gaudry could make his escape.

In spite of his reluctance, his sense of foreboding, Georges de Saint Pierre came to Paris on the night of the 12th, which he spent at the widow's apartment. He went to his own rooms on the morning of the 13th.

This eventful day, which, to quote Iago, was either to "make or fordo quite" the widow, found her as calm, cool and deliberate in the execution of her purpose as the Ancient himself. Gaudry came to her apartment about five o'clock in the afternoon. The widow showed him the vitriol and gave him final directions. She would, she said, return from the ball about three o'clock in the morning. Gaudry was then sent away till ten o'clock, as Georges was dining with her. He returned at half-past ten and found the widow dressing, arraying herself in a pink domino and a blonde wig. She was in excellent spirits. When Georges came to fetch her, she put Gaudry into an alcove in the drawing-room which was curtained off from the rest of the room. Always thoughtful, she had placed a stool there that he might rest himself. Gaudry could hear her laughing and joking with her lover. She reproached him playfully with hindering her in her dressing. To keep him quiet, she gave him a book to read, Montaigne's "Essays." Georges opened it and read the thirty-fifth chapter of the second book, the essay on "Three Good Women," which tells how three brave women of antiquity endured death or suffering in order to share their husbands' fate. Curiously enough, the essay concludes with these words, almost prophetic for the unhappy reader: "I am enforced to live, and sometimes to live is magnanimity." Whilst Georges went to fetch a cab, the widow released Gaudry from his place of concealment, exhorted him to have courage, and promised him, if he succeeded, the accomplishment of his desire. And so the gay couple departed for the ball. There the widow's high spirits, her complete enjoyment, were remarked by more than one of her acquaintances; she danced one dance with her lover, and with another young man made an engagement for the following week.

Meanwhile, at the Rue de Boulogne, Gaudry sat and waited in the widow's bedroom. From the window he could see the gate and the lights of the cab that was to bring the revellers home. The hours passed slowly. He tried to read the volume of Montaigne where Georges had left it open, but the words conveyed little to him, and he fell asleep. Between two and three o'clock in the morning he was waked by the noise of wheels. They had returned. He hurried downstairs and took up his position in the shadow of one of the pavilions. As Georges de Saint Pierre walked up the drive alone, for the widow had stayed behind to fasten the gate, he thought he saw the figure of a man in the darkness. The next moment he was blinded by the burning liquid flung in his face. The widow had brought down her pigeon.

At first she would seem to have succeeded perfectly in her attempt. Georges was injured for life, the sight of one eye gone, that of the other threatened, his face sadly disfigured. Neither he nor anyone else suspected the real author of the crime. It was believed that the unfortunate man had been mistaken for some other person, and made by accident the victim of an act of vengeance directed against another. Georges was indeed all the widow's now, lodged in her own house to nurse and care for. She undertook the duty with every appearance of affectionate devotion. The unhappy patient was consumed with gratitude for her untiring solicitude; thirty nights she spent by his bedside. His belief in her was absolute. It was his own wish that she alone should nurse him. His family were kept away, any attempts his relatives or friends made to see or communicate with him frustrated by the zealous widow.

It was this uncompromising attitude on her part toward the friends of Georges, and a rumour which reached the ears of one of them that she intended as soon as possible to take her patient away to Italy, that sounded the first note of danger to her peace of mind. This friend happened to be acquainted with the son of one of the Deputy Public Prosecutors in Paris. To that official he confided his belief that there were suspicious circumstances in the case of Georges de Saint Pierre. The judicial authorities were informed and the case placed in the hands of an examining magistrate. On February 2, nearly a month after the crime, the magistrate, accompanied by Mace, then a commissary of police, afterwards head of the Detective Department, paid a visit to the Rue de Boulogne. Their reception was not cordial. It was only after they had made known their official character that they got audience of the widow. She entered the room, carrying in her hand a surgical spray, with which she played nervously while the men of the law asked to see her charge. She replied that it was impossible. Mace placed himself in front of the door by which she had entered, and told her that her attitude was not seemly. "Leave that spray alone," he said; "it might shoot over us, and then perhaps we should be sprinkled as M. de Saint Pierre was." From that moment, writes Mace, issue was joined between the widow and himself.

The magistrate insisted on seeing the patient. He sat by his bedside. M. de Saint Pierre told him that, having no enemies, he was sure he had been the victim of some mistake, and that, as he claimed no damages for his injuries, he did not wish his misfortune to be made public. He wanted to be left alone with his brave and devoted nurse, and to be spared the nervous excitement of a meeting with his family. He intended, he added, to leave Paris shortly for change of scene and air. The widow cut short the interview on the ground that her patient was tired.

It was inhuman, she said, to make him suffer so. The magistrate, before leaving, asked her whither she intended taking her patient. She replied, "To Italy." That, said the magistrate, would be impossible until his inquiry was closed. In the meantime she might take him to any place within the Department of the Seine; but she must be prepared to be under the surveillance of M. Mace, who would have the right to enter her house whenever he should think it expedient. With this disconcerting intelligence the men of the law took leave of the widow.

She was no longer to be left in undisturbed possession of her prize. Her movements were watched by two detectives. She was seen to go to the bachelor lodgings of Georges and take away a portable desk, which contained money and correspondence. More mysterious, however, was a visit she paid to the Charonne Cemetery, where she had an interview with an unknown, who was dressed in the clothes of a workman. She left the cemetery alone, and the detectives lost track of her companion. This meeting took place on February 11. Shortly after the widow left Paris with Georges de Saint Pierre for the suburb of Courbevoie.

Mace had elicited certain facts from the porter at the Rue de Boulogne and other witnesses, which confirmed his suspicion that the widow had played a sinister part in her lover's misfortune. Her insistence that he should take her to the ball on January 13; the fact that, contrary to the ordinary politeness of a gentleman, he was walking in front of her at the time of the attack; and that someone must have been holding the gate open to enable the assailant to escape it was a heavy gate, which, if left to itself after being opened, would swing too quickly on its hinges and shut of its own accord—these facts were sufficient to excite suspicion. The disappearance, too, of the man calling himself her brother, who had been seen at her apartment on the afternoon of the 13th, coupled with the mysterious interview in the cemetery, suggested the possibility of a crime in which the widow had had the help of an accomplice. To facilitate investigation it was necessary to separate the widow from her lover. The examining magistrate, having ascertained from a medical report that such a separation would not be hurtful to the patient, ordered the widow to be sent back to Paris, and the family of M. de Saint Pierre to take her place. The change was made on March 6. On leaving Courbevoie the widow was taken to the office of Mace. There the commissary informed her that she must consider herself under provisional arrest. "But who," she asked indignantly, "is to look after my Georges?" "His family," was the curt reply. The widow, walking up and down the room like a panther, stormed and threatened. When she had in some degree recovered herself, Mace asked her certain questions. Why had she insisted on her lover going to the ball? She had done nothing of the kind. How was it his assailant had got away so quickly by the open gate? She did not know. What was the name and address of her reputed brother? She was not going to deliver an honest father of a family into the clutches of the police. What was the meaning of her visit to the Charonne Cemetery? She went there to pray, not to keep assignations. "And if you want to know," she exclaimed, "I have had typhoid fever, which makes me often forget things. So I shall say nothing more—nothing—nothing."

Taken before the examining magistrate, her attitude continued to be defiant and arrogant. "Your cleverest policemen," she told the magistrate, "will never find any evidence against me. Think well before you send me to prison. I am not the woman to live long among thieves and prostitutes." Before deciding finally whether the widow should be thrown into such uncongenial society, the magistrate ordered Mace to search her apartment in the Rue de Boulogne.

On entering the apartment the widow asked that all the windows should be opened. "Let in the air," she said; "the police are coming in; they make a nasty smell." She was invited to sit-down while the officers made their search. Her letters and papers were carefully examined; they presented a strange mixture of order and disorder. Carefully kept account books of her personal expenses were mixed up with billets dous, paints and pomades, moneylenders' circulars, belladonna and cantharides. But most astounding of all were the contents of the widows' prie-Dieu. In this devotional article of furniture were stored all the inmost secrets of her profligate career. Affectionate letters from the elderly gentleman on whom she had imposed a supposititious child lay side by side with a black-edged card, on which was written the last message of a young lover who had killed himself on her account. "Jeanne, in the flush of my youth I die because of you, but I forgive you.—M." With these genuine outpourings of misplaced affection were mingled the indecent verses of a more vulgar admirer, and little jars of hashish. The widow, unmoved by this rude exposure of her way of life, only broke her silence to ask Mace the current prices on the Stock Exchange.

One discovery, however, disturbed her equanimity. In the drawer of a cupboard, hidden under some linen, Mace found a leather case containing a sheaf of partially-burnt letters. As he was about to open it the widow protested that it was the property of M. de Saint Pierre. Regardless of her protest, Mace opened the case, and, looking through the letters, saw that they were addressed to M. de Saint Pierre and were plainly of an intimate character. "I found them on the floor near the stove in the dining-room," said the widow, "and I kept them. I admit it was a wrong thing to do, but Georges will forgive me when he knows why I did it." From his better acquaintance with her character Mace surmised that an action admitted by the widow to be "wrong" was in all probability something worse. Without delay he took the prisoner back to his office, and himself left for Courbevoie, there to enlighten, if possible, her unhappy victim as to the real character of his enchantress.

The interview was a painful one. The lover refused to hear a word against his mistress. "Jeanne is my Antigone," he said. "She has lavished on me all her care, her tenderness, her love, and she believes in God." Mace told him of her past, of the revelations contained in the prie-Dieu of this true believer, but he could make no impression. "I forgive her past, I accept her present, and please understand me, no one has the power to separate me from her." It was only when Mace placed in his hands the bundle of burnt letters, that he might feel what he could not see, and read him some passages from them, that the unhappy man realised the full extent of his mistress' treachery. Feeling himself dangerously ill, dying perhaps, M. de Saint Pierre had told the widow to bring from his rooms to the Rue de Boulogne the contents of his private desk. It contained some letters compromising to a woman's honour. These he was anxious to destroy before it was too late. As he went through the papers, his eyes bandaged, he gave them to the widow to throw into the stove. He could hear the fire burning and feel its warmth. He heard the widow take up the tongs. He asked her why she did so. She answered that it was to keep the burning papers inside the stove. Now from Mace he learnt the real truth. She had used the tongs to take out some of the letters half burnt, letters which in her possession might be one day useful instruments for levying blackmail on her lover. "To blind me," exclaimed M. de Saint Pierre, "to torture me, and then profit by my condition to lie to me, to betray me—it's infamous— infamous!" His dream was shattered. Mace had succeeded in his task; the disenchantment of M. de Saint Pierre was complete. That night the fastidious widow joined the thieves and prostitutes in the St. Lazare Prison.

It was all very well to imprison the widow, but her participation in the outrage on M. de Saint Pierre was by no means established.

The reputed brother, who had been in the habit of attending on her at the Rue de Boulogne, still eluded the searches of the police. In silence lay the widow's only hope of baffling her enemies. Unfortunately for the widow, confinement told on her nerves. She became anxious, excited. Her very ignorance of what was going on around her, her lover's silence made her apprehensive; she began to fear the worst. At length—the widow always had an itch for writing—she determined to communicate at all costs with Gaudry and invoke his aid. She wrote appealing to him to come forward and admit that he was the man the police were seeking, for sheltering whom she had been thrown into prison. She drew a harrowing picture of her sufferings in jail. She had refused food and been forcibly fed; she would like to dash her head against the walls. If any misfortune overtake Gaudry, she promises to adopt his son and leave him a third of her property. She persuaded a fellow-prisoner; an Italian dancer undergoing six months' imprisonment for theft, who was on the point of being released, to take the letter and promise to deliver it to Gaudry at Saint Denis. On her release the dancer told her lover of her promise. He refused to allow her to mix herself up in such a case, and destroyed the letter. Then the dancer blabbed to others, until her story reached the ears of the police. Mace sent for her. At first she could remember only that the name Nathalis occurred in the letter, but after visiting accidentally the Cathedral at Saint Denis, she recollected that this Nathalis lived there, and worked in an oil factory. It was easy after this for the police to trace Gaudry. He was arrested. At his house, letters from the widow were found, warning him not to come to her apartment, and appointing to meet him in Charonne Cemetery. Gaudry made a full confession. It was his passion for the widow, and a promise on her part to marry him, which, he said, had induced him to perpetrate so abominable a crime. He was sent to the Mazas Prison.

In the meantime the Widow Gras was getting more and more desperate. Her complete ignorance tormented her. At last she gave up all hope, and twice attempted suicide with powdered glass and verdigris. On May 12 the examining magistrate confronted her with Gaudry. The man told his story, the widow feigned surprise that the "friend of her childhood" should malign her so cruelly. But to her desperate appeals Gaudry would only reply, "It is too late!" They were sent for trial.

The trial of the widow and her accomplice opened before the Paris Assize Court on July 23, 1877, and lasted three days. The widow was defended by Lachaud, one of the greatest criminal advocates of France, the defender of Madame Lafarge, La Pommerais, Tropp-

mann, and Marshal Bazaine. M. Demange (famous later for his defence of Dreyfus) appeared for Gaudry. The case had aroused considerable interest. Among those present at the trial were Halevy, the dramatist, and Mounet-Sully and Coquelin, from the Comedie Francaise. Fernand Rodays thus described the widow in the Figaro: "She looks more than her age, of moderate height, well made, neither blatant nor ill at ease, with nothing of the air of a woman of the town. Her hands are small. Her bust is flat, and her back round, her hair quite white. Beneath her brows glitter two jet-black eyes—the eyes of a tigress, that seem to breathe hatred and revenge."

Gaudry was interrogated first. Asked by the President the motive of his crime, he answered, "I was mad for Madame Gras; I would have done anything she told me. I had known her as a child, I had been brought up with her. Then I saw her again. I loved her, I was mad for her, I couldn't resist it. Her wish was law to me."

Asked if Gaudry had spoken the truth, the widow said that he lied. The President asked what could be his motive for accusing her unjustly. The widow was silent. Lachaud begged her to answer. "I cannot," she faltered. The President invited her to sit down. After a pause the widow seemed to recover her nerve.

President: Was Gaudry at your house while you were at the ball?

Widow: No, no! He daren't look me in the face and say so.

President: But he is looking at you now.

Widow: No, he daren't! (She fixes her eyes on Gaudry, who lowers his head.)

President: I, whose duty it is to interrogate you, look you in the face and repeat my question: Was Gaudry at your house at half-past ten that night?

Widow: No.

President: You hear her, Gaudry?

Gaudry: Yes, Monsieur, but I was there.

Widow: It is absolutely impossible! Can anyone believe me guilty of such a thing.

President: Woman Gras, you prefer to feign indignation and deny everything. You have the right. I will read your examination before the examining magistrate. I see M. Lachaud makes a gesture, but I must beg the counsel for the defence not to impart unnecessary passion into these proceedings.

Lachaud: My gesture was merely meant to express that the woman Gras is on her trial, and that under the circumstances her indignation is natural.

President: Very good.

The appearance in the witness box of the widow's unhappy victim evoked sympathy. He gave his evidence quietly, without resentment or indignation. As he told his story the widow, whose eyes were fixed on him all the time, murmured: "Georges! Georges! Defend me! Defend me!" "I state the facts," he replied.

The prisoners could only defend themselves by trying to throw on each other the guilt of the crime. M. Demange represented Gaudry as acting under the influence of his passion for the Widow Gras. Lachaud, on the other hand, attributed the crime solely to Gaudry's jealousy of the widow's lover, and contended that he was the sole author of the outrage.

The jury by their verdict assigned to the widow the greater share of responsibility. She was found guilty in the full degree, but to Gaudry were accorded extenuating circumstances. The widow was condemned to fifteen years' penal servitude, her accomplice to five years' imprisonment.

It is dreadful to think how very near the Widow Gras came to accomplishing successfully her diabolical crime. A little less percipitancy on her part, and she might have secured the fruits of her cruelty. Her undoubted powers of fascination, in spite of the fiendishness of her real character, are doubly proved by the devotion of her lover and the guilt of her accomplice. At the same time, with that strange contradiction inherent in human nature, the Jekyll and Hyde elements which, in varying degree, are present in all men and women, the Widow Gras had a genuine love for her young sister. Her hatred of men was reasoned, deliberate, merciless and implacable. There is something almost sadic in the combination in her character of erotic sensibility with extreme cruelty.

VITALIS AND MARIE BOYER

I found the story of this case in a brochure published in Paris as one of a series of modern causes celebres. I have compared it with the reports of the trial in the Gazette des Tribunaux.

I In the May of 1874, in the town of Montpellier, M. Boyer, a retired merchant, some forty-six years of age, lay dying. For some months previous to his death he had been confined to his bed, crippled by rheumatic gout. As the hour of his death drew near, M. Boyer was filled with a great longing to see his daughter, Marie, a girl of fifteen, and embrace her for the last time. The girl was being educated in a convent at Marseilles. One of M. Boyer's friends offered to go there to fetch her. On arriving at the convent, he was told that Marie had become greatly attracted by the prospect of a religious life. "You are happy," the Mother Superior had written to her mother, "very happy never to have allowed the impure breath of the world to have soiled this little flower. She loves you and her father more than one can say." Her father's friend found the girl dressed in the costume of a novice, and was told that she had expressed her desire to take, one day, her final vows. He informed Marie of her father's dying state, of his earnest wish to see her for the last time, and told her that he had come to take her to his bedside. "Take me away from here?" she exclaimed. The Mother Superior, surprised at her apparent reluctance to go, impressed on her the duty of acceding to her father's wish. To the astonishment of both, Marie refused to leave the convent. If she could save her father's life, she said, she would go, but, as that was impossible and she dreaded going out into the world again, she would stay and pray for her father in the chapel of the convent, where her prayers would be quite as effective as by his bedside. In vain the friend and the Mother Superior tried to bend her resolution.

Happily M. Boyer died before he could learn of his daughter's singular refusal. But it had made an unfavourable impression on the friend's mind. He looked on Marie as a girl without real feeling, an egoist, her religion purely superficial, hiding a cold and selfish disposition; he felt some doubt as to the future development of her character.

M. Boyer left a widow, a dark handsome woman, forty years of age.

Some twenty years before his death, Marie Salat had come to live with M. Boyer as a domestic servant. He fell in love with her, she became his mistress, and a few months before the birth of Marie, M. Boyer made her his wife. Madame Boyer was at heart a woman of ardent and voluptuous passions that only wanted opportunity to become careless in their gratification. Her husband's long illness gave her such an opportunity. At the time of his death she was carrying on an intrigue with a bookseller's assistant, Leon Vitalis, a young man of twenty-one. Her bed- ridden husband, ignorant of her infidelity, accepted gratefully the help of Vitalis, whom his wife described as a relative, in the regulation of his affairs. At length the unsuspecting Boyer died. The night of his death Madame Boyer spent with her lover.

The mother had never felt any great affection for her only child.

During her husband's lifetime she was glad to have Marie out of the way at the convent. But the death of M. Boyer changed the situation. He had left almost the whole of his fortune, about 100,000 francs, to his daughter, appointing her mother her legal guardian with a right to the enjoyment of the income on the cap-

ital until Marie should come of age. Madame Boyer had not hitherto taken her daughter's religious devotion very seriously. But now that the greater part of her husband's fortune was left to Marie, she realised that, should her daughter persist in her intention of taking the veil, that fortune would in a very few years pass into the hands of the sisterhood. Without delay Madame Boyer exercised her authority, and withdrew Marie from the convent. The girl quitted it with every demonstration of genuine regret.

Marie Boyer when she left the convent was growing into a tall and attractive woman, her figure slight and elegant, her hair and eyes dark, dainty and charming in her manner. Removed from the influences of convent life, her religious devotion became a thing of the past. In her new surroundings she gave herself up to the enjoyments of music and the theatre. She realised that she was a pretty girl, whose beauty well repaid the hours she now spent in the adornment of her person. The charms of Marie were not lost on Leon Vitalis. Mean and significant in appearance, Vitalis would seem to have been one of those men who, without any great physical recommendation, have the knack of making themselves attractive to women. After her husband's death Madame Boyer had yielded herself completely to his influence and her own undoubted passion for him. She had given him the money with which to purchase a business of his own as a second-hand bookseller. This trade the enterprising and greedy young man combined with money- lending and he clandestine sale of improper books and photographs. To such a man the coming of Marie Boyer was a significant event. She was younger, more attractive than her mother; in a very few years the whole of her father's fortune would be hers. Slowly Vitalis set himself to win the girl's affections. The mother's suspicions were aroused; her jealousy was excited. She sent Marie to complete her education at a convent school in Lyons. This was in the April of 1875. By this time Marie and Vitalis had become friendly enough to arrange to correspond clandestinely during the girl's absence from home. Marie was so far ignorant of the relations of Vitalis with her mother.

Her daughter sent away, Madame Boyer surrendered herself with complete abandonment to her passion for her lover. At Castelnau, close to Montpellier, she bought a small country house. There she could give full rein to her desire. To the scandal of the occasional passer-by she and her lover would bathe in a stream that passed through the property, and sport together on the grass. Indoors there were always books from Vitalis' collection to stimulate their lascivious appetites. This life of pastoral impropriety lasted until the middle of August, when Marie Boyer came home from Lyons.

Vitalis would have concealed from the young girl as long as he could the nature of his relations with Madame Boyer, but his mistress by her own deliberate conduct made all concealment impossible. Whether from the utter recklessness of her passion for Vitalis, or a desire to kill in her daughter's heart any attachment which she may have felt towards her lover, the mother paraded openly before her daughter the intimacy of her relations with Vitalis, and with the help of the literature with which the young bookseller supplied her, set about corrupting her child's mind to her own depraved level. The effect of her extraordinary conduct was, however, the opposite to what she had intended. The mind of the young girl was corrupted; she was familiarised with vice. But in her heart she did not blame Vitalis for what she saw and suffered; she pitied, she excused him. It was her mother whom she grew to hate, with a hate all the more determined for the cold passionless exterior beneath which it was concealed.

Madame Boyer's deliberate display of her passion for Vitalis served only to aggravate and intensify in Marie Boyer an unnatural jealousy that was fast growing up between mother and daughter.

Marie did not return to the school at Lyons. In the winter of 1875, Madame Boyer gave up the country house and, with her daughter, settled in one of the suburbs of Montpellier. In the January of 1876 a theft occurred in her household which obliged Madame Boyer to communicate with the police. Spendthrift and incompetent in the management of her affairs, she was hoarding and suspicious about money itself. Cash and bonds she would hide away in unexpected places, such as books, dresses, even a soup tureen. One of her most ingenious hiding places was a portrait of her late husband, behind which she concealed some bearer bonds in landed security, amounting to about 11,000 francs. One day in January these bonds disappeared. She suspected a theft, and informed the police. Three days later she withdrew her complaint, and no more was heard of the matter. As Marie and Vitalis were the only persons who could have known her secret, the inference is obvious. When, later in the year, Vitalis announced his intention of going to Paris on business, his mistress expressed to him the hope that he would "have a good time" with her bonds. Vitalis left for Paris. But there was now a distinct understanding between Marie and himself. Vitalis had declared himself her lover and asked her to marry him. The following letter, written to him by Marie Boyer in the October of 1876, shows her attitude toward his proposal:

"I thank you very sincerely for your letter, which has given me very great pleasure, because it tells me that you are well. It sets my mind at rest, for my feelings towards you are the same as ever. I don't say they are those of love, for I don't know myself; I don't know what such feelings are. But I feel a real affection for you which may well turn to love. How should I not hold in affectionate remembrance one who has done everything for me? But love does not come to order. So I can't and don't wish to give any positive answer about our marriage—all depends on circumstances. I don't want any promise from you, I want you to be as free as I am. I am not fickle, you know me well enough for that. So don't ask me to give you any promise. You may find my letter a little cold. But I know too much of life to pledge myself lightly. I assure you I think on it often. Sometimes I blush when I think what marriage means."

Madame Boyer, displeased at the theft, had let her lover go without any great reluctance. No sooner had he gone than she began to miss him. Life seemed dull without him. Mother and daughter were united at least in their common regret at the absence of the young bookseller. To vary the monotony of existence, to find if possible a husband for her daughter, Madame Boyer decided to leave Montpellier for Marseilles, and there start some kind of business. The daughter, who foresaw greater amusement and pleasure in the life of a large city, assented willingly. On October 6, 1876, they arrived at Marseilles, and soon after Madame bought at a price considerably higher than their value, two shops adjoining one another in the Rue de la Republique. One was a cheese shop, the other a milliner's.

The mother arranged that she should look after the cheese shop, while her daughter presided over the milliner's. The two shops were next door to one another. Behind the milliner's was a drawing-room, behind the cheese shop a kitchen; these two rooms communicated with each other by a large dark room at the back of the building. In the kitchen was a trap-door leading to a cellar. The two women shared a bedroom in an adjoining house.

Vitalis had opposed the scheme of his mistress to start shop-keeping in Marseilles. He knew how unfitted she was to undertake a business of any kind. But neither mother nor daughter would relinquish the plan. It remained therefore to make the best of it. Vitalis saw that he must get the business into his own hands; and to do that, to obtain full control of Madame Boyer's affairs, he must continue to play the lover to her. To the satisfaction of the two women, he announced his intention of coming to Marseilles in the New Year of 1877. It was arranged that he should pass as a nephew of Madame Boyer, the cousin of Marie. He arrived at Marseilles on January 1, and received a cordial welcome. Of the domestic arrangements that ensued, it is sufficient to say that they were calculated to whet the jealousy and inflame the hatred that Marie felt towards her mother, who now persisted as before in parading before her daughter the intimacy of her relations with Vitalis.

In these circumstances Vitalis succeeded in extracting from his mistress a power of attorney, giving him authority to deal with her affairs and sell the two businesses, which were turning out unprofitable. This done, he told Marie, whose growing attachment to him, strange as it may seem, had turned to love, that now at last they could be free. He would sell the two shops, and with the money released by the sale they could go away to-

gether. Suddenly Madame Boyer fell ill, and was confined to her bed. Left to themselves, the growing passion of Marie Boyer for Vitalis culminated in her surrender. But for the sick mother the happiness of the lovers was complete. If only her illness were more serious, more likely to be fatal in its result! "If only God would take her!" said Vitalis. "Yes," replied her daughter, "she has caused us so much suffering!"

To Madame Boyer her illness had brought hours of torment, and at last remorse. She realised the duplicity of her lover, she knew that he meant to desert her for her daughter, she saw what wrong she had done that daughter, she suspected even that Marie and Vitalis were poisoning her. Irreligious till now, her thoughts turned to religion. As soon as she could leave her bed she would go to Mass and make atonement for her sin; she would recover her power of attorney, get rid of Vitalis for good and all, and send her daughter back to a convent. But it was too late. Nemesis was swift to overtake the hapless woman. Try as he might, Vitalis had found it impossible to sell the shops at anything but a worthless figure. He had no money of his own, with which to take Marie away. He knew that her mother had resolved on his instant dismissal.

As soon as Madame Boyer was recovered sufficiently to leave her bed, she turned on her former lover, denounced his treachery, accused him of robbing and swindling her, and bade him go without delay. To Vitalis dismissal meant ruin, to Marie it meant the loss of her lover. During her illness the two young people had wished Madame Boyer dead, but she had recovered. Providence or Nature having refused to assist Vitalis, he resolved to fall back on art. He gave up a whole night's rest to the consideration of the question. As a result of his deliberations he suggested to the girl of seventeen the murder of her mother. "This must end," said Vitalis. "Yes, it must," replied Marie. Vitalis asked her if she had any objection to such a crime. Marie hesitated, the victim was her mother. Vitalis reminded her what sort of a mother she had been to her. The girl said that she was terrified at the sight of blood; Vitalis promised that her mother should be strangled. At length Marie consented. That night on some slight pretext Madame Boyer broke out into violent reproaches against her daughter. She little knew that every reproach she uttered served only to harden in her daughter's heart her unnatural resolve.

On the morning of March 19 Madame Boyer rose early to go to Mass.

Before she went out, she reminded Vitalis that this was his last day in her service, that when she returned she would expect to find him gone. It was after seven when she left the house. The lovers had no time to lose; the deed must be done immediately on the mother's return. They arranged that Vitalis should get rid of the shop-boy, and that, as soon as he had gone, Marie should shut and lock the front doors of the two shops. At one o'clock Madame Boyer came back. She expressed her astonishment and disgust that Vitalis still lingered, and threatened to send for the police to turn him out. Vitalis told the shop-boy that he could go away for a few hours; they had some family affairs to settle. The boy departed. Madame Boyer, tired after her long morning in the town, was resting on a sofa in the sitting-room, at the back of the milliner's shop. Vitalis entered the room, and after a few heated words, struck her a violent blow in the chest. She fell back on the sofa, calling to her daughter to come to her assistance. The daughter sought to drown her mother's cries by banging the doors, and opening and shutting drawers. Vitalis, who was now trying to throttle his victim, called to Marie to shut the front doors of the two shops.

To do so Marie had to pass through the sitting-room, and was a witness to the unsuccessful efforts of Vitalis to strangle her mother. Having closed the doors, she retired into the milliner's shop to await the issue. After a few moments her lover called to her for the large cheese knife; he had caught up a kitchen knife, but in his struggles it had slipped from his grasp. Quickly Marie fetched the knife and returned to the sitting-room. There a desperate struggle was taking place between the man and woman. At one moment it seemed as if Madame Boyer would get the better of Vitalis, whom nature had not endowed greatly for work of this kind. Marie came to his aid. She kicked and beat her mother, until at last the wretched creature released her hold and sank back exhausted. With the cheese knife, which her daughter had fetched, Vitalis killed Madame Boyer.

They were murderers now, the young lovers. What to do with the body? The boy would be coming back soon. The cellar under the kitchen seemed the obvious place of concealment. With the help of a cord the body was lowered into the cellar, and Marie washed the floor of the sitting-room. The boy came back. He asked where Madame Boyer was. Vitalis told him that she was getting ready to return to Montpellier the same evening, and that he had arranged to go with her, but that he had no intention of doing so; he would accompany her to the station, he said, and then at the last moment, just as the train was starting, slip away and let her go on her journey alone. To the boy, who knew enough of the inner history of the household to enjoy the piquancy of the situation, such a trick seemed quite amusing. He went away picturing in his mind the scene at the railway station and its humorous possibilities.

At seven o'clock Vitalis and Marie Boyer were alone once more with the murdered woman. They had the whole night before them. Vitalis had already considered the matter of the disposal of the body. He had bought a pick and spade. He intended to bury his former mistress in the soil under the cellar. After that had been done, he and Marie would sell the business for what it would fetch, and go to Brussels—an admirable plan, which two unforeseen circumstances defeated. The Rue de la Republique was built on a rock, blasted out for the purpose. The shop-boy had gone to the station that evening to enjoy the joke which, he believed, was to be played on his mistress.

When Vitalis tried to dig a grave into the ground beneath the cellar he realised the full horror of the disappointment. What was to be done? They must throw the body into the sea. But how to get it there? The crime of Billoir, an old soldier, who the year before in Paris had killed his mistress in a fit of anger and cut up her body, was fresh in the recollection of Vitalis. The guilty couple decided to dismember the body of Madame Boyer and so disfigure her face as to render it unrecognisable. In the presence of Marie, Vitalis did this, and the two lovers set out at midnight to discover some place convenient for the reception of the remains. They found the harbour too busy for their purpose, and decided to wait until the morrow, when they would go farther afield. They returned home and retired for the night, occupying the bed in which Madame Boyer had slept the night before.

On the morning of the 20th the lovers rose early, and a curious neighbour, looking through the keyhole, saw them counting joyously money and valuables, as they took them from Madame Boyer's cash-box. When the shop-boy arrived, he asked Vitalis for news of Madame Boyer. Vitalis told him that he had gone with her to the station, that she had taken the train to Montpellier, and that, in accordance with his plan, he had given her the slip just as the train was starting. This the boy knew to be false: he had been to the station himself to enjoy the fun, and had seen neither Vitalis nor Madame Boyer. He began to suspect some mystery. In the evening, when the shops had been closed, and he had been sent about his business, he waited and watched. In a short time he saw Vitalis and Marie Boyer leave the house, the former dragging a hand-cart containing two large parcels, while Marie walked by his side. They travelled some distance with their burden, leaving the city behind them, hoping to find some deserted spot along the coast where they could conceal the evidence of their crime. Their nerves were shaken by meeting with a custom-house officer, who asked them what it was they had in the cart. Vitalis answered that it was a traveller's luggage, and the officer let them pass on. But soon after, afraid to risk another such experience, the guilty couple turned out the parcels into a ditch, covered them with stones and sand, and hurried home.

The next day, the shop-boy and the inquisitive neighbour having consulted together, went to the Commissary of Police and told him of the mysterious disappearance of Madame Boyer. The Commissary promised to investigate the matter, and had just dismissed his informants when word was brought to him of the discovery, in a ditch outside Marseilles, of two parcels containing human remains. He called back the boy and took him to view the body at the Morgue. The boy was able, by the clothes, to identify the body as that of his late mistress. The Commissary went straight to the shops in the Rue de la Republique, where he found the young lovers preparing for flight. At first they denied all knowledge of the crime, and said that Madame Boyer had gone to Montpellier. They were arrested, and it was not long before they both confessed their guilt to the examining magistrate.

Vitalis and Marie Boyer were tried before the Assize Court at Aix on July 2, 1877. Vitalis is described as mean and insignificant in appearance, thin, round-backed, of a bilious complexion; Marie Boyer as a pretty, dark girl, her features cold in expression, dainty and elegant. At her trial she seemed to be still so greatly under the influence of Vitalis that during her interrogatory the President sent him out of court. To the examining magistrate Marie Boyer, in describing her mother's mur- der, had written, "I cannot think how I came to take part in it. I, who wouldn't have stayed in the presence of a corpse for all the money in the world." Vitalis was condemned to death, and was executed on August 17. He died fearful and penitent, acknowledging his miserable career to be a warning to misguided youth. Extenuating circumstances were accorded to Marie Boyer, and she was sentenced to penal servitude for life. Her conduct in prison was so repentant and exemplary that she was released in 1892.

M. Proal, a distinguished French judge, and the author of some important works on crime, acted as the examining magistrate in the case of Vitalis and Marie Boyer. He thus sums up his impression of the two criminals: "Here is an instance of how greed and baseness on the one side, lust and jealousy on the other, bring about by degrees a change in the characters of criminals, and, after some hesitation, the suggestion and accomplishment of parricide, Is it necessary to seek an explanation of the crime in any psychic abnormality which is negatived to all appearances by the antecedents of the guilty pair? Is it necessary to ask it of anatomy or physiology? Is not the crime the result of moral degradation gradually asserting itself in two individuals, whose moral and intellectual faculties are the same as those of other men, but who fall, step by step, into vice and crime? It is by a succession of wrongful acts that a man first reaches the frontier of crime and then at length crosses it."

THE FENAYROU CASE

There is an account of this case in Bataille "Causes Criminelles et Mondaines" (1882), and in Mace's book, "Femmes Criminelles." It is alluded to in "Souvenirs d'un President d'Assises," by Berard des Glajeux. The murder of the chemist Aubert by Marin Fenayrou and his wife Gabrielle was perpetrated near Paris in the year 1882. In its beginning the story is commonplace enough. Fenayrou was the son of a small chemist in the South of France, and had come to Paris from the Aveyron Department to follow his father's vocation. He obtained a situation as apprentice in the Rue de la Ferme des Mathurins in the shop of a M. Gibon. On the death of M. Gibon his widow thought she saw in Fenayrou a man capable of carrying on her late husband's business. She gave her daughter in marriage to her apprentice, and installed him in the shop. The ungrateful son-in-law, sure of his wife and his business and contrary to his express promise, turned the old lady out of the house. This occurred in the year 1870, Fenayrou being then thirty years of age, his wife, Gabrielle, seventeen.

They were an ill-assorted and unattractive couple. The man, a compound of coarse brutality and shrewd cunning, was at heart lazy and selfish, the woman a spoilt child, in whom a real want of feeling was supplied by a shallow sentimentalism. Vain of the superior refinement conferred on her by a good middle-class education, she despised and soon came to loathe her coarse husband, and lapsed into a condition of disappointment and discontent that was only relieved superficially by an extravagant devotion to religious exercises.

It was in 1875, when the disillusionment of Mme. Fenayrou was complete, that her husband received into his shop a pupil, a youth of twenty-one, Louis Aubert. He was the son of a Norman tradesman. The ambitious father had wished his son to enter the church, but the son preferred to be a chemist. He was a shrewd, hard-working fellow, with an eye to the main chance and a taste for pleasures that cost him nothing, jovial, but vulgar and self- satisfied, the kind of man who, having enjoyed the favours of woman, treats her with arrogance and contempt, till from loving she comes to loathe him—a characteristic example, according to M. Bourget, of le faux homme a femmes. Such was Aubert, Fenayrou's pupil. He was soon to become something more than pupil.

Fenayrou as chemist had not answered to the expectations of his mother-in-law. His innate laziness and love of coarse pleasures had asserted themselves. At first his wife had shared in the enjoyments, but as time went on and after the birth of their two children, things became less prosperous. She was left at home while Fenayrou spent his time in drinking bocks of beer, betting and attending race-meetings. It was necessary, under these circumstances, that someone should attend to the business of the shop. In Aubert Fenayrou found a ready and willing assistant.

From 1876 to 1880, save for an occasional absence for military service, Aubert lived with the Fenayrous, managing the business and making love to the bored and neglected wife, who after a few months became his mistress. Did Fenayrou know of this intrigue or not? That is a crucial question in the case. If he did not, it was not for want of warning from certain of his friends and neighbours, to whom the intrigue was a matter of common knowledge. Did he refuse to believe in his wife's guilt? or, dependent as he was for his living on the exertions of his assistant, did he deliberately ignore it, relying on his wife's attractions to keep the assiduous Aubert at work in the shop? In any case Aubert's arrogance, which had increased with the consciousness of his importance to the husband and his conquest of the wife, led in August of 1880, to a rupture. Aubert left the Fenayrous and bought a business of his own on the Boulevard Malesherbes.

Before his departure Aubert had tried to persuade Mme. Gibon to sell up her son-in-law by claiming from him the unpaid purchase- money for her husband's shop. He represented Fenayrou as an idle gambler, and hinted that he would find her a new purchaser. Such an underhand proceeding was likely to provoke resentment if it should come to the ears of Fenayrou. During the two years that elapsed between his departure from Fenayrou's house and his murder, Aubert had prospered in his shop on the Boulevard Malesherbes, whilst the fortunes of the Fenayrous had steadily deteriorated.

At the end of the year 1881 Fenayrou sold his shop and went with his family to live on one of the outer boulevards, that of Gouvion-Saint-Cyr. He had obtained a post in a shady mining company, in which he had persuaded his mother-in-law to invest 20,000 francs. He had attempted also to make money by selling fradulent imitations of a famous table-water. For this offence, at the beginning of 1882, he was condemned by the Correctional Tribunal of Paris to three months' imprisonment and 1,000 francs costs.

In March of 1882 the situation of the Fenayrous was parlous, that of Aubert still prosperous.

Since Aubert's departure Mme. Fenayrou had entertained another lover, a gentleman on the staff of a sporting newspaper, one of Fenayrou's turf acquaintances. This gentleman had found her a cold mistress, preferring the ideal to the real. As a murderess Madame Fenayrou overcame this weakness.

If we are to believe Fenayrou's story, the most critical day in his life was March 22, 1882, for it was on that day, according to his account, that he learnt for the first time of his wife's intrigue with Aubert. Horrified and enraged at the discovery, he took from her her nuptial wreath, her wedding-ring, her jewellery, removed from its frame her picture in charcoal which hung in the drawing-room, and told her, paralysed with terror, that the only means of saving her life was to help him to murder her lover.

Two months later, with her assistance, this outraged husband accomplished his purpose with diabolical deliberation. He must have been well aware that, had he acted on the natural impulse of the moment and revenged himself then and there on Aubert, he would have committed what is regarded by a French jury as the most venial of crimes, and would have escaped with little or no punishment. He preferred, for reasons of his own, to set about the commission of a deliberate and cold-blooded murder that bears the stamp of a more sinister motive than the vengeance of a wronged husband.

The only step he took after the alleged confession of his wife on March 22 was to go to a commissary of police and ask him to recover from Aubert certain letters of his wife's that were in his possession. This the commissary refused to do. Mme. Gibon, the mother-in-law, was sent to Aubert to try to recover the letters, but Aubert declined to give them up, and wrote to Mme. Fenayrou:

"Madame, to my displeasure I have had a visit this morning from your mother, who has come to my home and made a most unnecessary scene and reproached me with facts so serious that I must beg you to see me without delay. It concerns your honour and mine. . . . I have no fear of being confronted with your husband and yourself. I am ready, when you wish, to justify myself. . . . Please do all you can to prevent a repetition of your mother's visit or I shall have to call in the police."

It is clear that the Fenayrous attached the utmost importance to the recovery of this correspondence, which disappeared with Aubert's death. Was the prime motive of the murder the recovery and destruction of these letters? Was Aubert possessed of some knowledge concerning the Fenayrous that placed them at his mercy?

It would seem so. To a friend who had warned him of the danger to which his intimacy with Gabrielle Fenayrou exposed him, Aubert had replied, "Bah! I've nothing to fear. I hold them in my power." The nature of the hold which Aubert boasted that he possessed over these two persons remains the unsolved mystery of the case, "that limit of investigation," in the words of a French judge, "one finds in most great cases, beyond which justice strays into the unknown."

That such a hold existed, Aubert's own statement and the desperate attempts made by the Fenayrous to get back these letters, would seem to prove beyond question. Had Aubert consented to return them, would he have saved his life? It seems probable. As it was, he was doomed. Fenayrou hated him. They had had a row on a race-course, in the course of which Aubert had humiliated his former master. More than this, Aubert had boasted openly of his relations with Mme. Fenayrou, and the fact had reached the ears of the husband. Fenayrou believed also, though erroneously, that Aubert had informed against him in the matter of the table-water fraud. Whether his knowledge of Aubert's relations with his wife was recent or of long standing, he had other grounds of hate against his former pupil. He himself had failed in life, but he saw his rival prosperous, arrogant in his prosperity, threatening, dangerous to his peace of mind; he envied and feared as well as hated him. Cruel, cunning and sinister, Fenayrou spent the next two months in the meditation of a revenge that was not only to remove the man he feared, but was to give him a truly fiendish opportunity of satisfying his ferocious hatred.

And the wife what of her share in the business? Had she also come to hate Aubert? Or did she seek to expiate her guilt by assisting her husband in the punishment of her seducer? A witness at the trial described Mme. Fenayrou as "a soft paste" that could be moulded equally well to vice or virtue, a woman destitute of real feeling or strength of will, who, under the direction of her husband, carried out implicitly, precisely and carefully her part in an atrocious murder, whose only effort to prevent the commission of such a deed was to slip away into a church a few minutes before she was to meet the man she was decoying to his death, and pray that his murder might be averted.

Her religious sense, like the images in the hat of Louis XI., was a source of comfort and consolation in the doing of evil, but powerless to restrain her from the act itself, in the presence of a will stronger than her own. At the time of his death Aubert contemplated marriage, and had advertised for a wife. If Mme. Fenayrou was aware of this, it may have served to stimulate her resentment against her lover, but there seems little reason to doubt that, left to herself, she would never have had the will or the energy to give that resentment practical expression. It required the dictation of the vindictive and malevolent Fenayrou to crystallise her hatred of Aubert into a deliberate participation in his murder.

Eight or nine miles north-west of Paris lies the small town of Chatou, a pleasant country resort for tired Parisians. Here Madeleine Brohan, the famous actress, had inhabited a small villa, a two-storied building. At the beginning of 1882 it was to let. In the April of that year a person of the name of "Hess" agreed to take it at a quarterly rent of 1,200 francs, and paid 300 in advance. "Hess" was no other than Fenayrou—the villa that had belonged to Madeleine Brohan the scene chosen for Aubert's murder. Fenayrou was determined to spare no expense in the execution of his design: it was to cost him some 3,000 francs before he had finished with it.

As to the actual manner of his betrayer's death, the outraged husband found it difficult to make up his mind. It was not to be prompt, nor was unnecessary suffering to be avoided. At first he favoured a pair of "infernal" opera-glasses that concealed a couple of steel points which, by means of a spring, would dart out into the eyes of anyone using them and destroy their sight. This rather elaborate and uncertain machine was abandoned later in favour of a trap for catching wolves. This was to be placed under the table, and seize in its huge iron teeth the legs of the victim. In the end simplicity, in the shape of a hammer and sword-stick, won the day. An assistant was taken in the person of Lucien Fenayrou, a brother of Marin.

This humble and obliging individual, a maker of children's toys, regarded his brother the chemist with something like veneration as the gentleman and man of education of the family. Fifty francs must have seemed to him an almost superfluous inducement to assist in the execution of what appeared to be an act of legitimate vengeance, an affair of family honour in which the wife and brother of the injured husband were in duty bound to participate. Mme. Fenayrou, with characteristic superstition, chose the day of her boy's first communion to broach the subject of the murder to Lucien. By what was perhaps more than coincidence, Ascension Day, May 18, was selected as the day for the crime itself. There were practical reasons also. It was a Thursday and a public holiday. On Thursdays the Fenayrou children spent the day with their grandmother, and at holiday time there was a special midnight train from Chatou to Paris that would enable the murderers to return to town after the commission of their crime. A goat chaise and twenty-six feet of gas piping had been purchased by Fenayrou and taken down to the villa.

Nothing remained but to secure the presence of the victim. At the direction of her husband Mme. Fenayrou wrote to Aubert on May 14, a letter in which she protested her undying love for him, and expressed a desire to resume their previous relations. Aubert demurred at first, but, as she became more pressing, yielded at length to her suggestion. If it cost him nothing, Aubert was the last man to decline an invitation of the kind. A trip to Chatou was arranged for Ascension Day, May 18, by the train leaving Paris from the St. Lazare Station, at half-past eight in the evening.

On the afternoon of that day Fenayrou, his wife and his brother sent the children to their grandmother and left Paris for Chatou at three o'clock. Arrived there, they went to the villa, Fenayrou carrying the twenty-six feet of gas-piping wound round him like some huge hunting-horn. He spent the afternoon in beating out the piping till it was flat, and in making a gag. He tried to take up the flooring in the kitchen, but this plan for the concealment of the body was abandoned in favour of the river. As soon as these preparations, in which he was assisted by his two relatives, had been completed, Fenayrou placed a candle, some matches and the sword-stick on the drawing-room table and returned to Paris.

The three conspirators dined together heartily in the Avenue de Clichy—soup, fish, entree, sweet and cheese, washed down by a bottle of claret and a pint of burgundy, coffee to follow, with a glass of chartreuse for Madame. To the waiter the party seemed in the best of spirits. Dinner ended, the two men returned to Chatou by the 7.35 train, leaving Gabrielle to follow an hour later with Aubert. Fenayrou had taken three second-class return tickets for his wife, his brother and himself, and a single for their visitor. It was during the interval between the departure of her husband and her meeting with Aubert that Mme. Fenayrou went into the church of St. Louis d'Antin and prayed.

At half-past eight she met Aubert at the St. Lazare Station, gave him his ticket and the two set out for Chatou—a strange journey Mme. Fenayrou was asked what they talked about in the railway carriage. "Mere nothings," she replied. Aubert abused her mother; for her own part, she was very agitated—tres emotionnee. It was about half-past nine when they reached their destination. The sight of the little villa pleased Aubert.

"Ah!" he said, "this is good. I should like a house like this and twenty thousand francs a year!" As he entered the hall, surprised at the darkness, he exclaimed: "The devil! it's precious dark! `tu sais, Gabrielle, que je ne suis pas un heros d'aventure.'" The woman pushed him into the drawing- room. He struck a match on his trousers. Fenayrou, who had been lurking in the darkness in his shirt sleeves, made a blow at him with the hammer, but it was ineffectual. A struggle ensued. The room was plunged in darkness. Gabrielle waited outside. After a little, her husband called for a light; she came in and lit a candle on the mantelpiece. Fenayrou was getting the worst of the encounter. She ran to his help, and dragged off his opponent. Fenayrou was free. He struck again with the hammer. Aubert fell, and for some ten minutes Fenayrou stood over the battered and bleeding man abusing and insulting him, exulting in his vengeance. Then he stabbed him twice with the sword-stick, and so ended the business.

The murderers had to wait till past eleven to get rid of the body, as the streets were full of holiday-makers. When all was quiet they put it into the goat chaise, wrapped round with the gas-piping, and wheeled it on to the Chatou bridge. To prevent noise they let the body down by a rope into the water. It was heavier than they thought, and fell with a loud splash into the river. "Hullo!" exclaimed a night-fisherman, who was mending his tackle not far from the bridge, "there go those butchers again, chucking their filth into the Seine!"

As soon as they had taken the chaise back to the villa, the three assassins hurried to the station to catch the last train. Arriving there a little before their time, they went into a neighbouring cafe. Fenayrou had three bocks, Lucien one, and Madame another glass of chartreuse. So home to Paris. Lucien reached his house about two in the morning. "Well," asked his wife, "did you have a good day?" "Splendid," was the reply.

Eleven days passed. Fenayrou paid a visit to the villa to clean it and put it in order. Otherwise he went about his business as usual, attending race meetings, indulging in a picnic and a visit to the Salon. On May 27 a man named Bailly, who, by a strange coincidence, was known by the nickname of "the Chemist," walking by the river, had his attention called by a bargeman to a corpse that was floating on the water. He fished it out. It was that of Aubert. In spite of a gag tired over his mouth the water had got into the body, and, notwithstanding the weight of the lead piping, it had risen to the surface.

As soon as the police had been informed of the disappearance of Aubert, their suspicions had fallen on the Fenayrous in consequence of the request which Marin Fenayrou had made to the commissary of police to aid him in the recovery from Aubert of his wife's letters. But there had been nothing further in their conduct to provoke suspicion. When, however, the body was discovered and at the same time an anonymous letter received denouncing the Fenayrous as the murderers of Aubert, the police decided on their arrest. On the morning of June 8 M. Mace, then head of the Detective Department, called at their house. He found Fenayrou in a dressing-gown. This righteous avenger of his wife's seduction denied his guilt, like any common criminal, but M. Mace handed him over to one of his men, to be taken immediately to Versailles. He himself took charge of Madame, and, in the first-class carriage full of people, in which they travelled together to Versailles, she whispered to the detective a full confession of the crime.

Mace has left us an account of this singular railway journey. It was two o'clock in the afternoon. In the carriage were five ladies and a young man who was reading La Vie Parisienne. Mme. Fenayrou was silent and thoughtful. "You're thinking of your present position?" asked the detective. "No, I'm thinking of my mother and my dear children." "They don't seem to care much about their father," remarked Mace. "Perhaps not." "Why?" asked M. Mace. "Because of his violent temper," was the reply. After some further conversation and the departure at Courbevoie of the young man with La Vie Parisienne, Mme. Fenayrou asked abruptly: "Do you think my husband guilty?" "I'm sure of it." "So does Aubert's sister." "Certainly," an-

swered M. Mace; "she looks on the crime as one of revenge." "But my brother-in-law," urged the woman, "could have had no motive for vengeance against Aubert." Mace answered coldly that he would have to explain how he had employed his time on Ascension Day. "You see criminals everywhere," answered Madame.

After the train had left St. Cloud, where the other occupants of the carriage had alighted, the detective and his prisoner were alone, free of interruption till Versailles should be reached. Hitherto they had spoken in whispers; now Mace seized the opportunity to urge the woman to unbosom herself to him, to reveal her part in the crime. She burst into tears. There was an interval of silence; then she thanked Mace for the kindness and consideration he had shown her. "You wish me," she asked, "to betray my husband?" "Without any design or intention on your part," discreetly answered the detective; "but by the sole force of circumstances you are placed in such a position that you cannot help betraying him."

Whether convinced or not of this tyranny of circumstance, Mme. Fenayrou obeyed her mentor, and calmly, coldly, without regret or remorse, told him the story of the assassination. Towards the end of her narration she softened a little. "I know I am a criminal," she exclaimed. "Since this morning I have done nothing but lie. I am sick of it; it makes me suffer too much. Don't tell my husband until this evening that I have confessed; there's no need, for, after what I have told you, you can easily expose his falsehoods and so get at the truth."

That evening the three prisoners—Lucien had been arrested at the same time as the other two—were brought to Chatou. Identified by the gardener as the lessee of the villa, Fenayrou abandoned his protestations of innocence and admitted his guilt. The crime was then and there reconstituted in the presence of the examining magistrate. With the help of a gendarme, who imper-

sonated Aubert, Fenayrou repeated the incidents of the murder. The goat-chaise was wheeled to the bridge, and there in the presence of an indignant crowd, the murderer showed how the body had been lowered into the river.

After a magisterial investigation lasting two months, which failed to shed any new light on the more mysterious elements in the case, Fenayrou, his wife and brother were indicted on August 19 before the Assize Court for the Seine-et-Oise Department, sitting at Versailles.

The attitude of the three culprits was hardly such as to provoke the sympathies of even a French jury. Fenayrou seemed to be giving a clumsy and unconvincing performance of the role of the wronged husband; his heavy figure clothed in an ill-fitting suit of "blue dittos," his ill-kempt red beard and bock-stained moustache did not help him in his impersonation. Mme. Fenayrou, pale, colourless, insignificant, was cold and impenetrable. She described the murder of her lover "as if she were giving her cook a household recipe for making apricot Jam." Lucien was humble and lachrymose.

In his interrogatory of the husband the President, M. Berard des Glajeux, showed himself frankly sceptical as to the ingenuousness of Fenayrou's motives in assassinating Aubert. "Now, what was the motive of this horrible crime?" he asked. "Revenge," answered Fenayrou.

President: But consider the care you took to hide the body and destroy all trace of your guilt; that is not the way in which a husband sets out to avenge his honour; these are the methods of the assassin! With your wife's help you could have caught Aubert in flagrante delicto and killed him on the spot, and the law would have absolved you. Instead of which you decoy him into a hideous snare. Public opinion suggests that jealousy of your former assistant's success, and mortification at your own failure, were the real motives. Or was it not perhaps that you had been in the habit of rendering somewhat dubious services to some of your promiscuous clients?

Fenayrou: Nothing of the kind, I swear it!

President: Do not protest too much. Remember that among your acquaintances you were suspected of cheating at cards. As a chemist you had been convinced of fraud. Perhaps Aubert knew something against you. Some act of poisoning, or abortion, in which you had been concerned? Many witnesses have believed this.

Your mother-in-law is said to have remarked, "My son-in-law will end in jail."

Fenayrou (bursting into tears): This is too dreadful.

President: And Dr. Durand, an old friend of Aubert, remembers the deceased saying to him, "One has nothing to fear from people one holds in one's hands."

Fenayrou: I don't know what he meant.

President: Or, considering the cruelty, cowardice, the cold calculation displayed in the commission of the crime, shall we say this was a woman's not a man's revenge. You have said your wife acted as your slave—was it not the other way about?

Fenayrou: No; it was my revenge, mine alone.

The view that regarded Mme. Fenayrou as a soft, malleable paste was not the view of the President.

"Why," he asked the woman, "did you commit this horrible murder, decoy your lover to his death?" "Because I had repented," was the answer; "I had wronged my husband, and since he had been condemned for fraud, I loved him the more for being unfortunate. And then I feared for my children."

President: Is that really the case?

Mme. Fenayrou: Certainly it is.

President: Then your whole existence has been one of lies and hypocrisy. Whilst you were deceiving your husband and teaching your children to despise him you were covering him with caresses.

You have played false to both husband and lover—to Aubert in decoying him to his death, to your husband by denouncing him directly you were arrested. You have betrayed everybody. The only person you have not betrayed is yourself. What sort of a woman are you? As you and Aubert went into the drawing-room on the evening of the murder you said loudly, "This is the way," so that your husband, hearing your voice outside, should not strike you by mistake in the darkness. If Lucien had not told us that you attacked Aubert whilst he was struggling with your husband, we should never have known it, for you would never have admitted it, and your husband has all along refused to implicate you. . . . You have said that you had ceased to care for your lover: he had ceased to care for you. He was prosperous, happy, about to marry: you hated him, and you showed your hate when, during the murder, you flung yourself upon him and cried, "Wretch!" Is that the behaviour of a woman who represents herself to have been the timid slave of her husband? No. This crime is the revenge of a cowardly and pitiless woman, who writes down in her account book the expenses of the trip to Chatou and, after the murder, picnics merrily in the green fields. It was you who steeled your husband to the task.

How far the President was justified in thus inverting the parts played by the husband and wife in the crime must be a matter of opinion. In his volume of Souvenirs M. Berard des Glajeux modifies considerably the view which he perhaps felt it his duty to express in his interrogatory of Gabrielle Fenayrou. He describes her as soft and flexible by nature, the repentant slave of her husband, seeking to atone for her wrong to him by helping him in his revenge. The one feature in the character of Mme. Fenayrou that seems most clearly demonstrated is its absolute insensibility under any circumstances whatsoever.

The submissive Lucien had little to say for himself, nor could any motive for joining in the murder beyond a readiness to oblige his brother be suggested. In his Souvenirs M. Berard des Glajeux states that to-day it would seem to be clearly established that Lucien acted blindly at the bidding of his sister-in-law, "qu'il avait beaucoup aimee et qui n'avait pas ete cruelle a son egard."

The evidence recapitulated for the most part the facts already set out. The description of Mme. Fenayrou by the gentleman on the sporting newspaper who had succeeded Aubert in her affections is, under the circumstances, interesting: "She was sad, melancholy; I questioned her, and she told me she was married to a coarse man who neglected her, failed to understand her, and had never loved her. I became her lover but, except on a few occasions, our relations were those of good friends. She was a woman with few material wants, affectionate, expansive, an idealist, one who had suffered much and sought from without a happiness her marriage had never brought her. I believe her to have been the blind tool of her husband."

From motives of delicacy the evidence of this gentleman was read in his presence; he was not examined orally. His eulogy of his mistress is loyal. Against it may be set the words of the Procureur de la Republique, M. Delegorgue: "Never has a more thorough-paced, a more hideous monster been seated in the dock of an assize court. This woman is the personification of falsehood, depravity, cowardice and treachery. She is worthy of the supreme penalty." The jury were not of this opinion. They preferred to regard Mme. Fenayrou as playing a secondary part to that of her husband. They accorded in both her case and that of Lucien ex-

tenuating circumstances. The woman was sentenced to penal servitude for life, Lucien to seven years. Fenayrou, for whose conduct the jury could find no extenuation, was condemned to death.

It is the custom in certain assize towns for the President, after pronouncing sentence, to visit a prisoner who had been ordered for execution. M. Berard des Glajeux describes his visit to Fenayrou at Versailles. He was already in prison dress, sobbing.

His iron nature, which during five days had never flinched, had broken down; but it was not for himself he wept, but for his wife, his children, his brother; of his own fate he took no account. At the same moment his wife was in the lodge of the courthouse waiting for the cab that was to take her to her prison. Freed from the anxieties of the trial, knowing her life to be spared, without so much as a thought for the husband whom she had never loved, she had tidied herself up, and now, with all the ease of a woman, whose misfortunes have not destroyed her self-possession, was doing the honours of the jail. It was she who received her judge.

But Fenayrou was not to die. The Court of Cassation, to which he had made the usual appeal after condemnation, decided that the proceedings at Versailles had been vitiated by the fact that the evidence of Gabrielle Fenayrou's second lover had not been taken ORALLY, within the requirements of the criminal code; consequently a new trial was ordered before the Paris Assize Court. This second trial, which commenced on October 12, saved Fenayrou's head. The Parisian jury showed themselves more lenient than their colleagues at Versailles. Not only was Fenayrou accorded extenuating circumstances, but Lucien was acquitted altogether. The only person to whom these new proceedings brought no benefit was Mme. Fenayrou, whose sentence remained unaltered.

Marin Fenayrou was sent to New Caledonia to serve his punishment.

There he was allowed to open a dispensary, but, proving dishonest, he lost his license and became a ferryman—a very Charon for terrestrial passengers. He died in New Caledonia of cancer of the liver.

Gabrielle Fenayrou made an exemplary prisoner, so exemplary that, owing to her good conduct and a certain ascendancy she exercised over her fellow-prisoners, she was made forewoman of one of the workshops. Whilst holding this position she had the honour of receiving, among those entrusted to her charge, another Gabrielle, murderess, Gabrielle Bompard, the history of whose crime is next to be related.

EYRAUD AND BOMPARD

There are accounts of this case in Bataille "Causes Criminelles et Mondaines," 1890, and in Volume X. of Fouquier "Causes Celebres." "L'Affaire Gouffe" by Dr. Lacassagne, Lyons, 1891, and Goron "L'Amour Criminel" may be consulted.

ON July 27, in the year 1889, the Parisian police were informed of the disappearance of one Gouffe, a bailiff. He had been last seen by two friends on the Boulevard Montmartre at about ten minutes past seven on the evening of the 26th, a Friday. Since then nothing had been heard of him, either at his office in the Rue Montmartre, or at his private house in the Rue Rougemont. This was surprising in the case of a man of regular habits even in his irregularities, robust health, and cheerful spirits.

Gouffe was a widower, forty-two years of age. He had three daughters who lived happily with him in the Rue Rougemont. He did a good trade as bailiff and process-server, and at times had considerable sums of money in his possession. These he would never leave behind him at his office, but carry home at the end of the day's work, except on Fridays. Friday nights Gouffe always spent away from home. As the society he sought on these nights was of a promiscuous character, he was in the habit of leaving at his office any large sum of money that had come into his hands during the day.

About nine o'clock on this particular Friday night, July 26, the hall-porter at Gouffe's office in the Rue Montmartre heard someone, whom he had taken at first to be the bailiff himself, enter the hall and go upstairs to the office, where he remained a few minutes. As he descended the stairs the porter came out of his lodge and, seeing it was a stranger, accosted him. But the man hurried away without giving the porter time to see his face.

When the office was examined the next day everything was found in perfect order, and a sum of 14,000 francs, hidden away behind some papers, untouched. The safe had not been tampered with; there was, in short, nothing unusual about the room except ten long matches that were lying half burnt on the floor.

On hearing of the bailiff's disappearance and the mysterious visitor to his office, the police, who were convinced that Gouffe had been the victim of some criminal design, inquired closely into his habits, his friends, his associates, men and women. But the one man who could have breathed the name that would have set the police on the track of the real culprits was, for reasons of his own, silent. The police examined many persons, but without arriving at any useful result.

However, on August 15, in a thicket at the foot of a slope running down from the road that passes through the district of Millery, about ten miles from Lyons, a roadmender, attracted by a peculiar smell, discovered the remains of what appeared to be a human body. They were wrapped in a cloth, but so decomposed as to make identification almost impossible. M. Goron, at that time head of the Parisian detective police, believed them to be the remains of Gouffe, but a relative of the missing man, whom he sent to Lyons, failed to identify them. Two days after the discovery of the corpse, there were found near Millery the broken fragments of a trunk, the lock of which fitted a key that had been picked up near the body. A label on the trunk showed that it had been dispatched from Paris to Lyons on July 27, 188—, but the final figure of the date was obliterated. Reference to the books of the railway company showed that on July 27, 1889, the day following the disappearance of Gouffe, a trunk similar in size and weight to that found near Millery had been sent from Paris to Lyons.

The judicial authorities at Lyons scouted the idea that either the corpse or the trunk found at Millery had any connection with the disappearance of Gouffe. When M. Goron, bent on following up what he believed to be important clues, went himself to Lyons he found that the remains, after being photographed, had been interred in the common burying-ground. The young doctor who had made the autopsy produced triumphantly some hair taken from the head of the corpse and showed M. Goron that whilst Gouffe's hair was admittedly auburn and cut short, this was black, and had evidently been worn long. M. Goron, after looking carefully at the hair, asked for some distilled water. He put the lock of hair into it and, after a few minutes' immersion, cleansed of the blood, grease and dust that had caked them together, the hairs appeared clearly to be short and auburn. The doctor admitted his error.

Fortified by this success, Goron was able to procure the exhumation of the body. A fresh autopsy was performed by Dr. Lacassagne, the eminent medical jurist of the Lyons School of Medicine. He was able to pronounce with certainty that the remains were those of the bailiff, Gouffe. An injury to the right ankle, a weakness of the right leg, the absence of a particular tooth and other admitted peculiarities in Gouffe's physical conformation, were present in the corpse, placing its identity beyond question. This second post-mortem revealed furthermore an injury to the thyroid cartilage of the larynx that had been inflicted beyond any doubt whatever, declared Dr. Lacassagne, before death.

There was little reason to doubt that Gouffe had been the victim of murder by strangulation.

But by whom had the crime been committed? It was now the end of November. Four months had passed since the bailiff's murder, and the police had no clue to its perpetrators. At one time a friend of Gouffe's had been suspected and placed under arrest, but he was released for want of evidence.

One day toward the close of November, in the course of a conversation with M. Goron, a witness who had known Gouffe surprised him by saying abruptly, "There's another man who disappeared about the same time as Gouffe." M. Goron pricked up his ears. The witness explained that he had not mentioned the fact before, as he had not connected it with his friend's disappearance; the man's name, he said, was Eyraud, Michel Eyraud, M. Goron made some inquires as to this Michel Eyraud. He learnt that he was a married man, forty-six years of age, once a distiller at Sevres, recently commission-agent to a bankrupt firm, that he had left France suddenly, about the time of the disappearance of Gouffe, and that he had a mistress, one Gabrielle Bompard, who had disappeared with him. Instinctively M. Goron connected this fugitive couple with the fate of the murdered bailiff.

Confirmation of his suspicions was to come from London. The remains of the trunk found at Millery had been skilfully put together and exposed at the Morgue in Paris, whilst the Gouffe family had offered a reward of 500 francs to anybody who could in any way identify the trunk. Beyond producing a large crop of anonymous letters, in one of which the crime was attributed to General Boulanger, then in Jersey, these measures seemed likely to prove fruitless. But one day in December, from the keeper of a boarding-house in Gower Street, M. Goron received a letter informing him that the writer believed that Eyraud and Gabrielle Bompard had stayed recently at his house, and that on July 14 the woman, whom he knew only as "Gabrielle," had left for France, crossing by Newhaven and Dieppe, and taking with her a large and almost empty trunk, which she had purchased in London. Inquires made by the French detectives established the correctness of this correspondent's information. An assistant at a trunk shop in the Euston Road was able to identify the trunk— brought over from Paris for the purpose—as one purchased in his shop on July 12 by a Frenchman answering to the description of Michel Eyraud. The wife of the boarding-house keeper recollected having expressed to Gabrielle her surprise that she should buy such an enormous piece of luggage when she had only one dress to put into it. "Oh that's all right," answered Gabrielle smilingly, "we shall have plenty to fill it with in Paris!" Gabrielle had gone to Paris with the trunk on July 14, come back to London on the 17th, and on the 20th she and Eyraud returned together to Paris From these facts it seemed more than probable that these two were the assassins so eagerly sought for by the police, and it seemed clear also that the murder had been done in Paris. But what had become of this couple, in what street, in what house in Paris had the crime been committed? These were questions the police were powerless to answer.

The year 1889 came to an end, the murderers were still at large. But on January 21, 1890, M. Goron found lying on his table a large letter bearing the New York postmark. He opened it, and to his astonishment read at the end the signature "Michel Eyraud." It was a curious letter, but undoubtedly genuine. In it Eyraud protested against the suspicions directed against himself; they were, he wrote, merely unfortunate coincidences. Gouffe had been his friend; he had had no share whatever in his death; his only misfortune had been his association with "that serpent, Gabrielle Bompard." He had certainly bought a large trunk for her, but she told him that she had sold it. They had gone to America together, he to avoid financial difficulties in which he had been involved by the dishonesty of the Jews. There Gabrielle had deserted him for another man. He concluded a very long letter by declaring his belief in Gabrielle's innocence— "the great trouble with her is that she is such a liar and also has a dozen lovers after her." He promised that, as soon as he learnt that Gabrielle had returned to Paris, he would, of his own free will, place himself in the hands of M. Goron.

He was to have an early opportunity of redeeming his pledge, for on the day following the receipt of his letter a short, well-made woman, dressed neatly in black, with dyed hair, greyish-blue eyes, good teeth, a disproportionately large head and a lively and intelligent expression of face, presented herself at the Prefecture of Police and asked for an interview with the Prefect.

Requested to give her name, she replied, with a smile, "Gabrielle Bompard." She was accompanied by a middle-aged gentleman, who appeared to be devoted to her. Gabrielle Bompard and her friend were taken to the private room of M. Loze, the Prefect of Police. There, in a half-amused way, without the least concern, sitting at times on the edge of the Prefect's writing-table, Gabrielle Bompard told how she had been the unwilling accomplice of her lover, Eyraud, in the murder of the bailiff, Gouffe. The crime, she stated, had been committed in No. 3 in the Rue Tronson-Ducoudray, but she had not been present; she knew nothing of it but what had been told her by Eyraud. After the murder she had accompanied him to America; there they had met the middle- aged gentleman, her companion. Eyraud had proposed that they should murder and rob him, but she had divulged the plot to the gentleman and asked him to take her away. It was acting on his advice that she had returned to France, determined to give her evidence to the judicial authorities in Paris. The middle-aged gentleman declared himself ready to vouch for the truth of a great part of this interesting narrative. There they both imagined apparently that the affair would be ended. They were extremely surprised when the Prefect, after listening to their statements, sent for a detective-inspector who showed Gabrielle Bompard a warrant for her arrest. After an affecting parting, at least on the part of the middle-aged gentleman, Gabrielle Bompard was taken to prison. There she soon recovered her spirits, which had at no time been very gravely depressed by her critical situ- ation.

According to Eyraud's letters, if anyone knew anything about Gouffe's murder, it was Gabrielle Bompard; according to the woman's statement, it was Eyraud, and Eyraud alone, who had committed it. As they were both liars—the woman perhaps the greater liar of the two—their statements are not to be taken as other than forlorn attempts to shift the blame on to each other's shoulders.

Before extracting from their various avowals, which grew more complete as time went on, the story of the crime, let us follow Eyraud in his flight from justice, which terminated in the May of 1890 by his arrest in Havana.

Immediately after the arrest of Gabrielle, two French detectives set out for America to trace and run down if possible her deserted lover. For more than a month they traversed Canada and the United States in search of their prey. The track of the fugitive was marked from New York to San Francisco by acts of thieving and swindling. At the former city he had made the acquaintance of a wealthy Turk, from whom, under the pretence of wishing to be photographed in it, he had borrowed a magnificent oriental robe. The photograph was taken, but Eyraud forgot to return the costly robe.

At another time he was lodging in the same house as a young American actor, called in the French accounts of the incident "Sir Stout." To "Sir Stout" Eyraud would appear to have given a most convincing performance of the betrayed husband; his wife, he said, had deserted him for another man; he raved and stormed au-

dibly in his bedroom, deploring his fate and vowing vengeance. These noisy representations so impressed "Sir Stout" that, on the outraged husband declaring himself to be a Mexican for the moment without funds, the benevolent comedian lent him eighty dollars, which, it is almost needless to add, he never saw again. In narrating this incident to the French detectives, "Sir Stout" describes Eyraud's performance as great, surpassing even those of Coquelin.

Similar stories of theft and debauchery met the detectives at every turn, but, helped in a great measure by the publicity the American newspapers gave to the movements of his pursuers, Eyraud was able to elude them, and in March they returned to France to concert further plans for his capture.

Eyraud had gone to Mexico. From there he had written a letter to M. Rochefort's newspaper, L'Intransigeant, in which he declared Gouffe to have been murdered by Gabrielle and an unknown. But, when official inquiries were made in Mexico as to his whereabouts, the bird had flown.

At Havana, in Cuba, there lived a French dressmaker and clothes- merchant named Puchen. In the month of February a stranger, ragged and unkempt, but evidently a fellow-countryman, visited her shop and offered to sell her a superb Turkish costume. The contrast between the wretchedness of the vendor and the magnificence of his wares struck Madame Puchen at the time. But her surprise was converted into suspicion when she read in the American newspapers a description of the Turkish garment stolen by Michel Eyraud, the reputed assassin of the bailiff Gouffe. It was one morning in the middle of May that Mme. Puchen read the description of the robe that had been offered her in February by her strange visitor. To her astonishment, about two o'clock the same afternoon, she saw the stranger standing before her door. She beckoned to him, and asked him if he still had his Turkish robe with him; he seemed confused, and said that he had sold it. The conversation drifted on to ordinary topics; the stranger described some of his recent adventures in Mexico. "Oh!" exclaimed the dressmaker, "they say Eyraud, the murderer, is in Mexico! Did you come across him? Were you in Paris at the time of the murder?" The stranger answered in the negative, but his face betrayed his uneasiness. "Do you know you're rather like him?" said the woman, in a half-joking way. The stranger laughed, and shortly after went out, saying he would return. He did return on May 15, bringing with him a number of the Republique Illustree that contained an almost unrecognisable portrait of Eyraud. He said he had picked it up in a cafe. "What a blackguard he looks!" he exclaimed as he threw the paper on the table. But the dressmaker's suspicions were not allayed by the stranger's uncomplimentary reference to the murderer. As soon as he had gone, she went to the French Consul and told him her story.

By one of those singular coincidences that are inadmissible in fiction or drama, but occur at times in real life, there happened to be in Havana, of all places, a man who had been employed by Eyraud at the time that he had owned a distillery at Sevres. The Consul, on hearing the statement of Mme. Puchen, sent for this man and told him that a person believed to be Eyraud was in Havana. As the man left the Consulate, whom should he meet in the street but Eyraud himself! The fugitive had been watching the movements of Mme. Puchen; he had suspected, after the interview, that the woman would denounce him to the authorities. He now saw that disguise was useless. He greeted his ex-employe, took him into a cafe, there admitted his identity and begged him not to betray him. It was midnight when they left the cafe. Eyraud, repenting of his confidence, and no doubt anxious to rid himself of a dangerous witness, took his friend into an ill-lighted and deserted street; but the friend, conscious of his delicate situation, hailed a passing cab and made off as quickly as he could.

Next day, the 20th, the search for Eyraud was set about in earnest. The Spanish authorities, informed of his presence in Havana, directed the police to spare no effort to lay hands on him. The Hotel Roma, at which he had been staying, was visited; but Eyraud, scenting danger, had gone to an hotel opposite the railway station. His things were packed ready for flight on the following morning. How was he to pass the night? True to his instincts, a house of ill-fame, at which he had been entertained already, seemed the safest and most pleasant refuge; but, when, seedy and shabby, he presented himself at the door, he was sent back into the street. It was past one in the morning. The lonely murderer wandered aimlessly in the streets, restless, nervous, a prey to apprehension, not knowing where to go. Again the man from Sevres met him. "It's all up with me!" said Eyraud, and disappeared in the darkness. At two in the morning a police officer, who had been patrolling the town in search of the criminal, saw, in the distance, a man walking to and fro, seemingly uncertain which way to turn. Hearing footsteps the man turned round and walked resolutely past the policeman, saying good-night in Spanish. "Who are you? What's your address?" the officer asked abruptly. "Gorski, Hotel Roma!" was the answer. This was enough for the officer. Eyraud was know{sic} to have passed as "Gorski," the Hotel Roma had already been searched as one of his hiding-places. To seize and handcuff "Gorski" was the work of a moment. An examination of the luggage left by the so- called Gorski at his last hotel and a determined attempt at suicide made by their prisoner during the night proved conclusively that to the Spanish police was the credit of having laid by the heels, ten months after the commission of the crime, Michel Eyraud, one of the assassins of the bailiff Gouffe.

On June 16 Eyraud was delivered over to the French police. He reached France on the 20th, and on July 1 made his first appearance before the examining magistrate.

It will be well at this point in the narrative to describe how Eyraud and Gabrielle Bompard came to be associated together in crime. Gabrielle Bompard was twenty-two years of age at the time of her arrest, the fourth child of a merchant of Lille, a strong, hardworking, respectable man. Her mother, a delicate woman, had died of lung disease when Gabrielle was thirteen. Even as a child lying and vicious, thinking only of men and clothes, Gabrielle, after being expelled as incorrigible from four educational establishments, stayed at a fifth for some three years. There she astonished those in authority over her by her precocious propensity for vice, her treacherous and lying disposition, and a lewdness of tongue rare in one of her age and comparative inexperience. At eighteen she returned to her father's house, only to quit it for a lover whom, she alleged, had hypnotised and then seduced her. Gabrielle was singularly susceptible to hypnotic suggestion. Her father implored the family doctor to endeavour to persuade her, while in the hypnotic state, to reform her deplorable conduct. The doctor did his best but with no success. He declared Gabrielle to be a neuropath, who had not found in her home such influences as would have tended to overcome her vicious instincts. Perhaps the doctor was inclined to sympathise rather too readily with his patient, if we are to accept the report of those distinguished medical gentlemen who, at a later date, examined carefully into the mental and physical characteristics of Gabrielle Bompard.

This girl of twenty had developed into a supreme instance of the "unmoral" woman, the conscienceless egoist, morally colour-blind, vain, lewd, the intelligence quick and alert but having no influence whatever on conduct. One instance will suffice to show the sinister levity, the utter absence of all moral sense in this strange creature.

After the murder of Gouffe, Gabrielle spent the night alone with the trunk containing the bailiff's corpse. Asked by M. Goron what were her sensations during this ghastly vigil, she replied with a smile, "You'd never guess what a funny idea come into my head! You see it was not very pleasant for me being thus tete-a-tete with a corpse, I couldn't sleep. So I thought what fun it would be to go into the street and pick up some respectable gentleman from the provinces. I'd bring him up to the room, and just as he was beginning to enjoy himself say, `Would you like to see a bailiff?' open the trunk suddenly and, before he could recover from his horror, run out into the street and fetch the police. Just think what a fool the respectable gentleman would have looked when the officers came!"

Such callousness is almost unsurpassed in the annals of criminal insensibility. Nero fiddling over burning Rome, Thurtell fresh from the murder of Weare, inviting Hunt, the singer and his accomplice, to "tip them a stave" after supper, Edwards, the Camberwell murderer, reading with gusto to friends the report of a fashionable divorce case, post from the murder of a young married couple and their baby—even examples such as these pale before the levity of the "little demon," as the French detectives christened Gabrielle.

Such was Gabrielle Bompard when, on July 26, exactly one year to a day before the murder of Gouffe, she met in Paris Michel Eyraud. These two were made for each other. If Gabrielle were unmoral, Eyraud was immoral. Forty-six at the time of Gouffe's murder, he was sufficiently practised in vice to appreciate and enjoy the flagrantly vicious propensities of the young Gabrielle. All his life Eyraud had spent his substance in debauchery. His passions were violent and at times uncontrollable, but unlike many remarkable men of a similar temperament, this strong animalism was not in his case accompanied by a capacity for vigorous intellectual exertion or a great power of work. "Understand this," said Eyraud to one of the detectives who brought him back to France, "I have never done any work, and I never will do any work." To him work was derogatory; better anything than that. Unfortunately it could not be avoided altogether, but with Eyraud such work as he was compelled at different times to endure was only a means for procuring money for his degraded pleasures, and when honest work became too troublesome, dishonesty served in its stead. When he met Gabrielle he was almost at the end of his tether, bankrupt and discredited. At a pinch he might squeeze a little money out of his wife, with whom he continued to live in spite of his open infidelities.

Save for such help as he could get from her small dowry, he was without resources. A deserter from the army during the Mexican war in 1869, he had since then engaged in various commercial enterprises, all of which had failed, chiefly through his own extravagance, violence and dishonesty. Gabrielle was quick to empty his pockets of what little remained in them. The proceeds of her own immorality, which Eyraud was quite ready to share, soon proved insufficient to replenish them. Confronted with ruin, Eyraud and Gompard hit on a plan by which the woman should decoy some would-be admirer to a convenient trysting-place. There, dead or alive, the victim was to be made the means of supplying their wants.

On further reflection dead seemed more expedient than alive, extortion from a living victim too risky an enterprise. Their plans were carefully prepared. Gabrielle was to hire a ground- floor apartment, so that any noise, such as footsteps or the fall of a body, would not be heard by persons living underneath.

At the beginning of July, 1889, Eyraud and Bompard were in London. There they bought at a West End draper's a red and white silk girdle, and at a shop in Gower Street a large travelling trunk. They bought, also in London, about thirteen feet of cording, a pulley and, on returning to Paris on July 20, some twenty feet of packing-cloth, which Gabrielle, sitting at her window on the fine summer evenings, sewed up into a large bag.

The necessary ground-floor apartment had been found at No. 3 Rue Tronson-Ducoudray. Here Gabrielle installed herself on July 24. The bedroom was convenient for the assassins' purpose, the bed standing in an alcove separated by curtains from the rest of the room. To the beam forming the crosspiece at the entrance into the alcove Eyraud fixed a pulley. Through the pulley ran a rope, having at one end of it a swivel, so that a man, hiding behind the curtains could, by pulling the rope strongly, haul up anything that might be attached to the swivel at the other end. It was with the help of this simple piece of mechanism and a good long pull from Eyraud that the impecunious couple hoped to refill their pockets.

The victim was chosen on the 25th. Eyraud had already known of Gouffe's existence, but on that day, Thursday, in a conversation with a common friend, Eyraud learnt that the bailiff Gouffe was rich, that he was in the habit of having considerable sums of money in his care, and that on Friday nights Gouffe made it his habit to sleep from home. There was no time to lose. The next day

Gabrielle accosted Gouffe as he was going to his dejeuner and, after some little conversation agreed to meet him at eight o'clock that evening.

The afternoon was spent in preparing for the bailiff's reception in the Rue Tronson-Ducoudray. A lounge-chair was so arranged that it stood with its back to the alcove, within which the pulley and rope had been fixed by Eyraud. Gouffe was to sit on the chair, Gabrielle on his knee. Gabrielle was then playfully to slip round his neck, in the form of a noose, the cord of her dressing gown and, unseen by him, attach one end of it to the swivel of the rope held by Eyraud. Her accomplice had only to give a strong pull and the bailiff's course was run.[17]

[17] One writer on the case has suggested that the story of the murder by rope and pulley was invented by Eyraud and Bompard to mitigate the full extent of their guilt, and that the bailiff was strangled while in bed with the woman. But the purchase of the necessary materials in London would seem to imply a more practical motive for the use of rope and pulley.

At six o'clock Eyraud and Bompard dined together, after which Eyraud returned to the apartment, whilst Bompard went to meet Gouffe near the Madeline Church. What occurred afterwards at No. 3 Rue Tronson-Ducoudray is best described in the statement made by Eyraud at his trial.

"At a quarter past eight there was a ring at the bell. I hid myself behind the curtain. Gouffe came in. `You've a nice little nest here,' he said. `Yes, a fancy of mine,' replied Gabrielle, `Eyraud knows nothing about it.' `Oh, you're tired of him,' asked Gouffe. `Yes,' she replied, `that's all over.' Gabrielle drew Gouffe down on to the chair. She showed him the cord of her dressing-gown and said that a wealthy admirer had given it to her. `Very elegant,' said Gouffe, `but I didn't come here to see that.'

"She then sat on his knee and, as if in play, slipped the cord round his neck; then putting her hand behind him, she fixed the end of the cord into the swivel, and said to him laughingly, `What a nice necktie it makes!' That was the signal. Eyraud pulled the cord vigorously and, in two minutes, Gouffe had ceased to live."

Eyraud took from the dead man his watch and ring, 150 francs and his keys. With these he hurried to Gouffe's office and made a fevered search for money. It was fruitless. In his trembling haste the murderer missed a sum of 14,000 francs that was lying behind some papers, and returned, baffled and despairing, to his mistress and the corpse. The crime had been a ghastly failure. Fortified by brandy and champagne, and with the help of the woman, Eyraud stripped the body, put it into the bag that had been sewn by Gabrielle, and pushed the bag into the trunk. Leaving his mistress to spend the night with their hateful luggage, Eyraud returned home and, in his own words, "worn out by the excitement of the day, slept heavily."

The next day Eyraud, after saying good-bye to his wife and daughter, left with Gabrielle for Lyons. On the 28th they got rid at Millery of the body of Gouffe and the trunk in which it had travelled; his boots and clothes they threw into the sea at Marseilles. There Eyraud borrowed 500 francs from his brother.

Gabrielle raised 2,000 francs in Paris, where they spent August 18 and 19, after which they left for England, and from England sailed for America. During their short stay in Paris Eyraud had the audacity to call at the apartment in the Rue Tronson- Ducoudray for his hat, which he had left behind; in the hurry of the crime he had taken away Gouffe's by mistake.

Eyraud had been brought back to Paris from Cuba at the end of June, 1890. Soon after his return, in the room in which Gouffe had been done to death and in the presence of the examining magistrate, M. Goron, and some fifteen other persons, Eyraud was confronted with his accomplice. Each denied vehemently, with hatred and passion, the other's story. Neither denied the murder, but each tried to represent the other as the more guilty of the two. Eyraud said that the suggestion and plan of the crime had come from Gabrielle; that she had placed around Gouffe's neck the cord that throttled him. Gabrielle attributed the inception of the murder to Eyraud, and said that he had strangled the bailiff with his own hands.

Eyraud, since his return, had seemed indifferent to his own fate; whatever it might be, he wished that his mistress should share it. He had no objection to going to the guillotine as long as he was sure that Gabrielle would accompany him. She sought to escape such a consummation by representing herself as a mere instrument in Eyraud's hands. It was even urged in her defence that, in committing the crime, she had acted under the influence of hypnotic suggestion on the part of her accomplice. Three doctors appointed by the examining magistrate to report on her mental state came unanimously to the conclusion that, though undoubtedly susceptible to hypnotic suggestion, there was no ground for thinking that she had been acting under such influence when she participated in the murder of Gouffe. Intellectually the medical gentlemen found her alert and sane enough, but morally blind.

The trial of Eyraud and Bompard took place before the Paris Assize Court on December 16, 1890. It had been delayed owing to the proceedings of an enterprising journalist. The names of the jurymen who were to be called on to serve at the assize had been published. The journalist conceived the brilliant idea of interviewing some of these gentlemen.

He succeeded in seeing four of them, but in his article which appeared in the Matin newspaper said that he had seen twenty- one. Nine of them, he stated, had declared themselves in favour of Gabrielle Bompard, but in some of these he had discerned a certain "eroticism of the pupil of the eye" to which he attributed their leniency. A month's imprisonment was the reward of these flights of journalistic imagination.

A further scandal in connection with the trial was caused by the lavish distribution of tickets of admission to all sorts and kinds of persons by the presiding judge, M. Robert, whose occasional levities in the course of the proceedings are melancholy reading. As a result of his indulgence a circular was issued shortly after the trial by M. Fallieres, then Minister of Justice, limiting the powers of presidents of assize in admitting visitors into the reserved part of the court.

The proceedings at the trial added little to the known facts of the case. Both Eyraud and Bompard continued to endeavour to shift the blame on to each other's shoulders. A curious feature of the trial was the appearance for the defence of a M. Liegeois, a professor of law at Nancy. To the dismay of the Court, he took advantage of a clause in the Code of Criminal Instruction which permits a witness to give his evidence without interruption, to deliver an address lasting four hours on hypnotic suggestion. He undertook to prove that, not only Gabrielle Bompard, but Troppmann, Madame Weiss, and Gabrielle Fenayrou also, had committed murder under the influence of suggestion.[18] In replying to this rather fantastic defence, the Procureur-General, M. Quesnay de Beaurepaire, quoted a statement of Dr. Brouardel, the eminent medical jurist who had been called for the prosecution, that "there exists no instance of a crime, or attempted crime committed under the influence of hypnotic suggestion." As to the influence of Eyraud over Bompard, M. de Beaurepaire said: "The one outstanding fact that has been eternally true for six thousand years is that the stronger will can possess the weaker: that is no peculiar part of the history of hypnotism; it belongs to the history of the world.

Dr. Liegeois himself, in coming to this court to-day, has fallen a victim to the suggestion of the young advocate who has persuaded him to come here to air his theories." The Court wisely declined to allow an attempt to be made to hypnotise the woman Bompard in the presence of her judges, and M. Henri Robert, her advocate, in his appeal to the jury, threw over altogether any idea of hypnotic suggestion, resting his plea on the moral weakness and irresponsibility of his client.

[18] Moll in his "Hypnotism" (London, 1909) states that, after Gabrielle Bompard's release M. Liegeois succeeded in putting her into a hypnotic state, in which she re-acted the scene in which the crime was originally suggested to her. The value of such experiments with a woman as mischievous and untruthful as Gabrielle Bompard must be very doubtful. No trustworthy instance seems to be recorded in which a crime has been committed under, or brought about by, hypnotic or post-hypnotic suggestion, though, according to Moll, "the possibility of such a crime cannot be unconditionally denied."

In sheer wickedness there seems little enough to choose between Eyraud and Bompard. But, in asking a verdict without extenuating circumstances against the woman, the Procureur-General was by no means insistent. He could not, he said, ask for less, his duty would not permit it: "But I am ready to confess that my feelings as a man suffer by the duty imposed on me as a magistrate. On one occasion, at the outset of my career, it fell to my lot to ask from a jury the head of a woman. I felt then the same kind of distress of mind I feel to-day. The jury rejected my demand; they accorded extenuating circumstances; though defeated, I left the court a happier man. What are you going to do to-day, gentlemen? It rests with you. What I cannot ask of you, you have the right to accord. But when the supreme moment comes to return your verdict, remember that you have sworn to judge firmly and fearlessly." The jury accorded extenuating circumstances to the woman, but refused them to the man. After a trial lasting four days Eyraud was sentenced to death, Bompard to twenty years penal servitude.

At first Eyraud appeared to accept his fate with resignation. He wrote to his daughter that he was tired of life, and that his death was the best thing that could happen for her mother and herself. But, as time went on and the efforts of his advocate to obtain a commutation of his sentence held out some hope of reprieve, Eyraud became more reluctant to quit the world.

"There are grounds for a successful appeal," he wrote, "I am pretty certain that my sentence will be commuted. . . . You ask me what I do? Nothing much. I can't write; the pens are so bad. I read part of the time, smoke pipes, and sleep a great deal. Sometimes I play cards, and talk a little. I have a room as large as yours at Sevres. I walk up and down it, thinking of you all."

But his hopes were to be disappointed. The Court of Cassation rejected his appeal. A petition was addressed to President Carnot, but, with a firmness that has not characterised some of his successors in office, he refused to commute the sentence.

On the morning of February 3, 1891, Eyraud noticed that the warders, who usually went off duty at six o'clock, remained at their posts. An hour later the Governor of the Roquette prison entered his cell, and informed him that the time had come for the execution of the sentence. Eyraud received the intelligence quietly. The only excitement he betrayed was a sudden outburst of violent animosity against M. Constans, then Minister of the Interior. Eyraud had been a Boulangist, and so may have nourished some resentment against the Minister who, by his adroitness, had helped to bring about the General's ruin. Whatever his precise motive, he suddenly exclaimed that M. Constans was his murderer: "It's he who is having me guillotined; he's got what he wanted; I suppose now he'll decorate Gabrielle!" He died with the name of the hated Minister on his lips.

Echo Library
www.echo-library.com

Echo Library uses advanced digital print-on-demand technology to build and preserve an exciting world class collection of rare and out-of-print books, making them readily available for everyone to enjoy.

Situated just yards from Teddington Lock on the River Thames, Echo Library was founded in 2005 by Tom Cherrington, a specialist dealer in rare and antiquarian books with a passion for literature.

Please visit our website for a complete catalogue of our books, which includes foreign language titles.

The Right to Read

Echo Library actively supports the Royal National Institute of the Blind's Right to Read initiative by publishing a comprehensive range of large print and clear print titles.

Large Print titles are in 16 point Tiresias font as recommended by the RNIB.

Clear Print titles are in 13 point Tiresias font and designed for those who find standard print difficult to read.

Customer Service

If there is a serious error in the text or layout please send details to feedback@echo-library.com and we will supply a corrected copy. If there is a printing fault or the book is damaged please refer to your supplier.

Lightning Source UK Ltd.
Milton Keynes UK
29 October 2009

145553UK00002B/101/A